FLESH & SPIRIT. A NOVEL

Published @ 2017 Trieste Publishing Pty Ltd

ISBN 9780649584925

Flesh & Spirit. A Novel by George James Atkinson Coulson

Except for use in any review, the reproduction or utilisation of this work in whole or in part in any form by any electronic, mechanical or other means, now known or hereafter invented, including xerography, photocopying and recording, or in any information storage or retrieval system, is forbidden without the permission of the publisher, Trieste Publishing Pty Ltd, PO Box 1576 Collingwood, Victoria 3066 Australia.

All rights reserved.

Edited by Trieste Publishing Pty Ltd.
Cover @ 2017

This book is sold subject to the condition that it shall not, by way of trade or otherwise, be lent, re-sold, hired out, or otherwise circulated without the publisher's prior consent in any form or binding or cover other than that in which it is published and without a similar condition including this condition being imposed on the subsequent purchaser.

www.triestepublishing.com

GEORGE JAMES ATKINSON COULSON

FLESH & SPIRIT. A NOVEL

A NOVEL.

BY THE AUTHOR OF "THE ODD TRUMP," "HARWOOD," "THE LACY DIAMONDS," Etc.

New York:
E. J. HALE & SON, PUBLISHERS,
MURRAY STREET.
1876.

Entered according to Act of Congress, in the year 1876, by
E. J. HALE & SON,
in the office of the Librarian of Congress at Washington.

PREFACE.

In criticising an American Novel, a late writer remarked that it was impossible to construct a Romance that should depict even a few distinguishing traits in American character. The diversities separating sections of this great country are, perhaps, as strongly marked as those that distinguish different nationalities in Europe. And in the social lives and habits of the many classes, constantly increasing in America, and constantly diverging more and more distinctly from any established standard, the romance writer may find types enough to fill a series of Novels, while he cannot exhaust the supply in an ordinary lifetime.

The present volume does not even attempt the analysis of character. In so far as ethical or philosophical questions are touched at all, they are only touched as incidental parts of the narrative. All temptation to descriptive writing has been steadfastly resisted, and the only effort has been to draw, in outline, a few characters for the reader's entertainment.

NEW YORK, *May*, 1876.

CONTENTS.

CHAPTER		PAGE.
I.	The Storm	7
II.	The Travelers	12
III.	Mrs. Norman	16
IV.	The Ruthvens	21
V.	Miss Abby Keith	25
VI.	Rupert's Commission	30
VII.	Two Soliloquies	34
VIII.	Helen	38
IX.	Dutchy	43
X.	Vendetta	48
XI.	Mr. Skillet	52
XII.	Moving	57
XIII.	Tige	62
XIV.	A Letter	66
XV.	At Work	71
XVI.	Nina	76
XVII.	The Meeting of the Worthies	81
XVIII.	Darcy's First Visit	86
XIX.	The Foremost Man of the Age	91
XX.	The Gold Room	96
XXI.	Title Deeds	100
XXII.	The Wanderer's Return	105
XXIII.	Watched	110
XXIV.	A New Departure	115
XXV.	Mr. Donis	120
XXVI.	Baffled	125
XXVII.	Nell Gaston	130
XVIII.	Cross Purposes	135
XXIX.	An Angry Household	139

CONTENTS.

		PAGE.
CHAPTER XXX.	Found	144
XXXI.	Mediums	149
XXXII.	The Sealed Envelope	154
XXXIII.	Mr. Skillet's Sympathy	159
XXXIV.	Miss Abby's Visit	164
XXXV.	Nina's Dilemma	169
XXXVI.	The Outlet	174
XXXVII.	Followed Again	179
XXXVIII.	A Declaration	184
XXXIX.	The Little Game	188
XL.	The Old Church	192
XLI.	Mr. Skillet's Plan	197
XLII.	The Red Spots in the Snow	202
XLIII.	The Friends' Parting	206
XLIV.	A New Relation	211
XLV.	Helen's Story	216
XLVI.	The Dark Chamber	222
XLVII.	The Partition	229
XLVIII.	Blake and Bloke	234
XLIX.	And Last	241

FLESH AND SPIRIT.

CHAPTER I.

THE STORM.

DARCY GASTON stood at the window, watching the whirling snow. The great flakes slanting from east to west, were interlaced with millions of erratic crystals, darting in all directions, and formed a white network that hid the dark pines skirting the garden. The windows on the eastern side of the room were blocked up by miniature drifts, and all the paths around the house were obliterated.

A horseman, powdered from head to foot, passed the window, and dismounted at the porch. Before he had done stamping, and shaking the snow from his hat and garments, Darcy opened the door to admit him. The horse had walked off soberly, in search of shelter and provender.

The new comer divested himself of overcoat and leggings, entered the warm room, and stood with his back to the roaring wood fire. A large, comely man, thirty-five, with kind eyes and smiling mouth. His name was Henry Gaston, but at college he had been nicknamed "Tiger," because he was so invariably sweet tempered and gentle. No man had ever known him to manifest temper, and no man ever dreamed of offering him an affront. The county would have risen, as one man, to resent an injury done to "Tige" Gaston. He was a lawyer, without practice, except in the way of gratuitous advice, which he gave freely to all applicants; a farmer, with five hundred acres, which he valued chiefly on account of the quail he shot in the broad fields in the autumn; a country gentleman, with a wife who believed in him without limit, and no kindred excepting the boy who watched him so anxiously, as he stood near the blazing hearth.

"Well, brother?" said Darcy, at last.

"All up, Darcy!" replied Tige, "and I'm glad of it! Suppose

we had won that suit, and turned out poor old Tom Phillips! Why the man has a dozen children."

"You will not appeal, brother?"

"Certainly not! What's the use? We have plenty. Since I left Covington, I have thought it over. I am going into the law, Darcy, and you must take this confounded farm. Hist! Here comes Nell!"

To them enters a bright little lady. Tige stoops down and kisses her, as a matter of course.

"Boots wet, Tige?" she said; "No? I tell you they are! Here, Nanny; bring Mr. Gaston's slippers. What about the verdict?"

"Gone against us, Nell, darling. It is all right. Darcy was more interested than I; but he would have given up the case, if he had heard the testimony."

"Well, I'm glad it is settled at last," said Mrs. Gaston. "I thought it would end in this way, and I have made a plan for Darcy."

"What is it, sister?"

"Splendid! Tige shall open a law office in Lexington, and you shall be a student a year or two, and then a partner."

"You and brother have been holding a caucus," answered Darcy, laughing; "but I think I shall spoil your scheme. I have expected defeat also, and have gradually perfected a plan. I am going——"

"Where?" said Tige and his wife, in a breath.

"Into commerce," said the youth, waving his hand, as if he would take in the visible horizon. "Commerce! That for your law," and he snapped his fingers contemptuously.

"I shot two ducks yesterday," interrupted Tige, "and the odour of dinner followed Nell when she entered. I am famishing. After dinner we will renew the discussion. I'll wash my hands, change my coat, and be down before you are ready."

They were all seated before the blazing logs an hour later, all thinking of the same thing, and each reluctant to break the silence. Tige was wondering if he had used due diligence in "working up the case," and was conscious of laxity of mind certainly, and perhaps of indifference as to the result of the trial. It was an old suit, and during Darcy's minority there had been a vague expectation that the verdict would give the youth a competency, as well as add to his brother's moderate estate. In their later conversations, Darcy had detected the doubt in his brother's mind concerning the justice of their claim, and had caught his feeling of indifference and non-expectation. And his thoughts were now busy with the purpose he had formed to enter the world, and contend for fortune in the marts of commerce. Nell was furtively watching the boy's countenance, looking for disappointment, and finding an expression of calm confidence instead. As the silence must be broken sooner or later, Mrs. Gaston, of course, broke it.

"Darcy," she said, drawing her chair nearer to him, "I have thought of all the merchants in Lexington, and if you are really going to make your fortune in that way, it must be in Milliken's."

"Milliken's?" said Darcy.

"Yes," she answered, decidedly; "he is a cross-grained old wretch, I know, but he is rich, and he has made his money since I was a girl. You can ride in—I'll give you luncheon to take with you—and you can ride back to dinner."

"Milliken's? Lexington?" replied Darcy. "What do you think about it, brother?"

"Whatever Nell thinks," said Tige; "she is always right, you know. Milliken was poor as a rat when he came."

"I don't think Milliken will do, brother. I thought of going further."

They were all silent again. Somehow, they all thought simultaneously of a little mound under the snow, where Tige and his wife had left their only child, a baby boy, ten years ago. He died while his age counted by days, and the scar made by his departure had not been very deep. It was disappointment rather than sorrow that troubled them when they remembered him.

"We have nobody but you, Darcy," said Mrs. Gaston, plaintively.

"And you will not lose me, sister dear," answered he, taking her hand; "I can and will write to you—as often as you say. Only a day or two between us——"

"A day or two!" said Tige; "are you going to open shop in London or Paris?"

"Do you remember that smart gentleman we met last week, brother? I mean at Judge Hammond's."

"You mean the Yankee, who talked of nothing all evening, except——"

"N'Yauk!" answered Darcy, laughing. "Well, sir, he won my heart. N'Yauk is the field for my genius."

Here was a bombshell! Mr. Gaston, whose knowledge of geography was not trustworthy, could not remember whether New York was a thousand or six thousand miles from Kentucky. He knew it was a vast wilderness, infested by ravenous beasts, and paved with dollars. He had an indefinite hatred of the locality, mingled with a dim apprehension of the fact that New York was certainly the most promising field for commercial enterprise on the continent.

Mrs. Gaston had a swift apprehension of numberless snares and pitfalls, constructed especially to entrap young gentlemen from Kentucky, all which were covered over with such skill as to defy scrutiny. Darcy was so good and gentle and unsuspecting! To think of this exemplary youth falling into habits of dissipation, losing his acute sense of honor, having his conscience seared with the hot irons that abounded in that Sodom, whence came those lovely silks which Mrs. Judge Hammond wore on great occasions.

"Darcy," said Tige, "you are old enough to know your own mind, and I suppose you have weighed all the chances. It seems to me that you will have great difficulties to encounter from the first. You know nobody in New York——"

"Excepting Mr. Foster, brother," said Darcy.

"Mr. Foster?"

"Yes. The gentleman at Judge Hammond's. I had a little talk with him. He was kind enough to say he would be glad to see me, should I visit his city."

"Do you know the nature of his business?" said Tige.

"Not accurately. Something about stocks. He says anybody in Wall street could direct me to him."

"And you were laying your plans a week ago," said Mr. Gaston with a touch of reproach in his tone.

"Not I!" answered Darcy; "it is true that I was attracted by Mr. Foster's stories of rapid money making. All my plans have been laid to-day. You know Judge Hammond gave me a hundred dollars—the only money I ever earned—for preparing his boy for college. I thought I should like to commence on that capital, and New York is my objective point."

"Why don't you say something, Nell?" said Mr. Gaston, after another pause. "What do you think about it?"

"I think Darcy has made up his mind," answered Mrs. Gaston; "it is dreadful! But if I could only know just what the poor boy was thinking and doing all the time, I might consent to let him try. When he gets fairly afloat in that whirlpool he will forget us."

"Sister!" said Darcy, "you two are the only friends I have in the wide world. None will ever love me as you two love me, and I will never love any mortal as I love you. When I forget you I will have no memory of anything else. When I conceal any thought or purpose from you two, I will be so utterly lost to all considerations of gratitude, of honor, of manhood, that you will be glad to forget *me*. Can you not trust me? I will promise to put aside enough money to pay my way back to you, and when I have no other money left I will return. I will write to you every night, and I will look every day for letters from you. If I fail——"

"Well?"

"If I fail—a hundred dollars will only last a few weeks. I will soon be able to decide as to my chances. I will not take one cent from you, brother. I have resolved to carve my way upon my own resources; and if I cannot win success with this beginning, I should fail with ten times as much. But go I must! Don't you see that I am obliged to go? Would you have me, with such abilities as you say I possess—with perfect health, with a liberal education, and with Gaston blood in my veins—would you have me live like a drone among your books, or vegetate among your sheep on the farm? I tell you, I fairly pant to encounter the discouragements, the disappointments, the 'hard knocks' that Mr. Foster warned me would be in my path! and I mean to triumph over all obstacles, or——"

"Or what?"

"Or come back and vegetate among the other sheep!"

"I think he will have to go, Nell," said Tige. "As soon as spring opens, Darcy, Nell and I will take you to New York."

"You mean, you and sister will pay me a visit?"

"When do you think of going?" said Tige, doubtfully.

"To-night! The train that leaves Lexington at eleven will take me."

CHAPTER II.

THE TRAVELERS.

THE snow storm which began in Kentucky worked its way eastwardly. After crossing the Ohio, the train that carried Darcy Gaston gradually fell behind time. On the second night it came to a full stop, half way between stations, and the conductor announced to the two hundred querulous passengers, that further progress was impossible. "The snow put out the engine fire." Another train would be due about daylight, and meantime there was nothing to be done, but keep up the fires in the cars and wait. Darcy listened to the comments of the passengers with eager curiosity.

"Misa'ble management!" said a gruff gentleman a few seats off. "This cussed corporation is a fraud! If they had put two ingines on to the train at Larkville, we'd a' ben in N'Yauk to-morrow noon. I'm bound to be in N'Yauk to-morrow!"

Nobody answered. There were sixty-four passengers in this car, and sixty-two of them thought the gruff gentleman had no right to monopolize the injury. Confound him! Did he suppose anybody cared whether he ever reached New York or not? Darcy alone gave him a grain of sympathy, and wondered how much he was bound to be in New York, and if the obligation were strong enough to overcome two feet of snow on the level, and ten feet in the drifts. After a short pause, he resumed his monologue.

"Narrer gauge road too! If we had took the other route we'd a' ben a good deal nearer home, and ben more comf able. Good sleepin' coaches too!"

"Must be long in Erie!" said a voice near the door; "long in Erie, and bullin' the stock!"

There was a titter first, and then a prolonged guffaw, in which the gruff gentleman joined. This had the effect to give a more cheerful tone to the conversation.

"Su'thin's got to be done!" said the gruff gentleman, rising; we can't set here five or six hours. I move that we send back to Scrabbletown, and try to git up another ingine. If we had two, we could push ahead. Let's look for the conductor." He walked down the aisle as he spoke, and catching Darcy's eye, nodded to him.

"Come, young gentleman, you and me will be a committee of two. We can't set here, like knots on a stump! Let's find the conductor."

Darcy rose at his invitation, and passing into the next car, they found the conductor, who was endeavoring to reassure an old lady, by promising relief at daylight.

"The express will bring two locomotives," he said, "and if we can get through this cut, the drifts will not be so heavy beyond."

"We've come to see you on that business, Mr. Conductor," said the gruff gentleman; "we're a committee from the next car."

"Well sir," replied the official, "what do you propose?"

"We think you might send back to Srabbletown, and git an ingine from there."

"I have to send a brakesman back to give warning," said the conductor; "but I don't know——"

"I'll go with him!" said a passenger, rising—"I want to stretch my legs anyhow."

This car was furnished with reclining seats. A young girl was in the chair next the window, apparently asleep. He looked round at her a moment, and then taking a ticket from his pocket, he slipped it into a satchel that lay on her lap.

"In case of accidents," he muttered, rebuttoning his overcoat—all ready, conductor!"

"Can I do anything?" said Darcy, touching his arm, as he followed the conductor; "shall I go with you?"

"Thanks! no use. The walking will be rough. You can do no good by going." He paused, and regarded Darcy intently by the dim light of the lamps. "Would you mind—have you any company?"

"None; I am alone."

"Well, suppose you take my seat? When she wakes you might tell her where I have gone. Would you mind?"

"I will do it with pleasure."

"If anything should happen—Pshaw! What foolery! The truth is, my whisky flask is empty—and I should get the horrors before morning without a nip. Just tell her where I have gone—that's all. Good night!" and he passed out.

Darcy quietly took the chair he had vacated, and looked curiously at the sleeping girl. Her hat was in the rack above, and a woollen hood was drawn over her head, concealing most of her face. One straggling curl of golden hair had escaped the hood and lay over her shoulder. Her head was resting upon her muff, a little white hand holding it in its place. She was sleeping profoundly.

Was she a child or a woman? The one hand visible was so small, that he concluded she must be a school girl. Tolerably well grown too. The other hand was gloved, holding the satchel. How fortunate that she was asleep! Perhaps she would not waken until her protector returned. By the bye, he had not said what relation he sustained to her. Father, of course. Too old for her brother. If anything should happen to awaken her, what the mischief should he say? Really this was a nice mess for a fellow to be in! Suppose the man did not come back at all!

Meanwhile the girl's protector was plodding through the deep snow, accompanied by the brakesman, who carried a red lantern that threw lurid streaks upon the white snow, looking like blood stains. The station they were seeking was some miles off, and part of the walk was exceedingly dangerous. The railway wound round a spur of the mountain range, and one curve was cut out of the face of the rock which rose fully a hundred feet, almost perpendicularly from the margin of the river that washed its base. In summer the trains went slowly over this part of the road, giving travelers an opportunity to take in the enchanting view of valley, river, and distant hills. Now everything was hidden by the whirling snowflakes. Fortunately, the wind had blown the snow from the track at this point, and they passed it safely. Scrabbletown was reached at last, and the solitary hotel opened its hospitable door to them after a brief delay. There was a stove in the barroom, and the passenger hovered over it while the landlord filled his flask and concocted a fiery compound for his present use. The brakesman steadfastly declined to partake of a similar draught, saying, he was "On dooty, and it was agin orders." If he had told the whole truth he would have added, he was a Son of Temperance.

Their journey was fruitless. The engine they expected to get had been sent back ten miles to meet the express train, and aid in pushing through the drifts further eastward. There was a telegraph station here, and, after sending warning to the next station of the whereabouts of the embargoed train, the brakesman announced his intention to retrace his steps.

One more hot toddy for the passenger, and then they began the return tramp.

When they reached the narrow ledge over the river, the brakesman, who was ahead, was startled by a sudden cry from his companion. He turned in time to see him disappear over the brink of the abyss! Another cry, far down the face of the rock, and then silence, except for the murmur of the river and the pulsations of his own heart.

He peered anxiously over the fatal edge of the precipice, but could see nothing beyond a few feet, where the unfortunate passenger had plowed his way to destruction. He had slipped on the rail, blinded by the snow, and probably the worse for his double dose of toddy, had staggered to his feet on the wrong side and shot over the edge, almost within reach of the brakesman's arm.

No possibility of giving aid. Nothing to be done, but get back to his train and report the disaster. Only one minute ago he had cautioned him to follow closely and keep near the face of the rock, towering up like a great wall on the left hand.

Darcy was dreaming of college days, drifting away from him into the Past, when he was roused by the conductor. He fumbled in his pocket for his ticket, but the man beckoned him away. As he left his seat he glanced at his companion sleeper, and met her calm, grey eyes. In the uncertain light, he half fancied he saw a wistful expression in them that he remembered afterwards.

At the end of the car the brakesman stood, his red lantern still in his hand. Two or three passengers with appalled faces were listening to his story.

"No chance for him, eh?" said one, as Darcy drew near.

"Not a grain!" replied the brakesman. "He went over just at the curve at High Bend. He must have been killed a dozen times before he got to the river."

"Of whom are you speaking?" said Darcy, the terrible truth beginning to dawn upon him; "not the gentleman who went with you?"

"Yes," replied the conductor; "I thought you would tell the lady. He sort o' left her in your care, didn't he?"

Darcy recoiled. He could not face those grey eyes with so horrible a story.

"He said," continued the conductor, "just as he was stepping down from this platform, that Mr. Gaston would explain to the lady."

"Mr. Gaston!" said Darcy, aghast.

"Yes; I heard him say that," put in the brakesman.

Darcy tried to recall the brief colloquy between the lost man and himself. Certainly he had not told his name. And how could the conductor learn it?

"Tell me exactly what has occurred," he said at last.

The man told the story of the walk to Scrabbletown, of the delay at the hotel, of the despatch to the next station, and of the return walk. In describing the fatal accident, his story was concise and direct. His eyes were upon his companion all the time, excepting the moment when he fell. He heard him cry out the second time after he disappeared over the verge.

"And then I *knowed* he was a goner!" he concluded.

Darcy walked back to the vacated seat. The girl was sitting upright, and wide awake. He endeavored to arrange in his mind the approaches to the catastrophe; but he was stunned and bewildered.

"Something has happened, sir!" she said, suddenly. "What is it?"

"I have a terrible story to tell you," he answered, "and I do not know how to begin. May I venture to tell you the exact truth?"

"Do not hesitate," she replied, steadily; "I shall not faint or cry out. I am accustomed to terrible stories. What is it?"

CHAPTER III.

MRS. NORMAN.

ON Fifth avenue, New York. Brown stone mansion, of course. The town residence of Mrs. Norman, widow; rich, old, bed-ridden. She had been ailing all summer, at Saratoga and Newport, and, since her return to the city, had not been out of her luxurious chamber. The medical attendant had informed her nearest relations, two grand-daughters, that the case was "serious," and suggested the propriety of calling in other physicians, to divide the responsibility. So others were invited to a consultation, and pronounced the treatment already employed precisely that indicated by the symptoms. Nothing to be done but sustain Nature.

Nature, however, had nearly reached her limit. That is to say, the time had arrived when Nature would perform an evolution, in accordance with her own inflexible laws, and disintegrate the particles of matter that were cognizable by the sensuous perceptions, and eliminate something that gave the atoms cohesion, and which could not be measured by the faculties that investigate the phenomena of matter. Mrs. Norman was taking her last look, with mortal eyes, at the sunlight. She was a good woman; her long life had been adorned by many deeds of kindness and charity; and she faced the messenger, whose dusky wings overshadowed her couch, with calm confidence.

Her grand-daughters stood at her bedside, vieing each with the other in watchful attention to the few wants of the invalid. The elder, Mrs. Bragdon, was a cheerful young matron, who had two new links in husband and baby attaching her to the things of earth, and who therefore looked with more composure upon the approaching separation from her life-long friend. Her sister, Nina Norman, had never left her grandmother, even for a day, and the prospect of her grandmother's death, which she knew was near and inevitable, filled her with horror and dismay. To her, perhaps more than to any one else in the world, the stealthy footfalls of the grim king sounded like the tramp of a cruel murderer, whose assault upon her friend and guardian was a menace addressed to herself; and she was conscious of a vague longing that her own life might terminate when the placid face of her grandmother should settle into cold rigidity.

"Children!" said the invalid, "I shall sleep presently. I do not suffer now, in mind or body. Nothing but weariness. You must remember that—hereafter——"

"Do not talk, Grandmother," said Nina, "if it tires you."

"It does not, child. I have only a word to say. Ruthven—if your Grandfather had not quarrelled with Ruthven——"

"Who is Ruthven, Grandmother?" said Nina.

"Ah! you do not know; and I cannot tell you now."

She closed her eyes, falling into a quiet sleep. Mrs. Bragdon, leaving her sister at the bedside, stole softly out. She had heard her husband's voice in the passage. Would return in a minute. Would make John exchange his boots for slippers, and bring him. The minute was multiplied by ten, and Mrs. Norman awoke before she returned. Nina was kneeling at her side.

"A drop of wine, Nina," she said.

"What did you wish to say about Ruthven, Grandmother?" said Nina, giving her the wine.

"Ruthven was your Grandfather's nephew. They quarrelled, and the boy disappeared. It was forty years ago. I have never heard of him but once since. If they had not quarrelled Mr. Norman would have left him——. I cannot tell the story. There is a packet in my writing desk. Take it and read the will. He made another will later, leaving me everything. There is the desk. Get the packet now."

Nina opened the desk, and after a short search found a bundle of legal looking documents.

"Here is one, Grandmother, marked 'Will.'"

"That is it. Replace the others. If I had lived, I thought I would find Ruthven and give him—— Ah! kiss me, Nina, my darling. I am going to sleep again. You and Mary can settle——" and she dozed again, leaving the sentence unfinished.

The house was on the corner, and the last beams of the setting sun came in at the west window. The faint ray, subdued by the lace curtain, flickered upon the face of the sleeper, and she awoke for the last time.

"Rupert is in the hall, Nina," she said, in low tones, clear and distinct; "call him. Stop!" she added, as Nina moved to the door. "It is too late. You had better send him—Kentucky. He will know. Poor child! Do not mourn! Obey the will!—the will!"

And, as Nina knelt by her, a solemn quiet spread over the pallid face. The sun was gone, and as the shadows gathered in the darkening chamber, Nina hid her face in her hands to shut out the sight.

They found her there a minute later, insensible, and carried her to her room, Mr. and Mrs. Bragdon, the Doctor, and Rupert. It was sudden, the Doctor said, but he had expected that termination and had warned them. It was a comfort to know that it was a painless death. Miss Norman was worn out by her prolonged vigils. Let her sleep if she would. It was only a swoon; she would be quite well in the morning. All that human skill and care could do had been done; but the case was utterly hopeless from the first. He would look in to-morrow and see Miss Norman.

Rupert had remained in the death chamber, while the others carried Nina to her room. When they returned, he was at the window. He did not mention the fact of his having explored the writing desk during their absence, or the further fact of his failure to find what he sought there.

"Can I serve you in any way, Mary?" he said.

"No, I think not; unless you will ask Doctor Blair to call. We ought to tell him, John."

"Oh, certainly!" replied Mr. Bragdon. "And Mr. Grey had better see him. It would be more decorous."

Mr. Grey walked soberly down stairs, and into the street, his handsome countenance grave and sad, as became the occasion. Stopping at the next corner, where the Reverend Dr. Blair resided, he sent in his card, and was speedily ushered into the study. Here he delivered his message in mournful accents, dwelling a moment upon the many virtues of the dear deceased, and left the venerable clergyman in a glow of sympathy, that was heightened by the stern composure wherewith Mr. Grey repressed his tears.

Proceeding down the avenue, he reached the hotel, and met an acquaintance at the entrance. The immediate consequences of the meeting were two glasses of whisky and bitters, and an invitation to dinner. The acquaintance was from Chicago, and after dinner added an invitation to Mr. Grey to accompany him to the theatre; but this last courtesy was declined, as there had been " a recent death in the family," and it "would not do" to indulge in ordinary frivolities until after the funeral.

Accordingly, left to his own resources, he found a seat in an obscure corner of the smoking-room, and, secure from interruption, smoked and meditated.

He was a showy looking man, about thirty-five, well formed and well dressed. A black moustache, hiding a mouth that was rather sensual, and contrasting with his sallow cheeks. Black eyes, that were keen and bold, a little insolent perhaps, defiant, certainly. Catching a glimpse of him in the corner as he sat there, moody, resolute, watchful—and being ignorant of his previous history, one would instinctively conclude that he was a man engaged in a warfare with society. A longer look would suggest the probability that the conflict had gone against him on the whole. Still, there was no indication of surrender. On the contrary, there were a calm consciousness of strength, and the ability to adapt himself promptly to the surrounding circumstances, whatever they might be, and a certain reliance upon his known powers, all of which were elements of ability. If Rupert Grey had been cast upon a desert island, he would have done all any mortal could do with the appliances he found there.

At the present juncture Mr. Grey was perplexed. He had been waiting with exemplary patience for Mrs. Norman's release from her sufferings. The old lady was ripe for translation, and she had been specially kind to him of late, and he had been specially attentive, calling every day to inquire as to the progress of the disease, and getting two good views of the packet in her writing-desk, when she dozed—he being alone with her in the chamber. Once, when she was sleeping profoundly, he ventured to glance through one of the papers in the packet, and saw his own name. He had not time to read all the particulars, as he heard a step on the stairs. This afternoon he had looked again, but the paper had disappeared. No matter. The lawyers had it, no doubt. After the funeral everything would come out. It would have been a bad business had there been no will. Mary and Nina would divide the entire estate. The thought made him shiver!

Among his other attainments, Mr. Grey included a good knowledge of law, especially that portion of the profession that related to inheritances. Mrs. Norman dying intestate, the entire estate would go to her only son's daughters. All collateral branches of the family were entirely and equally cut off, and the only expectations Rupert had, were founded upon late expressions of kindness from the old lady, the memory of sundry liberal gifts of money from her, when he had been in straits, and the sight of his name in the will. The enforced haste with which he had examined this document prevented the recognition of the fatal fact that it was legally worthless, as it was an old will of Rupert Norman's, which had been set aside by a later one, leaving all his possessions to his wife.

"I have made a mistake," he muttered, as he passed out into the street. "I should not have shocked Nina by showing her my liberal notions. She is terribly pious, and terribly obstinate, and has a terribly retentive memory. I suppose I might do some repenting, and all that sort of thing, upon this auspicious—I mean—melancholy occasion; but she will be cut up by the old lady's death, and would not listen to me for six months to come. Bragdon is sharp as a needle too, and would be quite apt to warn her against me. There must be something left to me. But my luck has been so uniformly against me, that I cannot place confidence in it now! And it will be a week before the will comes to light, anyhow."

Mr. Grey's ill luck consisted in a pair of fast horses in the earlier part of his business life—very expensive little dinners at Delmonico's, and very extensive wagers upon horse-races, pigeon-matches and elections, and a very cold-blooded set of creditors, who, dissatisfied with his offer of twenty-five per cent., had put him into bankruptcy, and left him, a helpless orphan, upon the cold charities of N' Yauk.

CHAPTER IV.

THE RUTHVENS.

TEN days after the funeral, Mr. Grey climbed the stairs which led to a number of lawyers' offices, far down Broadway. On the second floor, in the front room, he found Philemon Coke, Esq., the recognized legal adviser of the Norman family. He desired to know if a will had been left, and therefore he had concocted an introductory matter of business, that would naturally bring the facts in the case to the surface. Mr. Coke's table was filled with deeds and leases, and he seemed to be busy.

"Good morning, Mr. Coke!" he began, "may I trespass upon your valuable time long enough to ask a question or two?"

"Certainly," responded the lawyer,—"anything about the estate?"

"Yes! No! That is, I don't know. Grandmother Norman had arranged with me to get me out of this infernal bankruptcy business. You know I have not been discharged."

"Exactly;" replied Mr. Coke, "your assets failed to realize——"

"Yes; she understood the difficulty. It has only been a month since she proposed to relieve me from all entanglements, and I suppose her sickness prevented——"

"You call her grandmother," said Mr. Coke.

"Yes; she was not my real grandmother—my grandaunt in fact."

"Oh! ah!" said Mr. Coke.

Mr. Grey felt uncomfortable. Mr. Coke appeared to think the relationship was very distant, and it suddenly occurred to Rupert that Mrs. Norman might have left some documentary evidence of a slight inaccuracy in his statement. There had really been a proposition made to "fix up" his unfortunate bankruptcy, but Mrs. Norman had not made it. The lawyer took off his spectacles to rest his eyes.

Mr. Coke was near-sighted. When he removed his glasses he was practically blind. So, while he gazed blandly at Mr. Grey, he also gazed blindly, conscious only of the presence of a bulk of humanity sitting opposite. But his mental vision was not defective. It was his habit, when arguing knotty law points before the court, or addressing a somnolent jury, to escape distraction by removing his glass eyes, and thus, being oblivious of the phenomena of visible things, his mind worked with lucidity and precision. And in the present instance he looked into the mind of his visitor, and discovered the object of his visit.

"You are aware, Mr. Grey," he said, "that the estate of your grandaunt is inherited by her two grandchildren in the absence of a will."

"Yes, certainly; that is—I suppose so."

"There is no doubt about the law," responded Mr. Coke. "In volume four, New York Reports, page two hundred and six, the case of Snooks *versus* Snooks——"

"Oh, it is all right, Mr. Coke, you need not refer to cases. I suppose any agreement made by the deceased before death, would not bind the property?"

"Certainly;" said Mr. Coke, "a contract duly authenticated would be binding. It is of the nature of a debt, and can be enforced by process of law."

"Duly authenticated?" said Grey, "that is, signed and sealed, and referring to heirs, executors, administrators and assigns, and all that sort of thing."

"Not necessarily, my dear sir! Any one can present an account against the estate. I have quite a number of small bills on file here now, which will certainly be paid. Here is one from a dressmaker, which I shall pay to day, by Miss Norman's order."

"It is certain there was no will?" said Grey, after a pause.

"By no means certain," replied the lawyer, resuming his spectacles. "There may be a will, but having found none among the papers—and I may add—having drawn none, as the legal adviser of the family—I am inclined to think Mrs. Norman died intestate."

"If there had been a will," said Rupert, slowly, "you would have drawn it, of course. Yet she might have made one at Newport or Saratoga."

"In which event," said Mr. Coke, "it would probably have been entrusted to me on her return."

"She was bedridden, you know," persisted Mr. Grey.

"Yes," replied the lawyer, dryly, "yet I got her signature to a lease two days before her death."

"And she mentioned no will?"

"No." Mr. Coke did not think it necessary to say that Mrs. Norman had plainly stated there was no will. She desired her estate to fall into the hands of her granddaughters. That Grey had some decided expectations from the estate was evident, and the lawyer detected a tone of assurance that he was certain was based upon something more substantial than had yet appeared. He was too astute to ask any questions, knowing that Grey would reveal himself in due time, if not put upon his guard.

"Am I taking up too much of your time, Mr. Coke?" said he, after some quiet cogitation. "Speak frankly."

"Certainly not," replied the lawyer; "I am not busy to day. These papers will wait. Nothing urgent."

"I am almost emboldened to ask if I may smoke," continued Rupert.

"Undoubtedly! I do not smoke, but I like the odor, especially when the cigars are so good as yours are sure to be."

This was a gentle thrust. Mr. Coke thought Rupert could pay a better dividend if his habits were less expensive.

"Ah, that's the trouble!" said Grey, coolly, as he proceeded to light his cigar. "I can possibly do without smoke, but I cannot, possibly, smoke cheap weeds. If you will allow me to take a puff or two my mind will work more smoothly."

He puffed away a few minutes, packing a little cloud around his head, and trying to arrange his questions. He was after information, and the lawyer always closed his jaws with a kind of snap after exactly answering his interrogatories. The old gentleman had bewildered too many witnesses in his day to be voluble for nothing.

But while Rupert smoked his energies returned. The blank denial of Mr. Coke had settled the will business, and the shock of the disappointment affected him no little; but the man was a philosopher after a fashion, and, accepting the inevitable for the nonce, he reflected more calmly as he inhaled the fragrant smoke. Suppose Mrs. Norman had left him a few thousands. It was pretty certain the bankruptcy business would swallow them all up.

That cursed bankruptcy! It was clear that he could get no comfort from Mr. Coke. It was very doubtful whether he could gain any information either. Suddenly a thought struck him. Now proceed cautiously!

"Mr. Coke, do you happen to know anything about the Ruthvens?"

The lawyer started, and Grey saw it through the smoke.

"Ruthvens?" he answered, slowly. "What Ruthvens do you mean?"

"Indeed I don't know," said Grey, indifferently; "there is a fellow named Ruthven—must be related to me, I suppose—never saw him or heard of him until recently."

"What did you hear?"

"Very little. By-the-bye, he is *not* related to me; he was Mr. Norman's nephew or cousin. My relationship is to Mrs. Norman; that makes a difference."

"I do not understand," said the lawyer, dryly; "do you refer to any possible interest in the estate?"

"No! Yes! That is, I suppose the Ruthven interest would be excluded, as he was not related to Mrs. Norman."

"There is no possible interest either way. Mrs. Norman held her property under the will of her husband. She had one son, who died intestate in her life-time, leaving two daughters. These daughters inherit all the property, real and personal, and no possible claim could divert the inheritance from them. Mr. Ruthven has no more interest in the property than—Mr. Grey!"

Through the smoke Mr. Grey detected the spiteful snap of the near-sighted eyes. Decidedly, Mr. Coke was in favor of excluding both Grey and Ruthven. Rupert waited to hear more.

"Has Miss Norman mentioned the—the Ruthvens to you?" said the lawyer, after a brief pause.

"She did not send me to you," answered Grey. "I saw her yesterday, but she said nothing about the Ruthvens then."

The whole truth was—Miss Norman had never spoken to him on the subject; but he had seen the name in the same document that contained his own—that is, in the old will of Rupert Norman —and the half petulant dismissal of the possible claim of the "Ruthvens" by Mr. Coke, convinced Grey that their case had been debated before. His own knowledge of the family was very vague and unsatisfactory. There had been such people about New York years ago, but they had all disappeared. So he sat there, smoking and cogitating, when Mr. Coke brought matters to a crisis.

"The Ruthvens, as you call them, Mr. Grey," he said, "are all included, so far as I know, in the person of Mr. Darcy Ruthven, formerly of New York, but for long years a citizen of Kentucky. I obtained his address, in 1861, with some difficulty, and acting under instructions from the late Mrs. Norman, I wrote him, proposing to transfer certain property to him as a gift from her. The mails were unsettled at the time, and I had no reply from him for a month; but it came at last—shall I read it to you?"

"If you please," said Grey, much interested. The lawyer got up, and, taking a parcel of papers from a tin box, selected the letter, which he handed across the table to his visitor. Rupert opened and read:

"*To* PHILEMON COKE, Esq., *New York.*

"SIR: I have your letter of 3d ultimo, and in reply I have to say I decline the gift you proffer. To-morrow I shall begin a march, which I expect to end in your city, and I hope to set fire to the property in question.
"DARCY RUTHVEN,
"*Captain, C. S. A.*"

"Whatever intentions Mrs. Norman may have had," continued Mr. Coke, replacing the letter, "were entirely abandoned, of course. We have heard of Captain, or rather Colonel, Ruthven occasionally, since the war began, but his name has never been mentioned by the late Mrs. Norman since the receipt of that letter. Certainly, with her decided views, she would never have left her money to any of the name."

Mr. Grey took his hat to depart. There was some mystery about the business. He would have to investigate further. No information to be got from Mr. Coke. He would try Nina.

CHAPTER V.

MISS ABBY KEITH.

NINA NORMAN recovered slowly from the shock of her grandmother's death. The girl was sensitive and passionate—keeping her attendants in perpetual dread and anxiety, bothering the Doctor by the sudden presentation of new symptoms, half mental and half physical, with intervals of serene submission, the more noticed for their rarity. She refused all intercourse with the outside world, was not well enough to see Dr. Blair, and finally requested her sister, Mrs. Bragdon, to visit her only once in the day, and without nurse and baby.

"Nina's mind is certainly not right!" said Mrs. Bragdon, in confidential conversation with the last mentioned individual, "to refuse a 'ittle, peshus suga'-plum, who loves his Auntie Nina too !"

"A-goo !" replied John Bragdon, jr.

Thus confirmed in her suspicion of mental derangement, Mrs. Bragdon suggested to the Doctor the propriety of ministering to the mind diseased.

"Time, Mrs. Bragdon," said the Doctor, "is the great restorer. Miss Norman's symptoms are by no means alarming, though they are somewhat perplexing. If we could manage to get her a congenial companion——"

"I proposed sitting with her, and to take baby to amuse her with his little pranks, but she declined."

"Um, ah !" said the Doctor. "I think she would progress more rapidly with an older companion."

"Really, Doctor," replied Mrs. Bragdon, "if Nina would take any interest in anything, Johnny would amuse her. That child is perfectly won-der-ful ! He can almost talk !"

Johnny was five months old. His prose vocabulary was limited to the dissyllable above mentioned, and his poetry to a succession of howls, when suffering with colic. Nurse translated the latter into an instant demand for catnip tea.

"I cannot think of anybody," continued Mrs. Bragdon. "She seems to prefer her own society. It is enough to put her out of her senses to sit all day in that dull room. She don't even read— that is, the papers. She is quite devoted to Thomas-à-Kempis, however."

"Ah, well !" said the Doctor, "that will not last long. It very frequently takes that form, but it is a transient symptom. Possibly, the mental organism, being dyspeptic, takes that sort of— hum !—stuff—more safely than solid reading. Not that she would get much solid matter out of the papers, either. Does she take no interest in dress, for instance ?"

"Not the least," answered her sister, "and that is the next thing to being indifferent to baby ! I asked her about her mourning, and she said her dressmaker needed no instructions. She has not tried on any of her things."

"Without being exactly alarming," responded the Doctor, "that last mentioned symptom is certainly unusual. Are the dresses made in the latest fashion?"

"Of course!" said Mrs. Bragdon; "Madame O'Rafferty has not been from Paris over a month. There is a grenadine there that cost frightfully, I'm sure! Nina sent her a note consisting of two lines: 'Dear Mrs. O'Rafferty—Please make me some clothes!'"

There was something heinous about this. Mrs. Bragdon paused to recover breath. The Doctor was stunned.

"In the old practice, Mrs. Bragdon," said the Doctor, after some minutes of silent meditation, "I should have said quinine was indicated. Perhaps I should have alternated with tincture of valerian. But with better light, I am convinced that we are pursuing the proper treatment, rhus tox. and aconite! Good morning!"

As the Doctor passed out at the street door a lady passed in. She gave a card to the servant, saying,

"For Miss Norman."

"Walk in the parlor, mum," said the servant; "I don't think Miss Nina will see you, though. She is quite unwell. Shall I take your card to Mrs. Bragdon?"

"Miss Norman, first," replied the visitor, quietly.

There will be enough time to investigate this lady before the servant returns.

Under the fragment of straw and other fragments of lace and ribbons, which, when combined artistically, was called a bonnet in those days, you can see glossy black hair, smooth and even, over a smooth, white brow. You are perfectly certain that the hair is parted exactly in the middle. She does not know what "dishevelled locks" means. Black eyes—fearless, if not bold—corresponding with the firm lines of her mouth. You cannot deceive this lady with complimentary speeches. She looks underneath your polite smiles and sees what you think. She has no doubt about her own status. You cannot condescend when you talk to her, nor can you flatter her by pretending to recognize her superiority. Altogether, there is an air of hardness about her, modified somewhat by her round chin, slightly prominent. Prompt, decided and quiet; accustomed to rule. You can see that plainly enough. Her dress is perfectly neat, and so constructed as to escape notice; not extravagantly fashionable, yet not out of style.

This was Miss Abby Keith.

The servant returned. Miss Norman would be pleased to see Miss Keith. Would she please walk up stairs?

Miss Keith's face was a study, as she entered Nina's room.

First: There was a decidedly sympathetic expression. She had heard of Nina's seclusion, and her persistent refusal to see visitors. Mrs. Bragdon and Nina had been pupils in Miss Keith's select school, two or three years. They were favourites. Their recitations were generally faultless. The teacher was an accomplished teacher. She was mistress of all the branches she taught, and she admired Nina greatly, chiefly because she really studied for the sake of knowledge. The two girls had left her for a more pretentious institution, but the friendly relations between them and their first instructress were always maintained. Mrs. Bragdon was slightly afraid of her, but Nina, brave as a lion, knew no fear. She was her grandmother's idol, and Miss Keith fully appreciated the strength of the affection that bound these two. Hence her countenance recognized Nina's late loss.

Second: There must be a limit to mourning. There must come a time when Miss Norman should appear once more in society. So Miss Keith modified the sympathetic expression by raising one eyebrow in deprecation of too much prolonged grief.

Third: There was Miss Keith's habitual defiant air. She was always candid. Candour was her special weakness. No humbug with her, if you please. She was over thirty, and safe from all kinds of soft nonsense. She lived in Brooklyn, and enjoyed the ministrations of the Reverend Horatio Slam Dragger. Dragger was a foe to all sorts of pretence, theological or secular. Those little peculiarities, such as reverence for old forms or old creeds, that other reverend gentlemen, and all reverent people favoured, were a stench in the Dragger nostrils. It was unmanly to be tied up by these old leading-strings. Let every man make his own creed, out of the depths of his manhood, and cast Athanasius and the fathers of the Nicene Council to the moles and bats! Be manly! Yet some straight-laced old theologues in New York and elsewhere had a disagreeable habit of saying that Dragger doctrine was not only manly, but also slightly devilly. But Miss Keith swallowed Dragger without winking. It may be noted here, that she spoke two distinct languages. One, her habitual tongue, fairly pure English, that is, new English; and the other, the Dragger dialect, properly called Gush. The new English was for ordinary converse. The gush was only employed when metaphysical topics were discussed. It was rather hard on Miss Keith's interlocutors, as metaphysics ought to be bad enough, when presented in ordinary tongues. But the mixture of High Dutch philosophy, poetry, infidelity, Renan, Strauss and Herbert Spencer, all elements of the gush lingo, would drive any sane man mad if too much prolonged. But Dragger made it popular somehow, and his disciples in Brooklyn and Chicago are pouring out diluted streams of this same gush to-day to delighted auditors.

"How are you, Nina, my dear?" said Miss Keith, kissing Nina, with the sympathetic expression most prominent.

"I am glad to see you, Miss Abby," answered Nina; "it was kind of you to come; sit here beside me."

"It was a clear call of duty," replied Miss Abby; "I heard of your persistent seclusion"—here the sympathy dried up, and the candid Dragger philosophy became pronounced—"and I felt impelled to call and talk to you. My dear, you must go out!"

"I have almost decided to go out of the country, Miss Abby," said Nina, wearily. "If you will go with me, I will go to Europe."

Miss Keith made up her mind on the instant.

"My dear girls!" she said, shaking her head; "how gladly would I go with you, Nina, but my girls! I have twenty-two engaged for the next session, and most of them are in my bible-class, too!"

Nina made up her mind too.

"You cannot make a thousand dollars a year, Miss Abby. You told me so yourself. I will gladly pay a thousand dollars for your society. Say you will go, and I will begin my preparations at once."

"Don't you think, Nina," said Miss Keith, wisely dropping in a little opposition; "don't you think you have a mission here, in your own country?"

"Perhaps. But it will wait, I suppose. I must get away from all these surroundings for a year or two. Will you go? You shall not suffer any pecuniary loss."

Nina's maid entered, with a card. Nina glanced at it, and continued: "You must decide, Miss Abby, before I see this visitor. Will you go?"

"Yes."

"Ask him to walk up, Hannah."

CHAPTER VI.

Rupert's Commission.

MISS Norman's room was on the second floor. It was furnished with severe plainness, containing only a centre table, sofas, etageres and chairs—all of black walnut, antique and venerable. The new comer found Nina and Miss Abby seated on the large sofa.

"I am glad to see you, Rupert," said the former. "Miss Abby, this is my cousin, Mr. Grey; Miss Keith, Rupert, my old teacher and friend."

"I almost know Miss Keith," answered Grey, shaking hands with the ladies. "You have so often spoken of her, Nina, though we have not met hitherto. Ah! Miss Keith! you are to be envied; your vocation ennobles the worker."

"All work is honorable, Mr. Grey," responded Miss Abby, "unless it is work that injures another."

"Of course! of course! How are you, Nina?"

"Quite well. I have been anxious to see you—upon matters of business——" Rupert started, and Miss Abby rose.

"I will go down and look for Mrs. Bragdon," said she.

"Sit still, Miss Abby," replied Nina, "the business is not at all private, and I shall need your advice, probably. You have heard of the Ruthvens, Rupert?"

"Ruthvens? Yes, certainly. That is—a Mr. Darcy Ruthven—a Rebel colonel in the war—somewhere out West."

"Yes. He is the man. Do you think you could find him?"

"No doubt. That is, if he is alive. Have you heard from him since—since our sad bereavement?"

"No," answered Nina. "I have never heard from him. But I very much wish to see him. Indeed, I *must* see him. Can you aid me in the search?"

There was such an air of earnest determination about Miss Norman, that Grey swiftly concluded to acquiesce in any plan she proposed. He was very much bewildered, however.

"Have you consulted Mr. Bragdon?" said he, after a pause.

"No."

"Or Mr. Coke?"

"No."

"Or Mary?"

"No. I have sent for you, in order to escape consultations. I must see Colonel Ruthven. If you cannot find him and bring him to me, I shall go look for him myself."

"Are you in earnest, Nina?" said Grey.

"Dead earnest! I can know no rest, until I discharge a—an obligation—until I see and have speech with this man."

Grey reflected. He remembered the note he had read at the lawyer's office, every word of it. Defiant, truculent and scornful. Did Nina know of this letter? and if not, was it politic to tell her? Should he ask Philemon Coke, Esq.? Better not. Nina was difficult to manage alone. Nina and Coke combined would be totally unmanageable. How much did that sly looking schoolmistress know? She sat there with eyes half closed, apparently inattentive, or absorbed in the music of the spheres, yet certainly hearing every word and concocting schemes enough, no doubt. What a demure looking old grimalkin she was, to be sure!

"Can you tell me the nature or extent of this obligation?" he said, at last.

"No! certainly not;" replied Nina, decidedly. "Indeed, I do not myself know the extent of it. I think I can ascertain, however, in due time."

An expression of gushing candour overspread Rupert's handsome visage. Miss Abby suddenly decided that he was the handsomest man she had ever seen.

"I must tell you something, Nina;" said he. "This Mr. Ruthven—or Colonel Ruthven, was requested to communicate with grandmother Norman, five years ago, preparatory to a transfer of property of some sort——"

"Yes," answered Nina, "I know that."

"Well! he rejected the proposal rudely—I was going to say insolently; and so far as I know, his only motive was his hatred of everything Northern. He was a rebel, dyed in the wool!"

"And is so still, no doubt," replied Miss Norman, composedly. "But his political proclivities have nothing to do with the matter. I *must* see him."

"If he is still alive—" suggested Rupert, tentatively.

"And if not—his heir or heirs will do:" said Nina, firmly.

"Can you go?"

"Certainly, if you wish it. It seems to me this is not only a wild goose chase, but a very expensive one. It will cost two or three hundred dollars!" Nina walked over to the centre table, where there were writing materials, and wrote a line or two, handing the paper to Mr. Grey.

"Is that sufficient?" she asked, when he had read it.

"More than sufficient—I will account to you——"

"I don't want any account. I want Colonel Ruthven. When can you start?"

"To-morrow;" and seeing Nina's discontented expression, he added, "or to-night, if you prefer it. Shall I write to you?"

"If you meet with no unusual difficulties, you will be back within a week, but if your absence is necessarily prolonged, you had better write to me—care of Mr. Coke. You are very kind, Rupert, to undertake this service, and I am grateful. Please grant me one more favor. Keep this whole business secret for the present, until I give you leave to speak of it. Miss Abby, you and I know of it, and none besides. Mr. Coke may give you some information——"

"I know as much as Mr. Coke knows," answered Grey. "I will proceed with due caution, and the secret shall not be revealed by me." He took out his pocket book, wrote an address, and tore out the leaf. "Here is my address—'Galt House, Louisville.' I hope you will not need it. Good bye! Good morning, Miss Keith!"

"My dear," said Miss Keith, after Rupert's departure, "you seem to repose unlimited confidence in this gentleman. No doubt he is eminently worthy of it. I was greatly impressed with his air of candour. He is your cousin, is he not?"

"Yes; that is, he is related to my grandmother's family. You had better not place too much confidence in his candour, however; my trust in him is not unlimited."

"Yet you have sent him on this mission, which I do not clearly understand——"

"No, I suppose not. I can probably explain to you hereafter. But I was obliged to send him, first, because he was designated; and secondly, because I could find no other messenger; and I may add, he is thoroughly capable, and will find it more profitable to serve me faithfully in this business than to thwart me."

Wholly unconscious of this complimentary discussion, Mr. Grey entered a Broadway car and rode down to the Astor House. His first business was with Mr. Coke. This must be delicately managed! As he ascended the stairs leading to the lawyer's office, he arranged the mode of attack.

"Mr. Coke!" he began, after the preliminary salutations, "if I find a friend to purchase Squeeze and Skinnem's claim, is it probable that I can obtain my discharge in bankruptcy?"

"Very probable," answered the lawyer, taking off his spectacles.

"Their claim is nearly five thousand?"

"Forty-nine hundred and twenty-two," said Mr. Coke, consulting a schedule.

"They will accept fifty cents, I presume?"

"Not if they think they can get fifty-one," replied the lawyer.

"*I* don't think they can get fifty-one," said Rupert, with a melancholy smile. "By-the-bye, Mr. Coke, will you allow me to look at Colonel Ruthven's note once more? I want to see the signature."

"Certainly," and Mr. Coke produced the paper.

"Lexington, Kentucky," said Mr. Grey, mentally. "What a curious signature!" he added aloud. "It is very peculiar; I think I would know it again. Thank you! I will ascertain if I can make that offer to Squeeze and Skinnem; the assets will pay the others twenty-five at least. I *must* get out of that mess somehow." He took up his hat and moved to the door. "Ah! I had nearly forgotten!" he said, suddenly. "My memory is not worth a cent. Here is a commission that had almost escaped me!" and he presented Nina's paper to Mr. Coke.

The lawyer examined it carefully. It ran thus: "Mr. Coke will please pay Mr. Rupert Grey one thousand dollars for my use.
"NINA NORMAN."

"I do not understand this, Mr. Grey," he said at last. "Miss Norman has not advised ——"

"Oh! very well, Mr. Coke!" interrupted Rupert, heaving a sigh of relief. "If the thing is informal, please consult with Nina yourself. Of course, if I cannot get the money, I cannot comply with her instructions. Suppose you keep the paper? I will just write across the back that you decline payment ——"

"But I do not decline payment," answered the lawyer, testily. "I only require to know what use—how this money is to be employed."

"Very sorry I cannot enlighten you!" said Grey, coolly. "Nina requested me to get a thousand dollars from you in fifty dollar bills. If you haven't the money, or if she has none in your hands, the matter ends there."

"Suppose you leave the order and call to-morrow?"

"I shall leave New York this evening. I am going to dine with a friend at the St. Denis an hour hence, then pack my valise and start for Philadelphia at five. I will send a note to Nina from the hotel."

Mr. Coke produced his cheque book, wrote a cheque for the required amount, and handed it across the table to Rupert.

"I suppose it is all right!" muttered Mr. Coke. "But it is infernally irregular!"

"Never have money transactions with women!" said Rupert, irreverently. "They transgress business principles perpetually! Good morning!"

CHAPTER VII.

Two Soliloquies.

IN order to preserve the coherent drift of the story, it is necessary that the reader should know the secret thoughts of the two ladies from whom Mr. Grey parted in the previous chapter. Miss Keith was prevailed upon to stay and partake of luncheon, and Nina, as in duty bound, partook of a dose of St. Thomas-à-Kempis. While she perused the entertaining little volume, her thoughts wandered, which was a fortunate circumstance for her, mentally and morally.

"There can be no mistake," she thought, "about Grandmother's earnest desire to do what I purpose doing. It is the more certain because she was very emphatic in her dislike of Southern people. And there can be no doubt that I shall have to do whatever is done, alone. Mary would not be willing to part with so large a sum of money, and Mr. Bragdon would not be likely to permit such an outlay. I don't think I shall consult either of them. I don't think it would be right, either, as Mary is married, and I shall never marry. Never! Then it is certain that Rupert is the proper person to find the Ruthvens. Grandmother certainly told me to send him; and I have sent him, with no instructions whatever, except to find Darcy Ruthven and bring him here. What is Darcy Ruthven like? He must be fifty years old. How will I know that Rupert does not bring the wrong man? Does Rupert know or suspect what I intend, I wonder? Impossible!

"I must arrange for the division of the estate. Mr. Coke says it is important to fix ownership at once. I will write a note, telling him I am ready. I wonder if there are any disagreeable formalities, such as going into court.

"Dear me! I have read three pages of Kempis, and I do not remember a word. I must read them again.

"I wish Rupert were more trustworthy. No, I don't, either. The great struggle of my life will be to modify my hatred of that man. He is a wretch! But all men are wretches!

"I have done well to secure Miss Abby. I must make some provision for her, in case of my death. Shall I consult Mr. Coke? No. Grandmother has told me a dozen times to consult Mr. Skillet on all matters of business. He is a disagreeable old wretch. But she knew best. I will write to him, also, to-morrow.

"To-morrow will be Saturday. I'll go to church on Sunday.

"I have never examined my dresses! I'll do it this very day. That will be a treat to Miss Abby, also. She shall stay after luncheon. It was certainly wise to engage her. I can go where I please with her, and we will go to Europe as soon as I settle this Ruthven business. Mentone or Cannes for the winter. How can I get the special property I want? Mr. Coke can arrange—no, Mr. Skillet. How can I account to him for desiring this special property? I need not explain at all! Suppose it is a mere whim; who will question my right to indulge it? I will write to Mr. Skillet at once!"

She drew her chair to the table, and wrote the note. While she is thus employed, the reader can investigate the course of Miss Abby's reverie.

"It was a good spirit in attendance upon me this morning," thought Miss Abby, "that impelled me to call on Nina to-day. The prospect of visiting the classic shores of the Old World is very inviting. It is sad to miss Mr. Dragger's sermons, but I can read the old ones. I wonder what Nina is thinking about? She is evidently in deep thought. What will Mary think of this new move? But it makes little difference, as Nina was always the stronger, and she is free now to choose her own companions. Her share of the estate will be im-mense! No one knows the value of the Norman property. I am not going to give up the Institute, either. I will find some capable woman to take charge in my absence, and keep control in my own hands. I need not tell Nina. A thousand dollars, and all expenses of course. It is far better than twenty-two scholars, with rent and board to pay, especially as only half are in the first class, and half of the second class don't pay their bills! I can give a capable woman five hundred dollars a year, and make her responsible for the rent. That will be the plan.

"What elegant gloves Mr. Grey wears! He is certainly the handsomest man I ever met! Nina does not like him. That's a comfort! He seemed very eager to comply with her wishes. That was the money!

"I wish it was luncheon time!

"Of course it was the money! He looks like a man who could spend any amount of money. If I were to marry such a man, I would teach him to earn money too!

"They used to have splendid luncheons here, while the old lady lived!

"Nina will wear black at least a year. She must have any quantity of colored dresses. Probably she will give them away. She had a lovely ashes of roses at the concert last month—perfectly new.

"Really, I am half starved!

"European travel enlarges one's ideas amazingly. Anna Squills, who spent only a year abroad, is really a different girl. She actually speaks English with an accent! She was in Paris seven or eight months, and jabbers French on all occasions. I hope Nina will spend some time in the German capitals. I should like to become acquainted with some of the advanced thinkers of the Old World. Mr. Dragger admires them, I know. Really, theology is a science I must study a little more carefully. But with the higher spiritual insight, one does not need old-time creeds. There is Squizzim. He is a duck! And he makes himself a new creed as often as he likes. Mr. Dragger says he is a wonderful man! Won-der-ful! He seems so spiritual—ethereal! The fire of his genius lifts him above mere temporalities!

"I've a great mind to ask Nina for a cracker!

"Would it be possible to lead Mr. Grey to an appreciation of the capabilities of the spiritual life? Is there not in the profound depths of manly, human consciousness, the rich soil of native nobleness, some germ of the higher soul-life, recognizing the dynamical principle of affinities? And if so, might not the true soul of this man be reached, by persistent effort? The incrustation of selfishness, which the antagonisms of busy life and the chemical reactions of conflicting interests deposit upon the soul surface, may be dissolved or broken up by appeals to the affections! And then the limitless capacities of the diviner nature, that unfailing impress, which centuries of alienation have not entirely effaced, since the creation or development of man, would unfold and expand, beautifying the earth, and banishing to the moles and bats the figments of harsh creeds, resolving all questions by the unanswerable logic of Love.

"I should like to write that down, if I had paper and pencil. I don't see how any ordinary man could resist it.

"Nina will have to wait a week or two for Mr. Grey's return. In the meantime, I can arrange the affairs of the Institute. Where can I find a competent person? Let me see. First, I must find one whom the landlord will be willing to trust. I do not propose to incur responsibility for the rent.

"What in the world is Nina writing? A note to somebody. I never heard of her having any male friend, except Mr. Grey. She has addressed the note to mister somebody. I'll go over to the register to warm my feet, and can perhaps see the address. I took great pains with Nina, especially in penmanship, and she writes plainly. Ah! indeed! Mr. Timothy Skillet, Wall street, New York.

"Now, Mr. Skillet is the very man for me to consult. He has a niece at the Institute.

"Mr. Skillet has no appreciation of the inner light however. I think I shall consult a Medium. If I could only get Mr. Dragger to investigate spiritual phenomena! With his wonderful appreciation of character, he would make a grand conductor of spiritual seances. His antithetical references last Sunday were perfectly splendid. I intended to write that sermon down, but I have been *so* occupied. Perhaps I can remember it. Let me see! The reliance upon mere sensuous perception, is the common mistake of humanity. Those truths that we know most thoroughly, are not those that we have learned with our eyes or ears. But man is endowed with other faculties, by which he apprehends abstract truths, and truths of such dimensions as may not be compassed by the use of outward organs. Thus, we see the myriad stars, sparkling upon the midnight, numberless, and we even give names to clusters and constellations. Yet the ignorant Arab of the desert did this, before Anglo-Saxon civilization began. These nomadic tribes had a name for Sirius, corresponding with Dogstar, before Alfred reigned in England; and it may be, that the astrological lore of these children of the tropics, whereby they foretold, with amazing accuracy, the rise and overflow of the Nile, was an attainment a step higher than the astronomical knowledge of to-day. Who can tell the capacity of man for the reception of truth? Or who can estimate the power of this native insight? The anguished longing for higher attainments, springing up from the hidden depths of human nature, ennobled by suffering, breaks forth ever and anon, and through the long annals of the race marks the eras of progress. Contrasting Sherman with Attila, Grant with Sidney Johnston, Fizzlebacon with St. Augustine, or Squizzim with Solon, we may find where that spiritual perception which grasps unseen realities has most distinctly shown its power.

"Dear me! I have not forgotten a word of it. But the trouble is, to know exactly which of the worthies thus placed in contrast is the better. I would ask Mr. Dragger, only he would think I had not a grain of sense not to know. I must really read up ancient history. Mr. Dragger also spoke of beans, and made it very clear, that if their axils (I wonder what the axils are?) were properly managed, they might bear Bartlett pears. I wish I had about six Bartlett pears now.

"There is the luncheon bell at last. Nina looks as if she could live on air. Yes, my dear, certainly. I walked all the way from Fulton Ferry, and the exercise has given me quite an appetite."

CHAPTER VIII.

HELEN.

AT the opening of the year 1861, Darcy Ruthven, Esq., was practicing law in Cincinnati. By the time the spring buds made their appearance, the climate of that prosperous city had become unsalubrious to him and his household, simply because he was an outspoken man and very decided in his political opinions. Consequently, he sold his possessions in Ohio, and removed to Lexington, Kentucky, which was his wife's birthplace. The air was filled with warlike rumours, and when the sun began his return journey from the Northern tropic, Mr. Ruthven was captain of a cavalry company, enrolled in the service of the Confederate States

He was a colonel when he was brought back to Lexington to die of his wounds, in 1864, and before the grass appeared upon his last resting place, it was reöpened to receive the body of his heartbroken widow.

None of the other horrors of war can compare with its culminating horror of orphanhood. And Helen Ruthven stood by her mother's grave, filled with an unspeakable longing for death. She had been well instructed in those grand doctrines, under whose power all endurance is possible; and she would have answered her pastor's whispered consolations with meek submission, if the death she coveted had only been impending over her. But the consciousness of sound health, the conviction that she had a course prescribed for her, through a howling wilderness, wherein no mortal life could be found in sympathy with hers;—and the possibility of separation from her beloved, to be measured by scores of years,—rested upon her heart and mind. There was mingled with her sorrow a sense of gratitude also, that these dear ones would sorrow no more; and the calm, hopeless, purposeless drift of her life, had this much of promise in it. As the Giver of good had so tempered this double bereavement, that the death of her mother was a ground of thanksgiving, because of her deliverance from the woes of widowhood, Helen looked forward to a time in the near future, when the same peaceful end might possibly come to her.

There was a better promise than this, however. There were girls of her own age, hovering around her, with tearful eyes, and these also were suffering similar bereavements. Among her school companions and friends it might be said, as was said of Egypt at the date of her last plague—there was not a house in which there was not one dead! And Helen, touched by the unselfish sympathy of her companions in suffering, learned new lessons of endurance, as she mingled her tears with theirs.

A week after her mother's death, Helen learned her own utter poverty. She was alone in the world, and had to choose between a life of dependence or immediate exertion to win her daily bread. She was a guest at her pastor's house, and she reached the decision of the question in this wise: Henry Gaston, Esq., who had some legal business before the court then in session, called at the parsonage one afternoon, and requested an interview.

"I come with a message from my wife, Miss Ruthven," he said, after a preliminary greeting. "She begs you to return with me to-morrow to our country home. It will be dull in comparison with Lexington, but we will endeavour to make your time pass as pleasantly as may be."

"You are very kind, Mr. Gaston," answered Helen, " but I cannot visit Mrs. Gaston just now."

"Visit?" said Tige—"we don't invite you to visit, but to take up your abode permanently with us. You see," continued Tige, in answer to her perplexed look, "your father and mine were partners in Cincinnati. My brother is named Darcy Ruthven, after your father, so we are almost related."

"I don't think I quite understand you," she said, doubtfully.

"Oh, it is all plain enough. You have no relations nearer than my wife and myself, and there was never a final settlement of accounts between your father and mine."

"Do you mean to say your father was indebted to mine?"

"Yes. That is—there was no formal settlement. The law business in Cincinnati was left by Mr. Ruthven, in the charge of his partner. I was taken into the office just after your father came to Lexington, and I remember several cases that were afterwards tried in the courts in which Gaston and Ruthven were the attorneys."

"Well?"

"Well! Mr. Ruthven was clearly entitled to half the fees in all such cases. When we get home you and I will go over the records, and reach a settlement."

"I think I do understand you now, Mr. Gaston," said Helen. "My father had no possible claim upon any business done in Cincinnati after his departure. He has told me more than once that Mr. Gaston made him a handsome allowance at their separation, paying him far more than his just proportion for the unfinished business. You have imagined all you have told me, or you have invented the story to conceal your generous purposes."

"Really!" stammered Tige, "you are mistaken. I am sure *some* money is due to you—and anyhow, Nell and I are so lonesome that it would be a great charity to come. We have set our hearts upon it, and I would not know how to face Nell without you. We did not know until yesterday that you—that your mother——"

"That I was an orphan," said Helen, mournfully. "Ah, Mr. Gaston! I appreciate your kindness; but you know my father's daughter must earn her living by honest labour."

"I am sure I don't know what sort of labour you can make profitable," said Gaston; "can you plough, for example?"

"I can teach French and music, I think," answered Helen, with steady composure. "I have a list already prepared, of gentlemen whose influence I hope to secure. I have your name and Judge Hammond's, and I intended to apply to you for aid and advice to-morrow."

"That is it, exactly! Come out with me this evening and we will consult Nell?"

"I cannot go this evening, Mr. Gaston; Mrs. Crowder is coming here this evening to see me by appointment."

"Mrs. Crowder!"

"Yes. She has three daughters, and wants a governess."

"Governess?" said Tige, slowly. "I don't know how that will work, Miss Helen; Mrs. Crowder lives in Cincinnati."

"Yes; I should regret leaving Lexington, and all my kind friends here; but, if I should suit Mrs. Crowder, it would be very foolish to reject any offer she might make."

"I don't know what to say about this business!" said Mr. Gaston. "You are a mere slip of a girl, and the idea of your going out to service—I mean, taking charge of those abominable brats of Mrs. Crowder's—is perfectly absurd! You would die in a month!"

"Alas!" answered Helen, "I have been wicked enough to hope so. Don't encourage such evil thoughts in me, I pray you!"

"I'll bring Nell in to-morrow!" said Tige, desperately. "If she don't knock this Crowder matter in the head, I'm much mistaken."

An hour or two after Mr. Gaston's departure, Mrs. Crowder was announced, and Helen went down to the drawing-room with considerable trepidation. Her visitor was a meek looking little woman, dressed in funeral black. All her exterior indications were gentle. She was deeply pious, and her eyes were habitually half closed, as if to shut out the view of distracting temporalities, while her spirit indulged in heavenly musings. Helen's entrance called her down from the spheres.

"Well, my dear Miss Ruthven," she began with a preliminary sigh of sympathy, "I hope you feel resigned and submissive?"

"I am trying madam," answered Helen.

"This world is all a fleeting show!" said Mrs. Crowder, solemnly. "There is no such thing as happiness to be found here, except in the contemplation of a better one beyond the skies! When you reach my age, my dear, you will know how empty and unsatisfying all earthly joys must be!"

"Yes, ma-am!"

"I sometimes think," continued Mrs. Crowder, "that it is a sin to smile! But it is so natural! Yet Grace can overcome Nature! Add to your Faith, my dear! Keep adding! Faith without works is dead!"

"Yes, ma-am," said Helen, submissively.

"Add to your Faith Virtue!" continued Mrs. Crowder. "Virtue is the crowning grace! And as faith is a silent, unobtrusive grace, so virtue must be in the heart. The sentiments must be virtuous. Submission is a great virtue, and, no doubt, submission is the very grace referred to in the passage!"

"Dr. Graves says virtue means 'courage' in that passage," observed Helen.

"Does he?" answered Mrs. Crowder, with a sniff. "Ah, well! the courage of submission, probably. But my time is limited, my dear, and time is a talent which must not be buried in a napkin! I called to inquire if you would like to undertake the charge of my dear girls—in their studies, I mean. I cannot offer you a very large salary; but the duties will not be onerous. You sew remarkably well, I am told. I have a sewing machine—Singer's. I should like you to assist me with the sewing, when not engaged with the children."

"If you think I am competent, Mrs. Crowder," said Helen, "I will be very glad to instruct your daughters. I think I am equal to ordinary English studies—and French—and music——"

"Oh, we will make due allowance for your inexperience," said Mrs. Crowder, with a smile, subdued but cheerful. "You have been accustomed to Singer's?"

"Yes, ma-am."

"Well, then, Miss Ruthven, if a hundred dollars a year with your board, you know——"

"I will be very thankful, Mrs. Crowder," said Helen, when Mrs. Crowder paused, "to earn a hundred dollars a year, and I will do my best."

"And you don't object to the sewing?"

"Oh no, ma-am! I will sew as much as you like."

"Then," said Mrs. Crowder, rising, "the only point remaining to settle is the time; can you come at once?"

"Whenever you please, ma-am."

"I am going to Cincinnati this evening; do you think you could get ready to accompany me?"

"I will be quite ready in an hour——"

"You are very prompt, my dear. We shall get along famously! I will call for you at three o'clock; good morning! Give my regards to Dr. Graves. Perhaps you may as well let the terms be confidential at present—good morning! At three, punctually."

At half-past three o'clock there were two cards left at the parsonage for Miss Ruthven. One was inscribed "Darcy R. Gaston;" the other, "Mr. Rupert Grey." The servant, not knowing of Helen's final departure, merely informed the two gentlemen that Miss Ruthven was out.

CHAPTER IX.

DUTCHY.

NOBODY knew where Dutchy came from. He did not know himself. As far back as his memory extended he had been a New Yorker. He was a newsboy at first. He had a dim recollection of his inauguration into this vocation, and his first venture in the 'Erald and Trybune. He infested hotel corridors, ferry landings, and street corners, and sold his wares. At night he expended a large portion of his gains in the Bowery Theatre, where he refreshed himself with pea-nuts. When he outgrew the proportions to which newsboys are limited, he went into the petty larceny business, and was reasonably successful, getting "sent up" once and again, but coming down always with larger experience and increased ability. He knew all the "cops" that were dangerous, and as he could count them on his fingers, he easily avoided their beats. He was matured when the war began, and was quite prosperous as a bounty-jumper for a year. But he fell into a streak of ill-luck, and took his last bounty in a city regiment, where the corporals and sergeants knew him and his previous history, and, being carefully watched, failed to "jump" before his regiment started for the seat of war. His company was stationed at a little village on the border, to guard the railway that passed through it. Here he encountered the horrors of war, by getting into a fight at a political meeting, where he managed to murder one bucolic voter and maim another. To avoid scandal he was transferred to another station, where warrants could not reach him, and one fine night he deserted. Travelling on the railway was attended with difficulties, as he was adorned with the uniform that was not supposed to be journeying northward, and New York was his objective point. He got a coat and a straw hat without a brim from a scarecrow in a friendly cornfield one moonlight night, and walked ten miles before he found a barn with a window open. Here he was found by the farmer, while he was enjoying his beauty sleep, and promptly explained his trespass by telling the agriculturist a harrowing story of a widowed mother left destitute and sick, when the cruel draft tore him from her arms. He had received a letter from her a few days before, in which she depicted her privations in language which his sobs kept him from repeating. So he had crawled out of the hospital and started homeward. His trousers had betrayed him, and he thought it best to make a clean breast of the desertion part. The only drawback to the remainder of his narrative was his ignorance of the main facts he recited, as he really did not know that he had ever had a mother. The farmer (it was in Pennsylvania) was visibly affected by the dismal story of his unbidden guest. He took him to the kitchen and gave him a breakfast, which Dutchy pronounced "heavenly." After the meal his host gave him the choice between two days' work, without wages, in the cornfield, or immediate deliverance to a military station a mile off. Dutchy longed for work, and, armed with a hoe, went from the breakfast table to the cornfield. He did a man's work and ate a man's rations at meal time. At night the farmer escorted him to a garret room, and locked him in. Dutchy slept the sleep of the just, untroubled by dreams.

The next day the farmer worked by his side, and lightened the labor of both by cheerful conversation. He asked numberless questions about the war, and Dutchy gave him details as veracious as the cotemporaneous "extras" furnished the citizens of New York. At supper time Dutchy expressed himself so well content with agricultural employment, and so anxious to continue the peaceful, innocent life of the country, that the farmer was fairly captivated, especially as the soldier was indifferent about the matter of wages.

"Anything you please, boss," he said, in conclusion; "I am green about this here business, but I'm larnin'. Pay what you likes at the end of the week."

That night the farmer did not lock him in, and Dutchy, being somnambulic, wandered over the house, in the small hours. At early dawn the farmer sought him, but found only the scarecrow coat and hat, with the blue trousers which the Government had furnished Dutchy at the beginning of his military career. It was a curious coincidence that the farmer missed corresponding articles of attire from his own wardrobe, and he tore his hair in voiceless agony when he remembered that he had left United States currency, amounting to ten or twelve dollars, in the pocket of a missing garment. At the same moment Dutchy was exchanging some of this identical currency for breakfast at a smart restaurant in a railway station a dozen miles from the farmhouse.

To illustrate the far-reaching consequences of apparently trivial actions, it may be stated here, that the political complexion of that Pennsylvania district was materially affected by this little playful exchange of Dutchy's. That agriculturist had voted against "Jackson and liberty" all his mature life, before the fatal morning when Dutchy left the blue trousers. This useful, not to say ornamental part of the military dress of the period, had been furnished the Government, by a contractor, at six dollars and ninety-eight cents, and as they were composed, in the main, of shoddy, the profit of the contractor was about six dollars a pair. The acute judgment of the farmer quickly detected the flimsiness of the material, and by a swift process of reasoning, he pronounced sentence against the paternal authority that clothed Dutchy in habiliments so far inferior to those he had taken. The farmer tried on the blue garment, and being agitated as well as unpractised, he thrust his nether limbs entirely through the fragile material. In attempting to withdraw his limbs he made another grievous rent, like that of envious Casca, and involved the whole affair in remediless destruction.

"Dese pe Gov'ment preeches!" he muttered, sorrowfully surveying the wreck; "und dey vas made by New Yauk teifs, I schvear! I votes mit Shackson nex time. Sturmwetter!"

It was a sad sight to see that respectable father of a family, stalk up to the polls on the next election day, holding open in his hand one of those time-honored tickets adorned with a hickory tree, over which floated a scroll, bearing the inscription—"Jackson and Liberty." The Keystone State has been gradually growing Democratic ever since.

Wholly unconscious of the evil he had wrought, Dutchy took the first train running east and north. He saw the telegraph poles flitting by, as he sped along, and had uneasy visions of cops at the end of the journey. The train slackened speed, as it ran through Jersey City in the twilight, and Dutchy got on the rear platform and dropped safely on the track. An hour afterwards he crossed the river by the Hoboken ferry, and once in the great city, he was comparatively safe. Before he got off the train, he stumbled over a carpet bag belonging to a sleeping passenger, and desiring to save the other travellers from a similar stumble, he took the carpet bag with him. He found a change of raiment in it, when he had time to examine it in a cheap lodging-house in the Bowery. The bag itself, with a tooth-brush and comb, which were useless to him, and unpawnable, he carefully lost in a vacant lot, a mile distant from his lodgings. The bag needed some repairs, as he had been forced to cut it open, having no key to fit the lock.

Dutchy lived a virtuous and harmless life for several days. He ventured out after night fall, with his face wrapped up in a handkerchief, suffering from the memory of a toothache which had haunted his juvenile days. Cops passed him, glancing at him incuriously, as he plodded by. His habiliments were respectable, and fitted him reasonably well, but his supply of currency was diminishing. During the first week, he managed to make an honest living, by pawning all the articles of dress he had obtained in his homeward journey, excepting the one suit he wore. At the end of the week, in a private conversation with himself, he thus stated his condition.

"Flat busted! that's so! Last shirt gone, and on'y got two shillin' left. Landlord wants pay beforehand, and to-morrer ends the week I've paid for. Sumthin's got to be done! Had to take a ten cent hash to-day. Can't stand that long!"

He resolutely faced the situation, and brought into play all the keen logic of which such men have a stock. Not hampered by ethical considerations, the conditions of the problem were easily stated.

"Bounty-jumping is played out!" he thought—"it won't do to be cotched any more, and I don't want to git into no more guard houses. I might sew up one arm, and grind a organ—but I can't buy nary organ for two shillin'. It's a mean business anyhow, and some cussed cop would find me out. I'll go down 'long shore to-morrer, and git some work!"

No man who has been accustomed to useful occupation, can appreciate the heroism of this resolve. Since the day he gave up the newspaper business, Dutchy had never done anything like work, except upon compulsion. A brutal lieutenant had obliged him to carry a log of wood a half day, while he was a warrior, as the penalty for some breach of discipline. The sun was hot and the labour monotonous and profitless, and Dutchy promised to murder that lieutenant whenever he could do it safely. As work is the one beneficent provision against madness or idiocy, that has been implanted in the nature of humanity, Dutchy, who contradicted all normal instincts, hated work especially.

It was therefore a refreshing sight, to see him the next day cheerfully toiling on one of the piers. He had found work, on his first application. A steamer loading with cotton, was to sail within the week, and rather larger wages than usual were offered to any willing laborer who would meet the emergency " by doing his best." At the end of the week, he had more earned money in his pocket, than he had ever honestly owned before. The effect was to humanize the man, and he actually felt some respect for himself, as he sat on the edge of the pier, counting his currency. It might have been the turning point in the man's history; the first step from vagrancy to respectability, but for a sudden temptation which the watchful enemy passed swiftly before his startled eyes.

The ship was slowly moving, a tug drawing her out into the stream. The purser leaning over the bulwark, was talking to the stevedore who had just paid Dutchy his wages. There was some controversy between them, relating to the lading of the ship, and the stevedore, who had a bulky wallet in his hand, thrust it hastily into an outside pocket, just as he passed Dutchy, near the end of the pier. The latter saw the money wallet, coveted it greedily, and with practiced fingers twitched it out of the other's pocket and thrust it into his own. One minute later, he was on the next pier, hidden behind a long gangway, his heart thumping so loudly, that he thought it could be heard twenty yards off. But he was apparently sleeping soundly, when a watchman shook him roughly, and ordered him off the pier. He did not know how much time had passed, but he staggered on to the street, and with well counterfeited drunkenness, slouched along, across the entrance of the pier he had left—passed the stevedore, whose pale face glared upon him in the twilight, as he recounted the story of his loss to an attentive cop, unknown to Dutchy. Two or three streets further down the river, he was swallowed up in a throng of people rushing to a ferry house. He allowed himself to be carried on with the crowd, and imitating his "file leader" as they passed the window, bought a ticket for Newark.

A citizen of that prosperous city kindly directed him to a cheap boarding house, and here Dutchy philosophically rested, paying his board regularly, but speaking to no one.

CHAPTER X.

VENDETTA.

THE pocket-book that Dutchy found, almost ready to drop from the pocket of the chief stevedore, contained sundry memoranda relating to the lading of the ship. These, with the wallet itself, Dutchy cooked in a brisk fire. The wallet also contained three hundred and ten dollars in crisp, new greenbacks, mostly of the denomination of five dollars. These did not need cooking.

Dutchy read the New York *Herald* daily. For two weeks after his removal to Newark, that enterprising journal had something to say about him, more or less interesting. He learned first, that he had stolen the wallet some hours before the ship sailed, and had secreted himself in the hold, among the barrels and bales he had rolled into their places. Consequently he would not be heard of until the return of the *Hecla*, bound to Havre first, and thence to Port Elizabeth, Cape of Good Hope. She was to bring a return cargo of wool, already engaged, and would be due in New York in the early winter. The next report contradicted this statement, as he had been seen in New York, and the police were on his track. This did not disturb him much. The solitary consideration that affected him, almost to tears, and quite to profane ejaculations, was the knowledge that the "Boss" had paid fifty men, himself included, out of the same wallet only an hour before he had conveyed it. His knowledge of the exact sciences was limited, but he was able to estimate the loss to himself at about five hundred dollars, a loss caused by the premature payment of those fifty laborers.

"He had no call to pay in such a cussed hurry!" muttered Dutchy, day after day, as he brooded over the matter; "nobody axed him to pay before sundown. Cuss the luck!"

The next day brought a new development. The boss, who

was only the representative of a firm, had been arrested. Something had transpired to awaken the suspicion that he had robbed himself. The man had borne a good character hitherto, but the temptation to possess himself of " nearly a thousand dollars" was too much for him, and the pretext that his pocket had been picked was too transparent.

"Sarved him right !" commented Dutchy. "On'y he was too big a fool for that dodge. Anyway, he won't stay in long. Election first week in October. He knows too many woters. 'Thousand dollars'! Did he have *two* wallets? Cuss him !"

There were no more references to the "robbery on the pier" for several days. Dutchy read the paper carefully, and began to be uneasy. One day he saw a New York " cop" lounging down the street, in plain clothes. He knew the cop, and as he peeped through his shutter, he felt very grateful for its shelter. That night he left his lodgings, and walked on the railway track to Elizabeth. He took passage on a second-class train for Trenton, then walked again on the Philadelphia road through the day, reaching Kensington at nightfall, footsore and weary. He was devoured by a double dread. He feared the loss of his currency, and also the return to the unwholesome restraint of the army. His brief experience of military life satisfied him that he was not intended by nature to seek the bubble reputation at the cannon's mouth. He would like to be a sutler or a quartermaster, but these attractive vocations could not be had for the asking. He found lodgings at a carpet weaver's, and fed frugally at cheap eating houses, changing frequently. One morning he found a copy of the *Herald*, a day old, and while he waited for his breakfast, he studied the paper, and at last found a paragraph that took away his appetite full five minutes. It was headed, "The pier robbery," and ran thus:

"There is no doubt that the pocket of Mr. Lapp was picked by one of the labourers, and the police have positive information of his present whereabouts. He has been hiding in a neighboring city for some weeks, but mysteriously disappeared a few days ago. It is another case of police blundering, or perhaps of collusion, but he is certain to be caught before the week is out."

Dutchy tore the announcement out of the paper, and scattered the fragments of it over the sanded floor. Then he took his breakfast. It was raining; the wind from the east, and when he left the eating-house, he thought it would be safe to stretch his legs with a good walk. Taking the railway track once more, he walked out to the crossing of the North Pennsylvania road, arriving in time to see a freight train run off the track. He had been idle and housed so long, that work was a positive luxury, and throwing off his coat, he laboured heartily two hours or more. A brakesman had been hurt, and carried away, and the conductor touched Dutchy on the shoulder as he was resuming his coat.

"Say! Are you on this line?" said the conductor.

"Yes," answered Dutchy, promptly.

"I'm two hands short. Bill is hurt quite some, and I started with one man too little. Can you brake?"

"Dun'no," said Dutchy, doubtfully; "d'ye mean screw up them wheels atop of the cars?"

"Ezackly! Pooh! its nothin' to do. One whistle is for down brakes. Then you wind em up like blazes. Can't you come along? This is the through freight."

"And lose my place at the depot," said Dutchy, deceitfully. "Not if I knows it."

"You won't lose anything," replied the conductor. "I'll make it all right with the superintendent. He's my uncle. Mr. Grimes."

"Ya-as," drawled Dutchy. "I guess I know Mr. Grimes, and he'd blow me up prime, and stop my wages too."

"No danger!" persisted the conductor, eagerly. "Here! I'll write you a note at the first stop. It's allers allowed to take a man when we're short on brakes. Got thirteen cars, and all heavy. Here! I'll give you the rear brake—come along!"

Dutchy shook his head in outward discontent as he clambered up to the car roof. He kicked out the lever, releasing the brake, growling and muttering, while he inwardly chuckled. He rode all that day exposed to the storm, going farther and farther westward, with peace in his bosom, because no cop would dream of seeking him among the brakesmen of the "North Penn." The conductor wrote a formal document, addressed to the superintendent, exonerating John Smelzer (which was the name Dutchy took with his first brakes) from all blame, on account of absence from the main station. At the western terminus of the line he was regularly enrolled as brakesman, paid liberally for the service already rendered, and assured of prompt settlements at the end of each fortnight thereafter.

So passed the autumn. In addition to the new greenbacks, all of which he sewed up in the lining of his coat collar, Dutchy accumulated sundry greasy notes from honest wages. He had few opportunities, and no temptations, to spend. The letter to Superintendent Grimes he tore into small pieces, and sowed them along the line of railway one windy day in the early winter.

One day John Smelzer was detailed to assist in braking a long passenger train. He had the rear platform. The track was hidden beneath the snow, only a few inches deep, but sufficient to make the track slippery and braking troublesome. He was in an ill humour when night came, and disposed to be gruff and quarrelsome. A passenger came out upon the platform to smoke, and addressed some remark to Mr. Smelzer in a tone that was not conciliatory. The brakesman looked steadily at him, and recognized the lieutenant who had forced him to "nurse the log baby" at the far-off military station. The officer unfortunately had a retentive memory also, and being accustomed to quick obedience and the show of outward respect, swore at the brakesman first for his surly demeanor, and then recognizing him, exclaimed:

"Dutchy! Deserter! I'll fix your flint!"

As he turned to re-enter the car, Dutchy drew the iron pin from the coupling and struck him on the back of the head. As the warrior stumbled forward and fell senseless on the floor, Dutchy dropped deftly on the track, and by the time the startled passengers had raised the soldier and examined his cracked crown, the train was a mile or two beyond the scene of the "accident."

Because it *was* an accident. The lieutenant had a military cap on, and the wound was not visible, until a passenger found the blood dripping over his arm, supporting the officer's head. A doctor was found in the next car, and, after a hasty examination, he pronounced the hurt fatal. Dutchy had committed his second murder, though he did not know it. As soon as he had delivered the blow, he tossed the coupling-pin into the snow, and mechanically closed the car door before he dropped from the train.

"He struck his head agin this iron stanchion," said an on-looking passenger. "He came in from the rear platform and kind o' whirled round, and fell heavy like."

"Something must have knocked him," said the doctor; "his head looks like it had been smashed with a hammer."

"How long will he last, doctor?" asked the conductor.

"Last? He won't last at all. You had better carry him to the baggage car." He felt his wrist a moment. "It's about over with him—just a flutter. You had better get an inquest, I suppose.

These gentlemen, who saw him fall, can give their testimony what *made* him fall. That is the only question."

"Little tight, I guess," ventured another passenger. "These military men are hard drinkers! I noticed him a minute ago as he went past, and he was walking stiff and dignified; you'd a thought he was commander-in-chief."

"Only lef'tenant," said the conductor; "here's his shoulder strap. About two miles to Scrabbletown. We'll stop in five or six minutes, and have it all done regular."

"I'd like to have him on a table," observed the doctor, "to make a satisfactory examination. You might as well lay him down; he's done with all earthly troubles."

The sudden death, which would have cast a gloom over that car load of passengers a year or two before, was almost forgotten when the train stopped at Scrabbletown. The body was taken out and placed on a bench in the station house. A statement was hastily drawn up by the conductor, signed by half a dozen passengers, the doctor's certificate added—and the train only delayed about ten minutes.

"All aboard!" shouted the conductor, at last. "Jim, have you seen that new brakesman?"

"No."

"He's gone off somewhere for a drink, confound him!" Jim, take the rear brake; I'll not wait another minute! All aboard!" And he whirled his lantern in a circle—"All right!"—and the train plunged into the night with a prolonged shriek, as if wailing for the dead passenger.

CHAPTER XI.

MR. SKILLET.

WHEN Darcy Gaston sat down by the side of the young girl, with his mind oppressed with his dismal story, the conductor slipped away, to escape the coming fainting scene, and the cries of distress that were sure to follow the recital. On the contrary, the gruff gentleman, who had first accosted Darcy, quietly dropped into the seat behind him, evidently intending to hear the revelation, and doubtless intending to "assist" in any subsequent demonstration. There was sympathy in his countenance, certainly, and a business-like air of preparation, also. As Darcy glanced at him, over his shoulder, it occurred to him that the old gentleman was probably an undertaker.

"The gentleman who sat beside you," began Darcy, "put your ticket in your satchel, when he left his seat."

"Is he gone?" asked the girl, startled.

"Yes. He requested me to explain—You were sleeping——"

"No. I was awake. Where is he?"

"It is uncertain," said Darcy, slowly; "the brakesman who went with him cannot tell positively—he may be hurt—by his fall. He fell from the track, and down the hill side. Nobody can tell positively until daylight. My name is Darcy Gaston."

"Darcy Gaston," answered the girl mechanically.

"Yes. I don't know the name of the gentleman who was with you, but it seems he knew me. One or two of the officials tell me he mentioned my name, when he left the train."

"Did he?" There was a pause of some minutes, Darcy wondering at the quiet self-possession of the girl, and burning with curiosity to know her relationship to the missing man. The silence was broken by the gruff gentleman behind them.

"I think you ought to know, Miss," he said, "that the chances are agin your friend! He slipped over a high bank, and I guess he is some considerable hurted."

"What must I do?" said the girl, plaintively; "can I go to him?"

"Not by no means?" replied the gruff gentleman, heedless of grammar; "it is not possible—and anyway you could do nauthin'; in my opinion, he's past help!" The girl started, and looked to Darcy for confirmation. The boy's eyes answered her, as the old gentleman continued: "It's jest one of them cases, where nauthin' is certain, but where it is safe to expect the worst. Was he your father?"

"No."

"Oh! your uncle?"

"No."

"Um! Ah! your brother pr'aps?"

"No. Will you please tell me what I should do?" this was addressed to Darcy; "I know there is some terrible duty that I must perform: I am ready to do whatever you tell me, Mr. Gaston."

"You were certainly under this gentleman's protection," said Darcy; "may I ask his name?"

"His name—I am not sure that I am at liberty to tell you. Not now, certainly. Yes, I was going—am going to New York, in his charge, to meet relations that I have never seen, and scarcely heard of. I do not know where to look for them, or what to say, if I find them. All this, I am compelled to tell you, but I cannot explain anything that appears mysterious. I am under obligations to remain silent, at least at present. And I am so confused by this new calamity, that I do not, cannot think of the proper course for me to pursue!" While she said all this with outward composure, the tears were dropping over her cheeks and falling, unnoticed, upon her dress.

"If you will trust a stranger," said Darcy, earnestly, after he had looked back at the gruff gentleman who was apparently indulging himself in a peaceful nap; "if you will allow me to serve you, as I would serve my sister, I will do all a man may do in your behalf, without any explanation."

"If you are Mr. Darcy Gaston," answered the girl, "surely I will be glad to trust you. And I am grateful too. If you will allow me to think over the matter, a little, I will tell you as much as I dare. I may say this much: I bless the Divine mercy, that sent your father's son to me, in this dire emergency!"

Darcy looked at her in blank astonishment. He had all along been talking to her, feeling that she was inexperienced and decidedly young. And now there grew up in his mind, the conviction that she was a matured woman, capable of deep emotions, and acutely conscious of the delicacy of her situation. He was burning to ask her directly, what relation she sustained to the lost passenger, but something in her manner deterred him. He was bewildered by her reference to his father, and while he was trying to frame a question in answer to her last remark, she turned to him suddenly and continued:

"I know your family—that is—your brother. I think I remember your father also, but am not certain. But I know he was a gentleman of spotless honor. My name is—*not* Mary Harding, but I am not free to tell you what is my real name, and if you will please accept Mary Harding until—until I am released from the compulsion that keeps me silent, I will be very thankful. The name I have given you is on a grave stone, in my native town, and was borne by my earliest friend——"

"You are Helen Ruthven!" said Darcy, impetuously; "Oh, Miss Ruthven—do not answer me—I know all about it now. Tige told me. My brother, I mean." She covered her face with her hands as he went on; "I will call you Miss Harding—I will ask you no questions. You have no brother. If you will honour me so much, I pray you to consider me your brother. I will serve you in any way, and will relinquish the title whenever you bid me. And now I will say no more. Ah! remember only what my father was to yours and trust me."

She put out her hand which he seized and pressed, and when she withdrew it she leaned back in her seat and drew her hood over her face. Darcy felt it was a compact between them, and his heart beat a little faster as he reflected upon his new responsibilities.

"I must write all this to brother Tige!" he thought, "and ask his advice. But may be I am not at liberty to ask anybody! I will wait until we reach New York. I must take her to some hotel, of course. How ignorant and inexperienced I feel! Tige would know exactly what to do. Perhaps she will let me write to Nell—but that would be the same thing as writing to Tige. Dear me! She is going to sleep. Poor girl! Hillo! What the deuce—Oh! excuse me, sir."

The gruff old gentleman behind him had poked him in the back with his finger, startling him in the midst of his cogitations. He was standing up when Darcy turned, and beckoned him away to the other end of the car.

"Do you smoke?" said he, as Darcy followed.

"Sometimes, sir?"

"Wa-al, come into the smoking car. I've suthin' to say to you. You and me is responsible—that is, sorter responsible, for this business. And I'm going to see it out. I am, by thunder!"

Darcy followed him, and passing through two or three cars they reached the smoking car. The old gentleman pulled out his cigar case, presented it to Darcy very politely, and, seating themselves in a quiet corner, they blew a double cloud. No question about the quality of the weeds, Darcy thought.

"You see, Mr. Gaskins—that's your name?"

"No, sir; Gaston."

"Oh! ah! Wa-al, Mr. Gaston, let's come to business. You see, we was the committee that started this thing. And I was the primary caucus. Did you ask the young lady if she had any money?"

"Certainly not, sir!" answered Darcy, indignantly.

"Wa-al," said the other, composedly, "we must find out, somehow. If she's well to do we can symathize, and all that sort o' thing. But if she arn't, we must do suthin'. What do you propose?"

"Propose? I—I have made no proposition, sir."

"Exactly. But what *do* you propose?"

Darcy was learning a new lingo. He made a mental note—"Propose" meant "intend."

"You mean, what are my intentions?" he asked, doubtfully.

"Ezackly. What do you propose?"

"I hardly know, sir. I thought I would take the lady to a hotel——"

"Fi'th Av'noo, of course," said the old gentleman, nodding; "or the Brevoort is more nobby, and more expensive. I should think it would not be amiss to find out how long her purse is, first. P'raps you have plenty of beans yourself?"

"Beans?"

"Ya-as! beans—spondulies—stamps. But she don't look like a gal that would allow a stranger to pay her expenses. That chap arn't comin' back. He's tother side o' Jordan, and I guess he took his wallet with him. Did she tell you who he was?"

"No, sir."

"How does the weed smoke—pooty good, eh? Partagas. You come from down South somewhere, and so does the gal! I s'pose you air a rebbil?"

"I was in the Confederate army, sir," answered Darcy, stiffly; "but I was captured and released upon condition that I should take up arms against the United States Government no more."

"Ah! Wa-al, it's no consekense," said the old gentleman; "the foolishness is pooty nigh over, anyway. You did not git hurt in the war?"

"No, sir. I was captured in my first battle."

"That's lucky! What is the young lady called?"

"Miss Harding."

"Um! Miss Harding." He took a card from his pocket and wrote a few lines on the back of it. Darcy glanced at him while he was thus engaged, and the harsh accents, gruff manner, and general quaintness of the man, all faded from his memory while Darcy studied his countenance. There was an expression of genuine kindness in his eyes, blue and gentle; an air of unflinching determination about his mouth, and in spite of his gossiping manner, a quiet dignity in his *tout ensemble*, that impressed the youth strongly when the old gentleman handed him the card.

"Read it, please."

Darcy read: "Mrs. Camp, No. 96 Camden street. Mr. Gaston, the bearer, has a lady in his charge, whose protector was killed on the railroad this evening. Please give her a room and such attention as she may need, until she finds her relatives in New York, and oblige yours, T. S."

"My name is on the other side," said the old gentleman. "Mrs. Camp is the wife of my bookkeeper. He told me he would like to let a vacant room to some respectable lady, with board. It will be comfortable and safe and respectable. Don't make up your mind in a hurry! This is the sensible and right thing to do. And now go back to the young lady. I am going to smoke another cigar!"

Darcy turned the printed side of the card to the light as he walked down the aisle. The inscription was, "Timothy Skillet, Gold and Stocks, No. 55 Wall street, New York."

CHAPTER XII.

MOVING.

A LONG straight street, with flaring gas-lights on either side. A fog brooding over the city, which seemed preternaturally quiet. On the left-hand corner nearest him, Darcy noticed an old church with stone steps and an iron railing enclosing them. He walked over to examine it more closely, and by the dim light read the inscription on a square stone set in the brick wall. It was only the name of the sexton, "Patrick McGinn," and his place of abode. Darcy wondered at the strange quiet of the street, and suddenly remembered that it was past midnight. He had no definite purpose except to get to bed and rest. The charge of the girl, which he had so promptly assumed on the train, oppressed his mind, and he was revolving a dozen schemes, in all of which she played an important part. He had not asked her if she had any money, and had paid sundry small sums for her, merely remarking, in answer to some faint expostulation, that they "would settle hereafter." The condition of the girl was desolate enough, swallowed up in the great city, with no friend but himself, and he poor and a stranger. But while he reflected, there grew up within him a resolute purpose to find employment and make money. "Once engaged in some occupation," he thought, "the result is certain. The faithful discharge of duty will bring the proper reward."

He had not written to Tige. He would do that before he slept. Only a few lines to tell of his arrival. Nothing about the accident on the way, and the detention, and the charge. What would Tige do if he knew Helen Ruthven was in New York, looking for kindred, of whom they had never heard? By-the-bye, it was strange that Darcy had never met her, until he encountered her on the train. He remembered that he had called at Dr. Graves's house some months ago, with a message from Nell, but she was out. She had been out on two other occasions, when he called at her mother's house. Suppose he had met her four or five years ago, when they were both comparatively prosperous? Pshaw! They were mere children four or five years ago. Very likely they would have fought over each other's toys.

What is that at the other corner? Something moving in the misty street. With the prompt decision that was characteristic of the youth, he crossed the street, and found a bundle of old clothes crawling on the sidewalk. He could not see the crutch, but heard the dull thump on the pavement, as the creature shuffled along. As he drew back to give the cripple passage, he passed into the gaslight, and Darcy noticed the old blue overcoat and cape, and the military cap, before the newcomer disappeared down a side street. A soldier, wounded in the cruel war, no doubt. Perhaps he was needy, too. A dollar from an old enemy would get him food and lodging. He would follow and accost him.

As he turned down the street—it was on the corner where the old church stood—a man pushed open the iron gate and confronted him, with arm extended, as if to bar his progress, and Darcy thought his attitude was half menacing. The only remnant of his military equipment was the six-shooter on his hip, hidden by his coat. Darcy put his hand under the skirt, and with his thumb on the hammer, drew near the stranger.

"Good morning," said the unknown, courteously.

"Good morning, sir," responded Darcy.

"Will you excuse me if I detain you a moment? You are Mr. Gaston, I think?"

"Yes, sir," replied Darcy, trying to recall the voice.

"Ah! this is a fortunate meeting. I hope your charge has not been troublesome."

"I do not understand you," stammered Darcy, feeling certain that he did understand.

"Indeed!" responded the stranger, pushing his hat back. "Well, I think you were kind enough to take charge of—um!—um! —a young lady on the train, you know."

"Yes, I remember," said Darcy, feeling for the trigger of his pistol. There was an air of conscious strength and a mocking intonation in the voice of his interlocutor that irritated the youth. He suddenly resolved that he would not relinquish the charge, at least not just yet.

"I cannot thank you sufficiently," continued the stranger, smoothing his black moustache, with gloved hand, "but I can at least relieve you. I left rather suddenly."

"How did you escape?" said Darcy. "I thought you were certainly killed! That terrible fall!"

"Ah, yes!" said the other, quietly; "it was rather an adventure. But men like me are hard to kill. I came in by the next train. Where is she?"

Darcy heard the thump of the crutch as the cripple came round the corner and approached them. He did not appear to notice them, but halted by, passing between them. When he reached the lower end of the church railing, he turned and limped back. The stranger watched the lame man intently. The dull thud of the crutch on the hard pavement sounded louder, by reason of the quiet that prevailed. As the cripple came slowly and painfully towards them, Darcy drew back to the church rail, cocking his pistol silently. He had taken it from his pocket a moment before, feeling that a crisis was approaching.

"The girl!" said the stranger, imperatively. "The girl! Where is she, I say?"

"I cannot tell you," answered the youth, firmly. "Take care what you do. I am armed."

The lame man shook out his defective leg, then stood upright and raised his crutch. Darcy felt a hand seize his wrist, and his weapon was twitched from his grasp. At the same moment he heard a prolonged shriek, as he recognized Helen standing by his side, with his pistol in her hand. He awoke.

The train was moving, and the shriek came from the engine.

He gazed confusedly around him. The passengers were all talking at once, and rejoicing in the prospect of home and fireside. He closed his eyes again, and the brick wall of the old church, with the gray stone inscribed with the sexton's name; the cripple with uplifted crutch, grim and menacing; the tall stranger with black moustache and mocking smile, all came vividly into view. Then he turned cautiously to the girl at his side, and saw that she was watching him intently.

"You have been dreaming," she said.

"Yes," he answered; "I thought you had wrested my weapon from me and were taking sides with—with my enemy!"

"You called my name," she said, "and I saw this in your hand," and she handed his pistol. "What were you dreaming?"

"I thought he came back and demanded you."

"He? Of whom are you speaking?"

"Listen!" said Darcy, in strong excitement; "I will tell you now as coherently as I can. I thought I was in New York, where I have never been. I saw the long street—nay, I see it still when I close my eyes—with rows of gas lamps on either side; an old brick church on the corner; a lame man brandishing his crutch over my head, and—the man who left you to-night, and who fell over the brink of that terrible precipice, standing before me, demanding you—you! Some vague sense of danger to you impelled me to refuse, and his manner grew threatening. Then I drew my pistol, and you suddenly appeared and disarmed me. The feeling that most oppressed me was the conviction that he had the *right* to demand you, and that you recognized the right, and, therefore, aided him and opposed me. Ah! what a horrible nightmare! Perhaps," he continued, after a pause, during which he noticed the pallor spreading over her face—"perhaps I will forget all this vision, amid the busy realities that are probably before me; and, therefore, I tell it to you now, while the scenes and events are apparently so near. I am ashamed to confess how deep an impression it has made upon me. Never before have I had so life-like a dream. I have stood for hours in the midst of battle noises; have heard the roar of artillery, and the continuous snapping of musketry. I have seen men fall near me, shot to death, and have been compelled to stand idly waiting for some bullet to find me; but never before have I suffered torture to compare with the agony of this transient dream!"

She looked at him while he spoke, half in sympathy and half in terror.

"Do you know," he continued, impetuously, "that while the mere legality of this man's claim seemed beyond question, in my dream, there was a burning conviction in my thought that he had obtained the right by fraud! It was that overbearing conviction prompting me to desperate resistance! I felt that I was defying law and its penalties, but I had no thought of yielding. How can it be that such impalpable matter as the stuff that dreams are made of could excite me so desperately?"

"No one can account for dreams," she said; "you have been unusually excited by the events of this day, and—— "

"Pardon me!" he answered, interrupting her. "You are mistaken. There are just two theories. First: the dream is induced by the intercourse of other Intelligences with the human mind. I reject that theory. Second: the dream is the clearer vision of real events or circumstances—clearer, because the testimony of the senses does not hinder the working of the mind. This is far more plausible. Therefore, I conclude thus: My impressions, caught from such brief intercourse as I had with the lost man, came upon my mind freshly, when all surroundings were lost in sleep; and with swift intuition I detected meanings, motives, purposes that I could not have seen in my waking hours. And now, hear one final word: Should any such circumstance occur hereafter as that I have seen in my dream—do not be startled—I tell you once for all that I will remember you are Darcy Ruthven's child, and I will die a thousand deaths before I will see you wronged! We will never discuss this matter again, perhaps. By to-morrow, the impression that is now so distinct, will, perhaps, have faded, never to be recalled, unless some contingency lies in the future to reawaken it. But you will remember what I have said."

She sat silent as the train sped on. There was an air of weariness about her that was entirely different from that produced by physical fatigue. She had reached a conclusion, to wit: that life had for her nothing but sorrow, bereavement, doubt and anxiety. Nothing kept her from blank despair but the heroic faith of a Christian woman, which, in its normal exercise, more excites the wonder and admiration of angels than the noblest deeds of knightly prowess, shown by the stronger sex.

"Ladies and gentlemen," said the conductor, rapidly passing through the car. "We shall be in New York at ten o'clock this blessed morning. Four hours late!"

CHAPTER XIII.

TIGE.

HENRY GASTON, Esq., Attorney at Law, otherwise known as Tige Gaston, had an office in Lexington. He was trustee for half a dozen large estates, and his chief professional revenues were derived from these administrations. He was a lawyer of rare attainments, and once or twice in the year he had very important cases in charge; but he was careless about fees and not greedy of gain, and these yielded more reputation than emolument.

Two days after his visit to Miss Ruthven, armed with arguments and peremptory messages from his wife, he called again. Miss Ruthven had left Lexington. He asked for Dr. Graves, and being ushered into the study, found the reverend gentleman writing his next Sunday's discourse.

"I will only trespass a moment, Doctor," he said, shaking hands; "my business is with Miss Ruthven."

"Ah! she has gone to Cincinnati," replied Dr. Graves.

"Yes, sir; so I inferred. She told me two days ago that Mrs. Crowder had invited her to go there."

"She went the same afternoon. I did not like to part with the child—she is only nineteen, you know—but she seemed so eager to go. I thought change of scene and new occupations might divert her mind and make her less sensible of her recent bereavements, so I had no heart to resist her. Your brother called an hour after her departure."

"I sent him," said Tige.

"Another gentleman—I forget his name—from New York, also called," continued Dr. Graves; "he came again in the evening. He asked a number of questions about your brother, too. He had met him in the hall, he said, and was struck by his appearance. He is a handsome youth, by the bye, Mr. Gaston."

"Darcy, you mean?" replied Tige, absently. "Yes, sir. He is like Father in his young days, I am told. What did the New York man want?"

"Miss Ruthven. Some legal business. He took memoranda of the deaths of her parents, getting dates and circumstances. In fact, he got a formal statement from me, and brought a notary to take my statement down. The sum of the matter was to show that Helen was the sole representative of her father's family."

"Ah! indeed," said Tige, getting interested; "did he get her present address?"

"Oh! yes. Mr. Thomas Crowder, 10 River street, Cincinnati. He went there to-day."

"And I will go to-morrow," said Tige, rising. "There may be some Kentucky laws in the way, which this New York gentleman will not understand."

But Tige did not go the next day. A poor client had an important "case in court," and Mr. Gaston could not leave it. When this was brought to a triumphant conclusion, Mrs. Gaston was ailing, and Tige could not leave her. Then his own case came on —"Gaston *versus* Philips"—and this consumed some weeks. Then Darcy suddenly determined to seek his fortune in New York, and Tige went with him as far as Cincinnati, and so got the opportunity to seek Miss Ruthven.

At No. 10 River street he found Mrs. Crowder. Likewise, Mr. Thomas Crowder, who does not occupy a very important place in this history, and whose chief occupation was pork packing. Likewise, Miss Jane Crowder, aged sixteen, who was deeply pious, like her mother. After the usual exchange of greetings and such a settlement of the weather as would have been invaluable to Old Probabilities, Mr. Gaston asked for Miss Ruthven.

"Ah!" said Mrs. Crowder, with a sniff of pious resignation, "I am sorry to say Miss Ruthven has left us."

"Without notice, and giving no address," added Mr. Crowder.

"And without her last quarter's wages," said Miss Jane.

"The quarter is not out yet, my dear," observed Mrs. Crowder, "but I should not have refused payment for so much as she earned. She left yesterday, and I suppose she has gone back to Lexington. It is a very serious inconvenience to me, as the children are quite backward in their studies, and were getting along nicely."

"Perhaps she will return," suggested Mr. Gaston.

"Oh, no!" replied Mrs. Crowder, decidedly; "she told me she was dissatisfied, and desired to make a change. To be candid with you, Mr. Gaston, I must say, her conduct has not entirely pleased me, of late."

"Her conduct?" said Tige.

"Yes. You must know," she continued, with a gush of confidence, "a gentleman from New York—a Mr. Grey—has been visiting here, and the poor girl was evidently infatuated. He is quite handsome, and immensely rich."

"Did he pay any special attention to Helen?" said Tige, beginning to get angry.

"Oh, no!" replied Miss Jane. "He talked to her sometimes, of course. But she always managed to get near him and waylay him in coming from church, and walk home with him. And he talked to her in French a great deal, to improve her accent, he said. It was very kind of him, too. Only night before last they jabbered French here a full hour, and yesterday she told Mamma she was going."

Tige kept his temper down. He had a "case," and was about to put these witnesses under cross-examination.

"Why did you not expostulate with the girl, Mrs. Crowder?" he said; "you have experience and age on your side, and might have prevented——"

"Mamma expostulated enough, Mr. Gaston!" said Miss Jane, viciously; "she told her she would not have any such conduct in her house. You ought to have seen Miss Helen! she answered Mamma as if she owned Cincinnati!"

"Hush, Jane!" interposed her mother.

"Well she did, Mamma!" answered the young lady; "she as good as called you a Yankee! and she said she could get better wages for working on the sewing machine than you paid!"

"Do hush, child," said Mrs. Crowder, impatiently; "Miss Ruthven was your governess. You should not speak of her as a sewing-girl. And she behaved herself with perfect propriety until she became infatuated. Mr. Grey is deeply grieved, too!"

"Have you seen Mr. Grey since Helen's departure?" asked Gaston.

"Oh yes! he was here an hour after she left us. Jane told him she had gone."

"And where is he now?" said Tige.

"Gone to Chicago. He is a great friend of Professor Hang——"

"Professor Hang?" said Tige, aghast.

"Yes. You certainly know him. He has published a delightful book. There it is on the centre table. It is called Lies for To-morrow. You may take it and look over it."

"I don't think I will have time to read it to-day," said Gaston, rejecting the offered volume. "Can you describe Mr. Grey to me? I should like to know him, if—if I should happen to meet him."

"Jane, get your album. He gave his photograph to Jane several weeks ago. Ah, here it is. *Very* handsome, I think."

Tige examined the picture carefully. Black eyes, bold and

rather insolent. Black moustache, the ends waxed and sticking out like two little spikes. Rather large nose, slightly aquiline. The nether lip projecting, giving a pouting expression to the countenance. Still, there was an air of conscious strength about the face. Bad face, altogether, Tige thought.

"This picture is capitally taken," he observed at last; "was it done here, Miss Jane?"

"Oh, yes—Brixby, in Main street."

"Brixby? How long have you known Mr. Grey, Mrs. Crowder?"

"About three months, or less. We met him at church. He is quite serious, though not a professor. He seemed very anxious to converse on religious topics, especially with me. And he has spent his evenings here, generally. He has enjoyed Professor Hang's book immensely! I mean the Lies."

"Well," said Tige, putting his glove on; "if I address Mr. Grey in care of Professor Hang——by the bye, what does he profess?"

"Professor Hang? Oh, he is a minister," said Mrs. Crowder.

"Yes, ma'am, I understand. But does he profess anything besides the 'Lies for To-morrow?'."

"Of course!" replied Mrs. Crowder. "I suppose he was Professor in some Seminary. You really must read the book. Must you go? I heard you had lost the Philips suit."

"Yes, I'm thankful to say, I did. It was Darcy's case, not mine."

"I always hoped Darcy would turn his attention to the ministry," observed Mrs. Crowder, as Tige moved to the door; "he was so naturally pious when he was a child! But I suppose he will go into law?"

"Not he," answered Mr. Gaston. "Darcy has decided to try commercial life. He is on his way to New York now."

"And snow a foot deep!" said Mr. Crowder, "there will be some terrible accident in to-morrow's paper. "Did he go by the lower route?"

"Yes," answered Tige, startled; "why do you ask?"

"Ah! that road was cut up so often by both armies! It is in a dreadful condition——"

"But he was going by the North Penn., I remember," said Mr. Gaston. "I cannot tell where he changed—Pittsburg, probably."

"Ah, that is worse! Track good enough, but a bad line for snow-drifts. Well, a day or two will tell. Good morning!"

"This is a nice business," said Tige, as he strode down towards Main street. "What will that boy do if anything happens to his train! Confound old Crowder! He never speaks except to say something disagreeable—Hillo! here is Brixby's sign. I'll look at his pictures."

Mr. Brixby was idle that morning. Tige was hard to please in styles. He was going to take his carte home, as a present for Nell. So he turned over the great mass of pictures in Mr. Brixby's case. At last he selected one.

"Do you sell these?" he asked.

"Not usually. You can have that one, though, if you like. Stay! there is a companion picture—a young lady. Where the deuce is it? Oh! here it is. I took 'em together. Want both? a dollar. Will you be taken now? Walk in. I'll be ready in five minutes."

Tige placed the two cards in his pocket-book, and then sat in moody silence while Mr. Brixby "took him." Pictures would be ready in the afternoon. Would send them to the hotel—at five punctually. Very fine picture. He sat like a statue. Five dollars. Thanks!

Nell looked through the package of photographs a day or two afterwards, when Tige was not with her. A good fire was blazing on the hearth, and Mrs. Gaston placed the package in the warmest part of it.

CHAPTER XIV.

A Letter.

"New York, 15th December, 186–.

"My Dear Brother and Sister: One whole day gone since I arrived, and now it is near midnight. But I am wide awake, and have so many things to tell, that I cannot postpone my present pleasant duty. I have wished for you a hundred times, brother, since we parted. You have erred in teaching me to rely upon you so entirely. Don't you remember Looney, your Celtic client, who said his father had 'trated him with mistaken kindness when he kicked him out o' doors one fine mornin', and compelled him to depind upon his own resources.' I have thought of him several times in the past three days. And you too, sister, have done your 'level best,' as they say here, to spoil me. Positively, I am at a loss to decide, at times, what to eat, when I am in the midst of edibles.

"But while I am seated up here in my little room, with a bright gas burner over the table, and all the house quiet, I am momently getting nearer to you, dear friends, dear brother, dear sister. And it seems to me that we three are more closely bound together than any other three on the face of the earth. Sister Nell, if you will write me word that you are not anxious about me, but are satisfied and hopeful, I will promise to send you a camel's hair shawl about a year hence.

"Because I am in business. What do you think of that, brother Tige?

"It all came about thus: On the second night out, that is, last night, we were detained by snow-drifts. A passenger, Mr. Skillet, invited me to join him, and thus 'form a committee' to wait upon the conductor. I went, more from curiosity than any other motive, and the result of our conference with the conductor was to get a messenger sent back to Scrabbletown for assistance. Just before he left, a gentleman came forward and said he would go also, and he requested me to inform a lady, then asleep, why he had left her, and to promise his speedy return. He did not return, brother. The brakesman came back in two hours, with a horrid story of a bald precipice, a slippery path, and the sudden disappearance of his companion over the brink.

"I had to communicate this dismal intelligence to the lady, who was coming here in search of kindred, I believe. Mr. Skillet, who was very kind, aided me greatly, and he and I took her to a quiet boarding-house, where she now is. In a few days we shall learn something more definite about her relations. At present she is not able to get the luggage, as the lost man had the checks in his pocket, and she had only a small satchel with her. I suppose when the trunks are delivered (Mr. Skillet is looking after them), there will be some address found, and my little adventure will end with the discovery of her kindred. She calls herself Miss Harding.

"Mr. Skillet is in communication with the railway authorities, and will have some positive information from the scene of the accident to-morrow. The telegraph wires were down to-day, but we are assured that all will be repaired to-morrow.

"Sister Nell, you have always said I was superstitious. I have been dreaming about that lost man, and now that I am broad awake, cannot see what my dream portends. The man was my enemy. And there is upon my mind a constant conviction that I shall encounter him or his ghost hereafter, and try conclusions with him—or it.

"How can I tell you coherently about this man? When he spoke to me the other night, I recoiled from him. He was a stranger to me, of course, yet I felt sure that I had met him somewhere. I remember in that short conflict, hand to hand, before I was taken prisoner, that I noticed the expression in the faces of the men who were chopping at me with their sabres, and at first I thought I had encountered him there. But I was mistaken: They were all avowed enemies. But he, with his treacherous, smooth face; his black, bold eyes; his sleek, black moustache, waxed at the ends *a la Napoleon III*, nicely fitting kid gloves, and a *tout ensemble* indicative of cold-blooded badness, is totally different from the men I met in the heat of battle. Moreover, against these I harbour no thought of enmity, while towards this man I feel positive dislike that would ripen into deadly hostility if he were alive.

"For he is certainly dead. He fell five hundred feet, and encountered a dozen deaths before he reached the base of the cliff. The conductor told me there was not a spot on the line of his road where so fatal a precipice as this could be found. It is an old quarry, consisting of a succession of narrow ledges, beginning at the river bank, and running across the face of the hill about half way up. I expect to identify, or try to identify, his shattered body to-morrow or the next day.

"Mr. Skillet is from the Hub of the Universe. My knowledge of geography has been gathered from books that are no longer trustworthy. I have had a vague idea that this city was slightly larger and richer than any other American city, but this is a mistake. Boston is larger every way. You cannot lose yourself readily in New York, but in Boston you can get hopelessly lost, by turning any corner you please. Mr. Skillet tells me a New Yorker laid a wager that he could find his way unassisted from the old State House to his hotel, the Tremont, I believe. Well, he started, turning his back upon the State House, and after walking two days and nights, turning no corners, he found himself, on the third day, facing the State House again. It is a great city.

Seriously, if you make allowance for this harmless vanity, Mr. Skillet is one of the best men I have ever met. He affects a certain roughness of manner, but he is kind and considerate. He recommended the boarding-house to Miss Harding, and when we arrived this morning (or rather yesterday morning, as I just heard twelve sounded from a neighbouring steeple)—he took us in his carriage, which was waiting at the ferry, drove up to Camden street where Mrs. Camp lives, and where Miss Harding is; thence to Delmonico's, where we had breakfast, and while we were discussing that meal, he engaged me at a salary of eight hundred dollars, and you will please address me as indicated by the card I enclose.

"You will desire to know, Brother Tige, what my duties are, and I will recount my conversation with Mr. Skillet.

"I'd like to know what business you have in N'Yauk?" he began, over his second cup of coffee.

"My business, sir, is to look for business," I answered.

"Um! Ah!" he said. "What do you know?"

"Latin and Greek and mathematics."

"Very fine things!" said Mr. Skillet, coolly. "But there ain't no shop as I knows on, in N'Yauk, where they are specialties; do you know how to keep books, for instance?"

"Yes, sir; that is, I know the general principles of the science."

"And what will you do while you are learnin' how to apply your principles?"

"Any sort of work I can get. I intend to look for work, while my money lasts, every day. I thought I would go into all the offices in a certain street and ask for employment——"

"Got any references?" said Mr. Skillet.

"No—yes; I can refer to Judge Hammond."

"Does he live in N'Yauk?"

"No, sir, in Lexington."

"Wa-al, people ain't got time to write to Lexington for references, and if they had, they don't know Judge Hammond from a side of sole leather!"

"I never thought of references," said I, dismayed.

"I s'pose not! Young men from Kentucky mostly don't think of references; but they *du* think N'Yauk was built for them, and they have only to offer themselves on Broadway or Wall street to make all the merchants and bankers cut one another's throats to git the first chance at them!"

"You don't encourage me much, sir," said I.

"I s'pose not! That ain't in my line. I have a boy in my office who gets three dollars a week; he knows where the post-office is —where every bank in the city is—where all my customers are. He can't do any Latin or Greek or mathematics, but he can carry a straight message and bring back a straight answer. Have another chop?"

"Thank you, no," I said, pushing my plate back. "I am glad I had my breakfast before we began this business talk, as my appetite would not have been so vigourous otherwise."

Mr. Skillet laughed uproariously. He seemed to think my discomfiture the best joke of the season.

"Sorter took the starch outen you?" he said at last. "Wa-al, it won't do you any harm. And now I'll offer an amendment. S'pose you come into my office—say for a month—and see what you can do?"

"But I have no references," said I.

"Oh wa-al, we'll write for 'em later. I'll give you—let me see! —say eight hundred dollars a year."

"I am very grateful, Mr. Skillet," I answered; "I will serve you as well as I can, and I don't want any salary until I learn to be useful—find out the location of banks and offices——"

"All right, Mr. Gaston; I'll git the amount of your salary out of you, never fear."

"What will my duties be, sir?" I asked, doubtfully.

"To du things—I can't tell till the occasion arises. Eight o'clock in the mornin'; quit at five. Camp will put you through a course of sprouts, I guess! When 'll you begin?"

"Immediately, if you will allow me."

"All right! That's the grit!" He took out his pocket-book, selected a card, and wrote on the back:

"Mr. Camp. Set Mr. Gaston to work. Get more margin from Spriggins.   Yours,   T. S."

"There!" he said. "Go in and win! You can't swear to a man until you've summer'd him and winter'd him, but I guess you'll du. Don't be skeart. Talk like thunder to people, and say nauthin' all the time. Keep your mouth shet, as a general rule, but when you *must* talk, don't let the other fellow find out anything you know. If I don't have to raise you to fifteen hundred a year hence, I'm mistaken in you, that's all! And now go 'bout your business, please! Tell Camp to send my letters to the heouse!"

"That is all, Brother Tige. I have been working all day, and have become acquainted with multitudes of 'ropes' about the office. Chiefly, my work will consist of examinations of accounts, and I have learned numberless technicalities already. Mr. Camp is splendid! But I will reserve him for my next letter, only saying, that he was kind as possible, and when I asked his advice about getting lodgings, he offered me this comfortable little hall bedroom in his house, charging me three dollars a week. I get my meals at restaurants, and feel wonderfully elated at my success. Thankful also, dear sister Nell!

Your loving brother,   DARCY."

CHAPTER XV.

AT WORK.

ON the day following Helen's arrival in New York, Mr. Skillet called at No. 96 Camden street, and asked for Miss Harding. When she came into the little parlour she saw a well dressed, middle aged gentleman, with blue eyes full of kindness, and an expression of straightforward honesty that was reassuring. On his part, he saw a tall, slender girl, in a plain black dress, rather pretty, and if her sad, grey eyes could be lighted up with smiles, he thought she would "make any young fellow's heart bounce." But instead of smiles she wore a careworn expression, modified by an air of resignation, or rather unmurmuring submission, that had grown habitual through dismal experiences.

"Fine morning—cold!" said Mr. Skillet, when Helen was seated.

"Yes, sir."

"Have you been out to-day?"

"No, sir."

"Ah! wa-al. You hadn't ought to set about the heouse. You might walk down two blocks, and git in the cars. It'll do you good."

"I don't know the city," said Helen.

"Wa-al, you'll never learn while you set in the heouse. I've been to the depot."

"Yes, sir."

"There's nauthin' there. No baggage. They want checks. I s'pose we can make 'em show their hands, by law. Could you tell me the color of the trunk?"

"I could not, sir."

"There is nauthin' from the road, neither," continued Mr. Skillet. "No body found, nor nauthin'. The superintendent says there never will be any body found!"

Helen was silent. Mr. Skillet looked puzzled.

"You see, Miss Harding," he observed, after a little pause, "I hardly know how to talk to you on this subject. I've forgot what relation you said he was."

"I did not say anything about it, sir," replied Helen.

"Exactly!" said Mr. Skillet, not the least disconcerted; "the *Herald* has a pooty fair account of the accident, and says the gentleman was named Mr. Rupert Grey."

"Mr. Rupert Grey," repeated Helen.

"Ya-as. It says he was connected with some good family in N'Yank, but had no family of his own."

"Yes, sir."

"It seems to me," continued Mr. Skillet, "that you take the matter considerable cool. I was down to Alexandria a while back, and I seed a young woman there, who had travelled from Maine just to git a body. It was her husband, she said, and she was about as cool as you, and when I seed her, she was a quarrelling with the railroad men about the freight on her body."

"Yes, sir."

"She wan't quite sure of the body, she said, kind o' confidential like, to me, as it hadn't any head; but she took it. He didn't fall over a bank, neither, but had got killed in a battle. He was a kind o' third leftenant, or suthin'. Anyway, she got a Gov'ment pass for her body, and took it to Maine. I've thought since, she was considerable cool."

"Mr. Skillet," said Helen, "I don't want Mr. Grey's body, if he is really killed——"

"Killed!" said Mr. Skillet.

"Yes. I am not sure he was killed. But, dead or alive, I hope and pray that I may never see him again! I cannot tell you any more, because I do not know that he is dead. If his body is found and identified, I will tell you all my reasons. You have been so kind to me——"

"It's no consequence," said Mr. Skillet, starting up. "I see that s'uthin's wrong. Sorry I asked you. What do you propose?"

"Propose?"

"Ya-as. What do you intend to do?"

"Oh! I want to earn my living. I want to find work. I can teach; I can sew. Can't I get work in this great city?"

"Work—teach—sew? They do sewing by machinery now."

"Yes, sir. Can I find work of that kind?"

"Certainly. I know a place now. Do you understand all about machines?"

"Yes, sir."

"Wa-al! I'll go with you when you are ready. There is a man on Broadway who makes hoop skirts by hullsale. He has forty girls sewing in the top lofts, and they make as much clatter as a iron mill. Should you like to try him?"

"Oh! Mr. Skillet, if you will only get me such work as that, I would never forget your kindness. I am ready to go when you please."

"Git your hat," said Mr. Skillet.

"Mr. Skillet," said Helen, as they walked down Broadway, "I have brought my pocket-book with me; I have a little money, and I wish to pay Mr. Gaston some little expenses. Please take my pocket-book and settle the account."

"It's all right," answered Mr. Skillet, "I'll fix it with Gaston. It's no consequence. Young gentlemen always pay these little matters."

"But it is not all right," persisted Helen, pressing the book into his reluctant hand; "I am very uncomfortable about it. I don't know why I did not pay at the time."

"Wa-al, that's the true grit. Take back your money. I'll pay him, and you shall pay me—to-morrow. Did you know Mr. Gaston—out yonder," and he pointed westward, vaguely. "I mean, had you seen him before you met on the cars?"

"No, sir; I never saw him until he sat down by me that night."

"Oh, wa-al. I thought mebbe you could tell me suthin' about his people."

"They are all free now, sir."

"Free?"

"Yes, sir. He had a great many before the war."

"You mean his slaves! I was talkin' about his kin."

"Oh! they are the best people in Kentucky."

"Indeed! I thought you said you did not know him."

"I had never met him, sir. I know his brother, and his brother's wife. All the Gastons are good."

"Including Dassy?" said Mr. Skillet.

"Darcy. Darcy Ruthven Gaston. He was named for the best and noblest man that ever lived!" and the tears, so long repressed, gushed from her eyes.

"Dear me!" said Mr. Skillet, thoroughly miserable, "I've gone and put my clumsy foot into it agin! Never mind. It's no consequence. Here we are! Now we have seventy-two steps to climb. Take your time."

Mr. Tilter was in his office—five floors above the street. He was a little, bald headed man in spectacles. He wrote with a quill pen, and carried it in his mouth constantly, when he was not writing.

"Mornin'!" said Mr. Skillet, panting. "Them steps will be the death o' me, Tilter. This young lady wants a job; she knows all about them clatterin' machines. Great Cæsar! how they do clatter!"

"Much obliged, Mr. Skillet," answered Mr. Tilter, with the impediment in his speech. "We can find the work. Wages? Eight dollars a week. Eight to six. One hour to dinner. Satisfactory?"

Helen bowed her head.

"All right then; call this half a day. Mr. Donis!"

Mr. Donis appeared. He was a young man, with flaxen hair and moustache, gorgeously attired.

"Mr. Donis," continued Mr. Tilter, pointing to Helen, "a new hand. Understands the Singers. Show her in. Begins now. Call this half a day. Eight dollars."

"Yessir," said Mr. Donis. "This way, please."

Helen shook hands with Mr. Skillet, and followed the stunning youth.

"Tilter, you old miser!" said Mr. Skillet, when they were alone, "eight dollars is not enough."

"Regular wages, Mr. Skillet! Let's see what the young woman can do first. If she gets along well, we'll give her a rise."

"Ten hours a day, you old reprobate!" said Mr. Skillet.

"Only nine. One hour to dinner, you know."

"Wa'al! its no consequence. That's a slick lookin' fellow you've got for a boss."

"Donis? Yes. Pooty smart. Takes watching though. I think he likes to crook his elbow too much."

While Mr. Skillet retraced the seventy-two steps, Mr. Donis led Helen into the work room. One hundred feet by twenty-five; excepting the little office at the head of the stairs. The roar of twenty sewing machines, drowning out all other sounds. Twenty girls bending over the machines. Two others over a silent machine, with some complicated appliances. Mr. Donis motioned Helen to join these two.

"Can you see the difficulty?" roared Mr. Donis in Helen's ear.

She took the chair vacated by one of the girls, and tried the tension, rearranged some minor parts of the machinery, and then taking up the muslin, passed it rapidly through, sewing perfectly.

"Ah!" said Mr. Donis. "It's the new fangled feller! All right, you'll do!"

Helen worked away without reply, and he nudged her elbow.

"I say!" he continued, "if you can manage the fellers, you are all right you know! he! he!"

Helen looked at him in mute amazement, while he twisted his watch-key, smiling graciously.

"You had better keep this machine," he resumed; "number eleven. If you can teach one or two of these other girls—Here, Jane! This young lady—beg pardon! I did not catch your name to put in the books you know."

"Harding," said Helen, coldly.

"First name, please?"

"Mary; but I am called Miss Harding, usually.

"Oh! all right. Jane, Miss Harding will show you how to manage the fellers. He! he! When you are *aw fay*, you can take another machine;" and he swaggered grandly out of the workroom.

"Dang'd pooty gal!" he muttered, "but shy as a kitten in a strange garret! Must git her sociable. She'll come out all right."

At the same moment, Mr. Skillet, striding up Broadway, was meditating about Mr. Donis. And his thoughts ran thus:

"That simperin' young jackass will put his foot into it before the week is eout! He'll say s'uthin' sassy to the gal—and she'll put a mansard onto him quicker 'an litenin'!"

CHAPTER XVI.

NINA.

MR. SKILLET turned out of Broadway and walked briskly up Fifth avenue. Arrived at a corner house, brown stone front, he rang the bell, and, inquiring for Miss Norman, was admitted. Miss Norman would be down immediately. Would Mr. Skillet take a seat in the drawing-room? While he waited, he tried to remember what the sallow child he had known slightly several years ago looked like. And when Nina appeared at last, he found that she had entirely grown out of his memory. He must begin the acquaintance anew.

She was a slight girl, with brown hair and eyes, a healthy complexion, and an air of resolution in face and manner that modified the fragile suggestion of her slender form. Her black dress and quiet manner were set in opposition to the determined expression of a woman with a set purpose, and Mr. Skillet found himself involuntarily preparing to combat resolutions that might prove unwise or impracticable. He had been frequently consulted by Nina's grandmother, in matters relating to money investments, and the girl remembered that the old lady had always spoken of him as thoroughly honest and thoroughly sharp-witted.

"I am very much obliged to you, Mr. Skillet," said Nina, seating herself by his side, "for answering my invitation——"

"Ya-as!" said Mr. Skillet. "I was eont in Chicago, and only got back yesterday. I found your note last night."

"I knew grandmother always consulted you, and I was anxious to get your advice and help, perhaps—in the settlement of the estate."

"Oh! Ah! Ya-as!" said Mr. Skillet. "But you will have to git a lawyer to fix property things."

"No; I don't want any lawyer in this matter," answered Nina, "there is no will, and the property will be divided between my sister and me. I want certain pieces of property, which I will describe to you, and I very much desire to have them apportioned to me in the settlement."

"Oh, wa-al! There's no difficulty about that. You just git the hull property appraised, and then you can take turn about in choosin'."

"I thought," said Nina, after a momentary hesitation, "that

it would be more equitable to put up the separate properties at a kind of auction, and let us two bid; you know, I might fancy a certain piece of land that my sister would choose, if we had equal opportunities. But if the auction method is adopted, she who will pay the most can take it."

"Ezackly!" said Mr. Skillet. "I see. I see. Now, do you happen to know all the property?"

"No, sir; I only know there is one large parcel that I must have."

"*Must* have?"

"Yes," said Nina; "it is very probable that Mary or Mr. Bragdon would also prefer that special property. I am quite willing to pay, out of my portion of the estate, something more than they will be willing to pay."

Mr. Skillet mused. Was the girl going to speculate in corner lots?

"S'pose you make a list of the property—you mean the real estate, of course—and let me investigate a little?"

"Well, sir, when will you have the list?"

"To-morrow. I will send my clerk to see you."

"Let him ask for me, please; what is his name?"

"Dassy," said Mr. Skillet.

"Dassy? Very well. I will see Mr. Dassy to-morrow—say at eleven o'clock."

"Not Dassy neither!" said Mr. Skillet. "What a blunderin' old cuss I am, to be sure! Dassy is his given name—Mr. Gaston, I had ought to have said."

"Gaston. I will remember."

"You had better tell him jest what you want; he is true as steel, and close mouthed, and smart as a trap. I haven't summered him and wintered him yet, but I guess he'll do. I picked him up on the train t'other night. Oh! wa'nt Grey a relation of yourn?"

"Yes!" said Nina, startled. "What of him? Tell me instantly!"

"Oh, it's no consequence!" said Mr. Skillet, alarmed by Nina's vehement manner. "Dassy knows; you can put him through tomorrow. There was some story about his gittin' hurted—somewhere out West; don't know the particulars, for certain—Dassy can tell you. Bless my heart! Twelve o'clock! Gold room closes at three. Good mornin'! I'll send Dassy—eleven, prompt."

"Mr. Skillet!" said Nina, catching his arm as he rose. "You must tell me about Mr. Grey; did you see him out West?"

"No."

"Did Mr. Gaston see him?"

"Oh, ya-as; certainly."

"Can't you tell me anything about him; where he is, or what he is doing?"

"Them's the very p'ints I'm not posted on," answered Mr. Skillet. "I'd give a new hundred dollar greenback this minnit if I could git that information. It's no consequence! Better see what you can git out of Dassy—good mornin'."

While Mr. Skillet jolted down the avenue, in the omnibus, he arranged his plans.

"I must caution the boy to keep his eyes skun, and his jaws shet," thought he. "Bless my heart! The gal is sharp as litenin'! Now, it's a fair tussle between 'em, and I've a mind to let the young whelp tackle her without any warnin'—no harm to find out what he thinks, though. Seems to me that Mr. Grey was pooty much of a devil!"

Mr. Darcy Gaston was at his desk, immersed in debits and credits, and interest calculations, and charges for commission on purchases and sales. It was a long account of "gold operations," in which a highly respectable and substantial firm on Broadway had been "gambolling," as Mr. Skillet expressed it, for six months. This firm had suddenly discovered that it was not profitable, and Darcy was preparing the account for settlement. It was excellent discipline for him, but abominably perplexing. Mr. Camp, head bookkeeper, was at another desk, furtively writing poetry. It was the one amiable weakness, the solitary foil that served to set off the brightness of Mr. Camp's character. It is only just to add, that Mr. Camp always tore up the poetry into small fragments, and scattered it to the waste-basket. In most cases there were only three lines and a half, as Mr. Camp had a chronic impediment in rhyme or rhythm, which always forbade the completion of the fourth. In accordance with the invariable law of incongruities, under whose inexorable sway poets generally live, Mr. Camp was always unhappy in his selection of subjects, and more unhappy in his treatment of the subjects when selected. At present he had plagiarized the opening sentence, "Hail, gentle Spring," and had added from the recesses of his own imagination, "whose balmy breath." The stumbling block that corrugated his brow, was his inability to think of any other rhyming word than "death," which was objectionable, as he intended his poem to be cheerful, and suggestive of sweet repose in some rural paradise, which he usually kept in his mind's eye.

Your city man who deals in figures from morn to dewy eve always *does* have a rural paradise in his mind's eye. If he can get holiday at midsummer, for ten days or less, he seeks some leafy covert, and is always discomfited to find gnats and flies there before him. It is always hot in the shade too, and one cannot get ice water in the country. The roads are always dusty, except when it rains, and then they are quagmires. There are pigs and cows in the country, and they have no "realizing sense" of the importance of city people. So when the holiday is over, the city man heaves a sigh of relief, and flies back to counter or counting-room. There are arrears of work to get up. There are odours that differ from those of the country. So he dreams eleven months and two-thirds of some other rural paradise, where there shall be no cows or pigs, and next summer he disenchants himself again.

"Mr. Camp," said Darcy, looking up from his work, "when will you want this account?"

"Any time to-day will do," replied the bookkeeper, gently; "do you find a hitch anywhere? Ask me without hesitation whenever you are stumped."

"Thank you," said Darcy, "it is only this horrid interest."

"Dear me," said Mr. Camp, looking over Darcy's shoulder; "you have not been calculating all that interest, surely?"

"Certainly."

"Why, my dear sir, here are the tables. Any sum at five, six and seven per cent. for any length of time. Nobody dreams of calculating interest at this day. It's all done by machinery. You have only to find the sum, then the days, and here you have it to a fraction.

"Hail, gentle Spring, whose balmy breath—

"That is—never mind."

"No use to be hailing gentle spring," muttered Darcy, "with the thermometer at zero. Here comes Mr. Skillet."

Mr. Camp tore up gentle spring, and dived into a big ledger. Mr. Skillet passed into the back office, and divesting himself of hat and overcoat, called out:

"Gaston! Won't you come in here, please?"

"Got a nice job for you," he said, rubbing his hands together. "You must go up Fifth Av'noo to-morrow. Eleven A. M. Miss Norman. Stop! I'll write the address. There! I told her you would call at eleven to-morrow. How much does Miss Harding owe you? She offered me her pocket-book, and I said I'd settle with you. She's got a situation."

"A situation?" said Darcy, aghast.

"Ya-as. She's dyin' for work. Means to earn her livin', she says. I found her a place in a sowin' shop. Eight dollars a week. 'Taint much, but she is mighty glad to git it. Look here! You must be shady about that Grey man. S'uthin' wrong about him. It's no consequence. But I mean to find out what in thunder it is!"

"Grey man? something wrong? I don't understand, Mr. Skillet."

"No, I s'pose not. I don't understand myself. But she flew at me when I said he hadn't been found. You saw the *Herald* to-day?"

"No, sir."

"Oh! Wa-al, nobody has found any corpse or anything. He slid over the bluff, or else that brakesman was lyin', and there had ought to be some bones or s'uthin' found below. But there is nauthin."

"You are speaking of the man who was lost on the railway," said Darcy; "does the paper tell of any search for him?"

"Certainly. Here is the *Herald*. Better read it for yourself. But about Miss Norman. She wants to do s'uthin' about property—more law than finance. She hadn't ought to bother me with it. What the dickens have we to do with law?"

"I am a law student, Mr. Skillet. Perhaps I know enough to do what you require. What is the point?"

"Ah! there's the rub! I don't know exactly. She wants to secure certain parts of an undivided estate. So! You know law, do you? Wa-al, it's no consequence. I guess she has a lawyer already. Jest you go up there, and see what it is. You had better be shady there, too. What do you think of that sliding down hill? I mean out on the railroad. Read the *Herald*. Fifth page—second column."

Darcy rapidly ran through the article. It was a tolerably accurate account of the accident, and concluded with the announcement that Mr. Rupert Grey was connected with some of "our first families."

"Mr. Rupert Grey," said Darcy, as he laid the paper aside. "I'll remember."

"Remember what?" said Mr. Skillet, curiously.

"Remember to avoid the mention of his name," answered Darcy, slowly. "That is what you said."

"He was a nice man," said Mr. Skillet, "connected with first families. A great loss if he is dead, hey?"

"I don't know, sir," replied Darcy, bewildered; "if he is dead, let him rest. But the constant thought in my mind is, that he is alive, watchful, and devilish."

CHAPTER XVII.

The Meeting of the Worthies.

WHEN Dutchy alighted from the train, he stood a few minutes, watching the lights on the rear platform, that looked like two red eyes glaring at him, and threatening vengeance for his last crime. If the man had been of finer sensibilities, he would have felt the influence of the dismal portent. But he was not troubled with childish superstitions.

"Cuss his hide!" he said, savagely, "I did not knock him half hard enough. Wish I had him out here! How it snows! About two miles from Scrabbletown. I'll walk back to the shanty. It's a mile, cuss him!"

As he plowed his way through the accumulating snow, Dutchy meditated. Man's inhumanity to man, was the thing that made this angel mourn. The fierce assault of the lieutenant, with no provocation on his part, hurt his feelings. He endeavoured to account for it, upon some rational grounds, in vain. Zeal for the public service did not enter into Dutchy's estimates of motives. There was no sufficient cause for the officer's harsh manner. Dutchy had been insubordinate in camp, and had exhausted the penalty. So that account was balanced.

"It was pure cussedness!" he thought; "he had no call to rear on me. S'pose I did desert? it didn't cost him nothing. And here I was earnin' my livin' honest and square, and he had to turn up and blow! cuss him!"

The shanty was a rude structure near the track, built of rough boards, to shelter the workmen who had been repairing the bridge spanning a ravine near by. There was a little stove here, and plenty of fuel. Dutchy collected some splinters and soon had a glowing fire. While he smoked, squatted down before the stove, he concocted various schemes for the future.

"Must git out of this; nothin' to do but git up and git. He will come stompin' down the road to-morrow, with a file o' men on the hunt o' me. He's got a blessed sore head, I'm thinkin' too, but that will only make him madder. Can't go to Scrabbletown, not much! Can't go anywheres on this line. Must cut across country. Will start by daylight."

He stretched himself out on the floor, when his pipe was finished, and fell asleep. He dreamed the lieutenant was coming after him by rail, followed by a brigade of soldiers, and he heard the roar of the train as it approached. Then, wakened by the noise, he pushed the door ajar, and, sure enough, a train was passing the shanty, going East. He watched it passing down the line, and saw it stop, less than a mile below the shanty. Looking for him, doubtless! His fire had gone out, and he dared not rekindle it. Nothing to do at present but watch the train.

How long he watched he could not tell, but after a time he saw a light moving towards him. Some one coming back from the train. Ah! they knew the shanty was there, and were coming for him! As he pushed the door open he was surprised to see the depth of the snow. It had increased a foot since he fell asleep. But there was a snow shovel on the engine and the track was comparatively free. Leaving the shelter he darted upon the track and raced away, looking back once and again at the red light, which gradually fell behind. They were not gaining on him.

Half a mile from the shanty the ground fell away, and Dutchy remembered that the track passed over high ground, a little further on. He turned off, plunging through the deep snow, and at last stopped, panting, under the shelter of the cliff, far below the iron road. Here was present safety.

He was greatly demoralized. The snow swept by him in gusts, sometimes being caught up from the ground near him, and sometimes coming down the face of the rock in fine powder. In exposed places the earth was bare for a few short minutes, and then, as the wind came roaring round the crag, bearing great clouds of flakes, a miniature drift would pile up, growing into a little mountain, to be levelled and blown away by the next blast. Just below his shelter, the river ran by, tossing ice islands upon its bosom, or wrecking them on the rough bank. Watching the current, and wishing for an ice-floe large enough to bear his weight, Dutchy suddenly remembered that he had noticed a boat hauled up on the shore near the shanty. If he could get that boat and push off, he might manage to float or paddle across to the other side. It was a *terra incognita* to him, but it would be out of the line of the present pursuit.

But that lieutenant would scour the whole country! He was passably mad before Dutchy struck him, and he had always been vindictive and morose. Guard-house and log babies would be nothing in comparison with the new torments the officer would invent if he caught him. And if he got away at last, there would still remain the "civil" process. Would he never know peace again? Cops and sogers! Would the world never get rid of these pests?

Perhaps he was threatened with that stevedore Nemesis! Suppose the soldiers had tracked him from the old camp, through Pennsylvania into New York and finally to the pier where he had made his latest "financial arrangement?" Suppose, by some fiendish ingenuity, the two forces, civil and military, should be brought to bear against him at once? He might escape the former by crossing State lines. But the army regarded no lines, and Dutchy was filled with the common conviction among soldiers, that officers were above all law and absolute in authority.

"The cussed little whelp could hang me up, and no questions axed!" he murmured, "and if he wanted law, he could git that stevedore to swear my life away! I wish there wasn't no law, no leftenants, no stevedores! Hollo! what's that!"

The red lantern swinging to and fro, as the man who carried it crunched over the snow. Another man with him. Both up on the hill top on the railway level. They are moving slowly and cautiously; must lie close up against the rock, lest they should look over and see the blot his body made on the white snow.

Looking for him? of course. What else would stop the train out there. No station within a dozen miles.

He crawled along cautiously, hidden by the rock, but in a lull of the wind he heard their voices distinctly, and holding his breath, he listened.

"The snow blinds me," said one, "and your lantern makes it worse. I can scarcely tell whether I am on the track or no."

"Keep a sharp lookout, sir;" replied the other, this is a narrow cut. Once apast High bend, we can see the train. They'll wait for us, he! he!"

"Where is High bend?" said the first speaker.

"Right here. Rock runs straight down to the river. Fine view in summer time. Keep close, sir! Track runs close to the edge."

They were overhead now. Dutchy crouched down in the snow at the very base of the cliff.

"I believe I see the river, and—ah! Help!"

The snow had piled itself in great drifts against the face of the rock, resting on ledges that traversed the surface in horizontal lines, from the river bank to the summit. The masses of snow overhung the narrow pathway where Dutchy crouched, and with the cry came the rustling sound of the avalanche, as it slipped from ledge to ledge; then a ton weight of snow, rushing over and around him, striking him down, and burying him in an instant. If he had not been resting upon a drift, two or three feet deep, which gave way as he fell, he would have been killed outright. Then came a solid mass, crushing through the snow that covered him, and flattening him out with the weight and shock. And while he debated in his mind the question as to whether he were killed or no, this solid mass seemed to rear up, and Dutchy shouted out in terror. Then a pair of gloved hands came out of the mass, grappling him by the shoulder and throat, and Dutchy rolled over, dragging the new comer out of the debris with him. The soft hands still clutched him with the tenacity of death.

"Lem'me go!" murmured Dutchy, half strangled. "Lem'me go, cuss you! I surrender! Got nary knife, nary pistol. Who would guess that a cussed cop would come for a feller over the rock!"

The stranger released the terrified rascal, and stood apart, coolly surveying him.

"Air you goin' back to the train?" said Dutchy.

"We will consider the point," replied the other; "what have you been up to?"

"Guess you know well enough," said Dutchy; "what do you want me for?"

"Ah! one never knows! Here! brush the snow from my coat. Are you cold?"

"Freezin'!"

"Well, take a drop of this. Stop, I'll take a taste myself first.

Excuse me!" and he put the flask to his mouth and indulged in a long swallow. "There! you may have the rest; plenty left to warm you."

"You ain't nary cop!" said Dutchy, as he returned the empty flask. "Cops don't give away that sort o' stuff—you're a cappen!"

"Well?"

"And the leftenant sot you on, cuss him!"

The stranger meditated. He was shaken and bruised by his tumble, and had escaped instant death only because the snow drifts had broken his fall from ledge to ledge; and because he had fallen upon Dutchy at the bottom. The last words of Dutchy recalled some story he had heard at Scrabbletown, of a dead officer whose body then lay in a side room in the station. It would do no harm to connect Dutchy with his death, tentatively.

"The lientenant will not bother you any more," he said; "he is lying cold and quiet at Scrabbletown."

"What killed him?" said Dutchy, huskily.

"You mean *who* killed him. Well, nobody knows. What is your opinion?"

"I don't know nothin' about it. What did he say?"

"He did not indulge in any conversation after the—accident. Come! I am not a cop; I am not an officer. I shall not interfere with you. How did you do it—and why?"

"I don't know nothin' about it," repeated Dutchy. "What air you goin' to do? We can't stand here shiverin' all night."

"I am a stranger in this part of the country," replied the other, after a short pause; "we need shelter and warmth at present. Where can we go?"

"Is anybody lookin' for me, or anybody, on the train?"

"No."

"Well, there's a shanty half a mile off with a stove in it; I work on this road. I can make a fire, and we can get thawed."

"And afterwards?"

"I dunno!" replied Dutchy, irresolutely.

"Let us go to the shanty first," said Mr. Grey; "I have a plan half formed. I will develope it as we smoke. Come on! I feel pretty stiff after that slide! It seems to me that I fell on your carcase?"

"Mashed the life out'en me!" growled Dutchy. "What did you choke me for, after mashin' me fust?"

"I did not know that I had reached bottom," said Grey, apologetically. "Excuse me! I only caught at the first thing my hands touched. It was quite providential that you were reposing just there! Only think of it! A foot distant on either side, and you would not now be enjoying this conversation! Nor I, either."

"Well! you're a cool one, you air!" said Dutchy.

"Quite cool; indeed, rather too cool for comfort. How far off is that infernal shanty?"

"Jist round the bend. Don't you want to catch your train agin?"

"I believe not. We'll think about it. I have a scheme; wait until we get fire. Any sleeping accommodations at your shanty?"

"A fust rate floor!" said Dutchy, with a grin. "Never mind! There's plenty o' blocks around. We can set up awhile. I've got my pipe."

"Pipe!" answered Grey, disdainfully. "Partagas, my friend! If you have never indulged in that weed, prepare yourself for a surprise! Ah! this is the shanty, is it? Accommodations somewhat limited. Walk in!"

CHAPTER XVIII.

DARCY'S FIRST VISIT.

NINA NORMAN knew Mr. Skillet's punctuality, and when Darcy sent his card in she was waiting in the drawing room. Darcy was a thoroughbred, and his demeanour was perfection. This was the first thought that shot through Nina's mind when he bowed and took the seat she indicated. He waited a few minutes for her to begin the conversation, and as she maintained silence, he was forced to take the initiative.

"I am instructed by Mr. Skillet to receive your commands, Madam," he began.

"Yes, sir. Mr. Skillet said he would send a gentleman this morning. Did he tell you the nature of the business?"

"He told me nothing, except——" and Darcy paused, remembering Mr. Skillet's exact words.

"Except," said Nina.

"Except some cautionary suggestion, that was purely personal." Nina looked surprised, and a slight color appeared on her cheeks and forehead. "Mr. Skillet perplexes me sometimes," continued Darcy, "as I am not yet familiar with his idioms. But the sum of his caution, as I understood him, was, that I should be discreet——"

"Have you any objection strong enough to prevent your telling me his exact language?" said Nina; "because I understand him perfectly well."

"He said," replied Darcy, slowly, "that I was coming to see a lady of no ordinary sharpness—pardon me, but I am giving his own words—and therefore it would be advisable to—to——"

"I am all attention, sir," said Nina, mercilessly.

"Keep my eyes open and my mouth shet!" blurted out Darcy, "which I am doing with a vengeance! Really, Miss Norman, you have forced me to say exactly the wrong thing!"

Nina laughed. Darcy had unconsciously imitated Mr. Skillet's voice and manner, and had extorted the first laugh from Nina since her grandmother's death.

"There is no need for extraordinary caution, Mr. ——," and she glanced at the card which lay on the table, "Mr. Gaston. Darcy Ruthven Gaston! Is it possible that this is your name?"

"Yes, Madam," answered Darcy, astonished at her excitement.

"Darcy Ruthven!" she continued; "surely this is an uncommon name. Are you a native of this State?"

"I am from Kentucky," replied Darcy, with a certain intonation, which meant, being translated into English, "I do not take on any airs on that account, however."

"Kentucky!" echoed Nina, "and your kindred are named Ruthven?"

"No, Madam. Colonel Ruthven was my father's law partner and friend, and I am named for him."

"And not related?"

"Not related," and Darcy suddenly remembered Mr. Skillet's caution. Perhaps this very topic was one that he should avoid.

"And can you tell me anything about the Ruthvens?" said Nina.

"Very little. I saw Colonel Ruthven only once since my boyhood, and then—I had no conversation with him."

"Where was it?" said Nina, imperatively.

"In Kentucky, Madam."

"Yes. So I suppose. What part of Kentucky? if you please."

"Near the Tennessee line. I am not sure of the county."

"What was he doing when you saw him? Excuse me, but I have particular reasons for all my questions. Do not answer any that are improper."

"He was riding at the head of his regiment, and about to attack a redoubt. I have not seen him since."

"Were you in the same regiment?" persisted Nina.

"No. I was in the cavalry. I was taken prisoner half an hour later, and though we won that fight, I was carried away in the retreat."

Miss Norman had always cherished the conviction that rebels were children of the devil. She was accustomed to think of them as truculent savages in red flannel shirts, long knives in their belts, and bearded like the pard. There was in her mind a mingled sentiment of horror and wonder when she reflected upon the desperate stand they had maintained through four years of warfare. And she looked at the smooth face of the youth before her with an astonishment that she did not attempt to conceal.

"May I ask how it happens that you are free now?" she said after a short silence. "Excuse me, if I should not ask; but I have never seen a rebel before, and you do not look like my conception of them."

Darcy laughed. Something like the reality of her conceptions dawned upon his mind.

"I was sick, Madam," he answered, "and the doctor said I would die in the prison. My brother obtained my release, upon my promise to take up arms against the Government no more. I was only eighteen, and when he bade me take the pledge, I was forced to obey."

"Your brother?"

"Yes. He is the head of my house, the representative of my Father, and I could not disobey him. He is loyal, as you call it."

"And yet you entered the army with his consent?"

"Oh, no! I ran away from college. He did not know I was in the army until I wrote to him from prison. Pardon me! But you cannot be interested in such matters, and I am neglecting my duties. How can I serve you, Madam?"

"One more word, please," said Nina; "what have you done since your release?"

"Studied law."

Nina arose, and with a word of apology, left the room. She returned in a few minutes, accompanied by Miss Abby Keith.

"My friend, Miss Keith, Mr. Gaston," she said. "Take a seat, Miss Abby. I have brought you down to introduce you to an actual rebel. Mr. Gaston has been in arms against the Government!"

Miss Abby looked at the young stranger, her countenance expressive of pious horror.

"Do not look aghast, Miss Keith," said Darcy; "I was only a short time a soldier, and did not kill anybody, though several fellows tried to kill me."

"I suppose," said Miss Abby, "that rebellion is a pardonable sin. But there should be a very hearty repentance first."

"Well, I have not had time to do much repenting," answered Darcy, stoutly. "But I have promised to rebel no more, and I will keep my word."

"Rebellion," said Miss Abby, quoting Dragger feloniously, "is a sin that is akin to witchcraft. Such is the testimony of Scripture. But the *gravamen* of the offence consists less in its defiance of Divine authority than in its contradiction of the civilization of the nineteenth century. In this age, when humanity is emerging from the tyranny of creeds and confessions, and when the mental and moral development of the race is so rapidly progressing, a warfare that is avowedly waged for the perpetuation of a barbarous institution, is a high crime against humanity. No excuse can palliate the turpitude of the crime. The age demands obedience to its sentiment. The crowning virtue of the age is Love; and any organization, any institution, any code of morality, any antiquity of custom that may be athwart the path of Love, must perish beneath her chariot wheels. Her divine mission is to elevate, to ennoble, to enfold in her comprehensive embrace all the families of earth. And as age follows age, through the long annals of time, she has gradually but steadily enlarged the borders of her wide dominion. Not much longer will she tolerate the existence of those who resist her gentle sway. The time is near when the cultivated scholar, surrounded by all the appliances of modern civilization, will spontaneously seek the companionship of the bushman, because the cardinal principle of this heaven-born affection is the essential equality of the race. It levels all distinctions. And as we find the tokens of high sentiment in the domestic animals around us, it may be that the approaching Golden Age will dawn upon this sphere, when man ceases to recoil from his nearest link in the great chain of development, and with cheerful composure takes the gorilla to his bosom."

"I had never thought of all that," answered Darcy, stunned.

"No," said Miss Abby; "moral questions of that nature are not often discussed in your latitude. Have you ever heard Mr. Squizzem's lecture on the cultivation of the species?"

"No, I never heard of Mr. Squizzem."

"Never heard of Mr. Squizzem? Nina, my dear, he never heard of Mr. Squizzem. Mr. Gaston, you can scarcely be abreast of the age if you don't know Mr. Squizzem. It is conceded, I believe, in all civilized countries, that Squizzem is the foremost thinker of this century. Stay! Here is Mrs. Bragdon's album! She has his photograph, of course. Ah! yes. Look at that countenance, Mr. Gaston, and tell me what you think."

Darcy studied the picture, with the direct purpose of estimating the character of the original. A beardless face, surmounted by a profusion of wavy hair, brushed backward, intellectually. A prominent nose, something like that part of the sun-dial that casts the shadow, and over all a thick layer of egregious conceit and self-assertion.

"Well?" said Miss Abby.

"He looks like he wrote verses," replied Darcy, doubtfully; "that is, he looks like he *thinks* he can."

"Would you not take him for the foremost man of his generation?" said Miss Abby.

"I cannot say that I would. But I am sure he takes himself in that way; so it's no consequence, as Mr. Skillet says."

"I don't know whether you are serious or not, Mr. Gaston," said Miss Abby; "but you are the first gentleman I have met who did not think Mr. Squizzem has a striking countenance."

"I think it is quite striking, Miss Keith. And I am sure he is either an intellectual giant, or else"——

"Or else what?"

"Or else very much mistaken."

Miss Abby closed the album with a snap, and Nina once more indulged in a good healthy laugh.

"I will only say a word more, Mr. Gaston," observed Miss Abby. "Laying aside all prejudice, please tell me your estimate of the African mind."

"African mind! Do you mean the American negro?"

"Yes."

"I am hardly competent to judge," said Darcy, musingly. "My life has been spent among these people, servants mostly, born in my father's house. Under tutelage and restraint, I think they make the best peasantry on the face of the earth. But while they have quick intuitions, I think they have none of the logical power that belongs to the white race. I have never known one that could apprehend the syllogism."

"And this mental condition is the result of generations of bondage," said Miss Abby.

"Hardly," replied Darcy. "So far as known, the African in his native land is no wiser than his descendants here. I foresee that he is about to enter a new sphere, and I have none other than kindly feelings for him, but I have not much hope for him."

Miss Abby was about to answer, when the door opened, and admitted the original of the photograph. He shook hands impressively with the ladies, and was presented in due form to Darcy.

"Mr. Gaston, Mr. Squizzem!"

CHAPTER XIX.

The Foremost Man of the Age.

"OH, Mr. Squizzem!" said Miss Keith, rapturously, "I am so glad you have come! Mr. Gaston has just asserted that the African mind is incapable of the apprehension of the syllogism!"

"Indeed!" said Mr. Squizzem, loftily; "we must introduce Mr. Gaston to Frederick Douglass."

"Who is Frederick Douglass?" said Darcy.

"Do you *really* not know?" asked Mr. Squizzem, surveying Darcy incredulously; "well, Mr. Douglass is one of the foremost men of this age! With most acute perceptions of truth, and with few opportunities for culture, he has attained the front rank among the master-minds of this century. I look forward to the time, in the near future, when he will occupy the Presidential chair! and I should be proud to be his Foreign Secretary."

"There are so many foremost men," observed Darcy, "that I fear the standard is not very high. How large is the master-mind, for example?"

Mr. Squizzem rested his elbow on the mantle and struck an attitude. He expanded his manly bosom. He straightened out his elongated legs and brought his right boot handsomely to the front. This young man must be exterminated.

"Perhaps you have never heard my lecture on the 'Euclid of Mortality?'" he began.

"No. I have but recently arrived. That pleasure is in store for me. The title is very striking."

"In that lecture," continued Mr. Squizzem, "I have endeavoured to demonstrate, with mathematical accuracy, the falsity of the general idea of property. Ownership in anything that interferes with the voluntary methods by which the human race finds happiness, is so near akin to robbery, that the differential points are too infinitesimal for scrutiny."

"Pardon me!" said Darcy, "am I to understand that lands, houses, moneys, inherited by legitimate children, are included in this sweeping postulate?"

"Around the world, yes!" answered Squizzem, in thunder tones.

"I don't mean around the world. I mean here, in New York."

"And I mean," retorted Mr. Squizzem, severely, "that the last development of human wisdom is in the formation of a league that ignores all property titles. The commune is the hope of the world. In all the down-trodden governments of Europe this bright spirit of liberty is cabined, cribbed, confined. And on these shores, the hospitable retreat for the oppressed of every clime, the true principles of liberty are destined to find their legitimate outgrowth. The beneficent genius of the age has stricken the shackles from the free limbs of manhood, and now invites the rapt attention of the universe to the apotheosis of Freedom! In this free land, the former slave to creeds and customs will find the true scope of his normal powers, in possessing himself of all the good within reach of his hand, without the irksome restraints of law. Do you not see there could be no thefts if there were no property? All through the long epochs of the dismal past, the smothered wail of humanity teaches the same lesson. The noble spirits, that have been the very off-scouring of society, tabooed or banished, or held back by gyves and prison gratings, to prevent their violation of some absurd feudal monstrosity called law, are now calling to us from their dishonored graves to take up the battle gage!"

"There must be truth in what you say," said Darcy, as the

orator paused for breath; "I have noticed that officials, in various places throughout the land, are literally fulfilling your words, and taking whatever their hands can reach. Pray go on, sir. I am deeply interested."

The orator glanced at his watch. It was not profitable to deliver his lecture gratis, and he did not like Darcy's prompt agreement with his gushing doctrines.

"Some other time," he said; "at present I am hurried. I called to see Mary. Is she at home?"

Nina touched the bell, and when the servant appeared, asked for Mrs. Bragdon. She was in the library. Would Mr. Squizzem please walk in there? Mr. Squizzem walked in, and Miss Abby followed. The lofty utterances of Squizzem were too precious to be lost.

"What do you think of Mr. Squizzem?" asked Nina, when she and Darcy were once more alone.

"I have not known him long enough to judge him," replied Darcy, cautiously. "He is a very ready speaker."

"You are remarkably conservative, Mr. Gaston!" said Nina. "What do you know about Mr. Grey?"

"Mr. Grey?"

"Yes."

"I saw in the paper yesterday, that some Mr. Grey had disappeared——"

"You were on the train with him, Mr. Skillet told me."

"Was I? Well, if it was Mr. Grey who fell from the cliff, I hardly saw him. It was in the night, and we exchanged a few words only. I believe I never saw him before that night."

"You believe?"

"One cannot be certain," replied Darcy. "It seems to me now that his face was familiar. We may have met somewhere. Was he in the army?"

"Oh, no!" said Nina, disdainfully; "men of that sort don't go into the army!"

"I did not mean in *our* army," said Darcy; "I thought he might have been among the two or three hundred men that rode down upon me and over me, down there in Kentucky."

"Oh no!" said Miss Norman.

"Well, then, I cannot account for the impression that we have met somewhere; he certainly knew my name."

"Some one told him, perhaps."

"No; that was not possible. No one on the train knew my name. I never heard his until yesterday."

"Then you can tell me nothing about him?" said Nina.

"If you could trust me enough to tell me what you desire to know, I would gladly serve you. Mr. Skillet sent me here for that purpose, and it is my clear duty. Besides, I would be bound to serve any lady, to the best of my ability, whenever she honoured me by demanding service. Can you not consider me Mr. Skillet for the nonce?"

"I think not," replied Nina, smiling. "But I will do better. I will tell you something that Mr. Skillet does not know; it was I who sent Mr. Grey to the West. It was a special mission, and he was cautioned to keep the object secret. I have had but one letter from him; here it is. Read it, and tell me precisely what you think it means."

Darcy took the letter and read it carefully. It was written on a sheet of note paper in a dainty hand:

"CINCINNATI, *Tuesday.*

"DEAR COUSIN NINA: I have not found that for which you sent me; but I have found the next. The first does not exist; the second I will present to you within a week.   RUPERT."

"Cousin Nina!" said Darcy, returning the letter. "I did not know that Mr. Grey was related to you."

"Yes," replied Miss Norman; "but you do not say what he means."

"How should I know?" said Darcy.

"Have you no theory upon the subject?" persisted Nina. "Listen! I am the seventh child of my father, and he was the seventh child of my grandfather. There is some superstition that gives special insight to the seventh child of a seventh. Have you never heard it? You have! Well, I believe in it so strongly that I never distrust my instincts; and now I have two. The first is, that a man is bent with desperate determination upon the solitary purpose to deceive me; the second is, that you will aid me in my desperate determination to thwart him! And I seem to see that you know the man, and are at this moment hiding from me the extent of your knowledge. I have inherited great wealth, some part of which I hold in trust for—another. I seem to see that this watchful, relentless adversary is intent upon securing for himself that identical property. I am sure you are a gentleman; I am certain you will not deceive me, though you may refuse to enlighten me. But I can never be happy until I dispose of this property, and the first thing for you to do is, to devise a plan whereby I can obtain possession of it; it is part of an estate not yet divided. If I should avow my purpose to part with it, those who have a joint interest in it would take steps to prevent me, no matter why. Now, sir, can you and will you undertake this case?"

"Mr. Skillet," began Darcy, strangely moved by her words and manner—"Mr. Skillet instructs me to render you whatever service you may require. But, surely, this is a matter for lawyers——"

"The only lawyer I know, or desire to know, is Mr. Coke, and he is the legal adviser of my family. I cannot engage him to assume a position that even appears antagonistic to other interests. No; you are lawyer enough for this emergency."

"If I should attempt to meddle," said Darcy, rising and standing before her, "your friends and kindred would say you were misled by an unknown adventurer. How long would you be able to resist the multitude of innuendoes they would launch at you? And when you finally yielded, and dismissed me, your case would be worse for my interference; besides, I am only the clerk of Mr. Skillet——"

"That is precisely the strong point. Let Mr. Skillet be the ostensible adviser and friend, and do you manage all the details. Do not tell Mr. Skillet any of your plans——"

"Madam," said Darcy, interrupting her, "you require impossibilities. I am sent by Mr. Skillet; I am in his service. He pays me for the hour I have spent here. It is not possible to conceal one word from him, if he should question me."

"Suppose 'my friends and kindred' should not be able to make me distrust you," said Nina, "what effect would injurious suggestions, affecting your integrity, have upon you?"

"If a man should openly charge me with fraud," replied Darcy, slowly, "I should be bound to resent the insult——"

"And if a woman?"

"If a woman, I should be equally bound to endure the imputation in silence."

Miss Norman tore off the blank leaf from the letter she still held, and rapidly wrote a few lines upon it with a pencil. Folding the missive, she addressed it to "Mr. Skillet."

"I will not detain you longer now," she said, rising; "please give this to Mr. Skillet Here comes Miss Abby. Good morning, Mr. Gaston!"

CHAPTER XX.

The Gold Room.

"THIS is a nice business, I don't think!" said Mr. Skillet, after reading the note brought by Darcy; "kinder cool and collected like, too! Did you read this note?"

"Certainly not, sir!" said Darcy, insulted.

"Why, it warn't sealed! Did she tell you not to read it?"

"No, sir," replied Darcy, coldly.

"It's cu'rous," observed Mr. Skillet, still perusing the note. "I'd like to know what you said to her and what she said to you."

"I will recount the entire conversation, sir. First, Mr. Squizzem; no, first, Miss Keith was presented——"

"Miss Keith! Schoolmarm! What did Miss Keith say?"

"A great deal, sir. She must have studied the speech. It was about rebellion and love——"

"Ya-as! About love. Go on!"

"I cannot remember the words. She concluded by saying I ought to hug a gorilla."

"Bully for Miss Keith!" ejaculated Mr. Skillet. "She got that from Dragger. I seed it in one of his printed sermons. Great man, Dragger! Pews rent same price as a four-story brown stone front on Fi'th Av'noo! A feller ran off with another feller's wife; t'other feller shot him. Before he died he wanted to be married to t'other feller's wife, and Dragger and Fizzlebacon fixed 'em up. Bully for Dragger! Go on."

"Then, Mr. Squizzem came," continued Darcy, rather stunned by this outflow of contemporaneous history; "and he lectured me on the foremost man of the age. I thought he meant himself, but he said he meant some Mr. Douglass."

"Oh, aye! Fred Douglass! First class barber, I guess. Bright mulatter. Smart, too. Go on, please!"

"Well, sir, Mr. Squizzem left the room, and Miss Keith followed——"

"Of course!" said Mr. Skillet, rudely; "the women all believe in Squizzem. He kisses 'em, bless you, right and left! Pop'lar lecturer. Leonidas Squizzem! They do say he is goin' into the spiritual dodge, now. Go on, please!"

"Then Miss Norman requested me to undertake some partition of property in which she is interested; to form plans, and keep my plans secret, even from you——"

"Stop, please!" said Mr. Skillet, holding up his hand, "you've got to the jumpin' off place, I guess. Now, read this note."

Darcy took the open paper and read:

"Miss Norman presents her compliments to Mr. Skillet, and requests that Mr. Gaston may call on her to-morrow, at the same hour, and also that Mr. Skillet will allow Mr. Gaston to maintain, for the present, *perfect silence* in relation to the business matters under consideration."

"Now," said Mr. Skillet, "do you suppose she means to include me, when she says 'perfect silence,' underscored?"

"Yes, sir; in fact, she said as much."

"And what did you say?"

"I told her I could have no secrets from you; that I was acting as your representative, under salary, and I advised her to employ some competent lawyer instead of me."

"Wa-al! it's no consequence," observed Mr. Skillet, after a pause, during which he had a mental struggle, and achieved a victory; "you will have to humour her, I guess. The case is in a nut shell. The young woman is full of whims, but her grandfather raised me. I was clerk in his office ten years, and then he set me up when he retired. Then her father stood by me when I had no capital to speak of. He gave me lots of business, and brought other customers. Her grandmother always sent for me to consult about investments. It's a risky business, though, and you must keep your eyes skun and your mouth shet, pooty generally. It's a safe rule. You can talk like thunder two hours, if you're smart, without saying anything. Don't write anything. You can do all by talking. And if any writing has to be done, in the way of memorandums, you can jest let her do it herself. And now, please keep your jaw! If I should forget, and ask you any questions, jest remind me that you are on confidence. Two o'clock! Go round to the gold-room, please, and see what you can find out about the market. Here, you must have a pass—'Mr. Gaston, attorney for T. Skillet.' That'll do."

Darcy gained admission to the Gold Exchange, and found himself suddenly in the midst of a room full of maniacs. There was a fountain in the centre of the room, with an iron railing around it. Two or three dozen maniacs were leaning over the rail, with outstretched arms, wildly gesticulating, and shouting out bids and offers. The presiding officer sat in an enclosed desk, reading a newspaper as composedly as though he were reposing in some sylvan solitude. The circle of "operators" was three or four deep, and nine-tenths of them were bawling offers to buy or sell fabulous sums. Enough millions to pay the national debt were offered by seedy looking individuals, who would not sell for ten dollars apiece in any second hand clothing shop. "I'll give a quarter for any part of a million!" shouted one, whose exterior did not indicate the ownership of five cents. "I'll sell any part of a million for three-eighths!" said a madman on the opposite side of the circle, who looked wealthy enough to go into partnership with the other.

Darcy walked around the circle, looking with great curiosity at the faces of the people, so intent upon their traffic that they did not notice him. A bright looking youth standing near him, when he stopped, touched his arm.

"Can't get her up," he observed, in reply to Darcy's inquiring look.

"Get her up?" repeated Darcy.

"Yes! All Bull dodge! Hasn't been a real sale to-day over a naith."

"A naith?"

"Yes. Seventy-four bid; seventy-four and a naith, asked. Jings took twenty at a naith. Had an order. All them bids is bogus."

"How can that be?" said Darcy, beginning to understand. "There is a man bidding a quarter for a million. Listen how eagerly he bawls!"

"Oh, yes. That is Spang's attorney. Hillo! There goes the president's hammer! Let's see what's up?"

The president pounded on the block about five minutes. The room gradually became quiet.

"Gentlemen!" said the president, "Mr. Jings claims a purchase of one hundred thousand at a quarter, of Mr. Spang. Mr. Spang claims the purchase of the same amount from Mr. Jings. All those who saw the transaction will please vote. Those who give the purchase to Mr. Spang will please hold up their hands. Eleven! Those who give the purchase to Mr. Jings will please hold up their hands. Four! Spang has it." And he took up his newspaper and was absorbed in two seconds, while the room resumed its uproar in the same space of time. Darcy's interlocutor nodded triumphantly.

"Told you so," he said.

"I do not understand," replied Darcy.

"Come over here and sit down, and I'll explain. You see, Spang and Jings are both bullin' the metal. They made up that little dispute, just to fix a quotation. Now listen! There's ten voices offering to sell it at a quarter. Only three or four bidding a nalth."

"How does the market look?" said Darcy, remembering that this was the point in which he was interested.

"Down! Be off two points to-morrow. Gov'ment going to tilt ten millions. I'm five hundred thousand short at a quarter."

"And do you feel no apprehensions?" said Darcy. "Suppose it should go up a point or two to-morrow?"

"Ah! well," replied the other, "I should only have to wait a day or two. Sure to come down. Gov'ment bound to sell. Hillo! there is a real sale at three-eighths!"

Darcy walked across the room, and accosted a sober looking old gentleman, who seemed to be watching "the market" very intently.

"Excuse me, sir," he said, "but I am so confused by this uproar, which is entirely new to me, that I can form no judgment as to the tendency of the market! Will you favour me with your opinion?"

"Ah!" said the old gentleman, politely, "you are new at the business?"

"Yes. This is my first visit here."

"And you find it difficult to decide which way to operate?"

"Operate?"

"Yes. You want to speculate, I suppose."

"Not I," answered Darcy, with a shudder. "I should go mad if I were to incur the frightful risks that are so lightly regarded here. That dilapidated gentleman yonder has sold five hundred thousand at a quarter, and now three-eighths is bid. There! It is selling at a half."

"That dilapidated gentleman is worth two millions. He is the coolest operator in the room. Always wins. See! He is selling now at a half."

"Where can he find the gold to deliver to-morrow?" asked Darcy, in wonder. "I have counted more millions sold here this morning than could be found in the whole country."

The old gentleman looked at the youth in surprise.

"Why, my dear sir, none of this gold is delivered. They pay

the difference between the sale and to-morrow's quotation. Or they borrow or lend as the case may be, if they desire to continue the risk. As for the probable course of the market, the old apple woman sitting at the entrance there, knows just as much as the best operator in the room. If you want to win here, always bet against your judgment."

Darcy went back to the office with a very unsatisfactory report. The Government was going to tilt uncounted millions upon the market to-morrow. And while everybody seemed to know the fact, the quotation had increased. It was seventy-four and three quarters when he left. Mr. Skillet received the news with a grin and without comment.

That night the gold-room sat on Darcy's breast, a huge nightmare. The presiding officer pounded him on the head with his mallet, calling him to order, though he was quiet as a mouse. A little red haired man, with eyes that were constantly threatening to pop out of their sockets, was swinging his arms over an iron rail, and roaring in a voice totally out of proportion to his size,

"I'll sell any part of a hundred thousand billions at an aith!"

CHAPTER XXI.

TITLE DEEDS.

ON the succeeding day, Miss Norman gave Darcy sundry documents relating to the Norman estate; consisting of attested copies of title deeds to real estate, and schedules of stocks, bonds and other personal property. With these, she also placed in his hands an envelope, sealed and addressed to Darcy Ruthven Gaston, Esq.

"I will be greatly indebted to you," she said, "if you will make a list of the personal property, affixing to each portion the present value. If you can discover, without direct inquiry, the approximate value of the real estate, I should be glad to know that also, in detail. You cannot question property agents without exciting suspicion, and inducing the very discussion I wish to avoid. Do not open the sealed package, until you finish the other papers. And please return all to me, with any comments or suggestions you may think requisite."

Darcy took the papers, glanced at the titles, and put them in his pocket.

"How long a time will you require?" said Nina.

"I cannot say until I examine the papers;" replied he.

"I am going to Europe on the 22d; two weeks from to-day. In the mean time, I very earnestly desire to—to obtain exclusive possession of my portion of the estate. It is by no means indispensable, however, and if you find any reason for delay, do not hesitate to inform me."

"I will do my best, madam," replied Darcy. "I understand you to say that I must tell no one what these papers may reveal?"

"No one," said Nina, promptly.

"Mr. Skillet kindly consents to that arrangement," said Darcy. "I will begin to-night, in my own room. It is possible that I can give you the needed information within the time you mention. I may go now?"

"I should tell you," said Nina, as he took up his hat, "that the names in the sealed paper are all fictitious. That is, the initials do not indicate the real persons."

"They will reveal nothing to me, certainly," answered Darcy, smiling, "as I am a stranger to all parties. May I ask if your stay in Europe will be prolonged?"

"I don't know," she replied; "I only know that I am dying to get away from New York. Away! Anywhere!"

Darcy looked with surprise at her flushed countenance.

"I beg your pardon!" he said; "good morning, madam."

She held out her hand to him, amused at his penitent look.

"You were surprised at my vehemence. Nothing in your question induced it. You are very courtly, or—very kind. I am sure you would not pain me intentionally. Good morning. Please come one week from to-day."

"If I were impressible," thought Darcy, as he walked down the avenue, "I could fancy myself ready to fall in love with this impulsive young lady. What a soft little hand she has! I wonder if it is the New York fashion to shake hands with a lady the second time one meets her? She put out her hand to me, certainly. Now, I cannot write a word of this business to brother Tige, either, as I am 'on confidence.' What can be in this sealed envelope? This day week I am to go back, she says. That means I am not to go sooner. Perhaps it also means that I must not presume upon my business acquaintance. Don't be alarmed, my lady!

"Fall in love, indeed! Not I. Too many title deeds and too large a schedule of personals. Too decided in her opinions. Too resolute and self confident. Strong minded, I suspect. A friend of that Squizzem, probably, with his nose in the air. He is the kind of fellow we used to call a 'sucker,' at college. What an unlimited ass he is, to be sure!

"The girl interests me greatly! She has some scheme in her mind that she does not reveal. Once or twice she has halted in the midst of a sentence; and she has been tortured by some devil of a man. Aha! I see it. That Grey fellow.

"No! She never cared a straw for him. But he may have cared for her. She is not the sort of woman a man would go mad about; but if she liked a fellow at all she would like him tremendously! and if she knew a fellow was a sucker she would be apt to tell him so. Evidently, that is her estimate of Grey.

"She has not pitched into me once about rebellion and all that sort of stuff. I am totally bewildered whenever I try to make her out. I wish I could ask Tige. How would it do to state a hypothetical case? Won't do! Tige is so sharp he would smoke me out in two minutes.

"I wonder what Mr. Skillet thinks about it. He would naturally resent Miss Norman's cool manner and her request to mind his own business. He is a regular old brick, though. Kind and thoughtful as he can be.

"I intended to have an interview with Miss Ruthven to-night, but I must get at these papers. But I will find out how she likes that sewing place and how they treat her there. The idea of Colonel Ruthven's daughter making her living by sewing! Yet, why not? She looked better satisfied last night—quite composed and dignified. 'She is not going to live on anybody's charity.' That is what her manner said. I'll ask Mr. Skillet if he cannot find a more congenial vocation for her, though. If she could outgrow that mournful expression she would be positively lovely! Somehow, when I look at her I am filled with grief. I mean to have a little talk to-night, anyhow."

But the fates were against him. Miss Harding had a headache, and was not visible. Darcy dined down town, and consequently missed seeing her at dinner. He thought he would ask Mr. Camp, the next day, if he might board as well as lodge at his house, and then he went to his room and unfolded his papers.

The personal property was soon disposed of. He had a list of late quotations, and could easily affix the estimates of value. Then he made a list of the real estate. Numerous stores, some on Broadway, and some in the vicinity of Wall street. A large parcel of unimproved ground, far up town, and a separate parcel of three acres called " Ruthven's Folly."

This was the last deed, and he had reserved it for the last, because it was bulky. He was attracted by the description, which was very elaborate, giving the streets that passed through it, and the numbers of the lots on the city map, and then, quoting from former transfers, gave the courses and distances as of a farm, and finally referred to a still prior deed, in which the name of the tract was given, "Ruthven's Folly." The deed recited the transfer, "being the same land conveyed by Arnold Grey and wife to Norman Ruthven, and recorded, &c."

Here was a discovery! The Normans, and Greys, and Ruthvens, had made these transfers two or three generations ago.

He read the deed all over again. It was a transfer from Norman Ruthven and wife, Helen, to John Norman, and referred to a mortgage debt due by the former, which was cancelled by the transfer. It also referred to a bond of conveyance from Norman to Ruthven, by which provision was made for the re-transfer of "Ruthven's Folly," upon the fulfilment of the bond, the terms of which were not recited; and at the bottom of the deed there was a formal relinquishment of the rights conveyed in the said bond, for the consideration of ten thousand dollars, duly paid, receipt of which was therein acknowledged. This was signed by Helen Ruthven, widow, and Darcy Ruthven, heirs of Norman Ruthven, deceased, and witnessed by Philemon Coke, and then the signature of the Surrogate.

Darcy was devoured with curiosity to see that bond of conveyance and learn its provisions. He knew enough law to infer that these late signatures were added twenty years after the original deed had been made, for the purpose of perfecting a title that was possibly defective without them. While he pondered these matters, he heard Helen's voice in the hall below, and sweeping all the papers into the drawer, he went out and met her on the stairs.

"I am glad to meet you, Miss Harding," he said; "I heard you had headache. I hope it is gone."

"It is better."

"Will you please come down into the parlor; that is, if you are well enough. I want some information, which you can probably give me."

She followed him down stairs, and into the parlor. Mrs. Camp was sewing, and Mr. Camp was seeking a rhyme for "breath" with knitted brows. He had read "Hail, gentle Spring," to his wife forty-eight times, and she, good woman, had listened attentively every time, and smiled approval at each dismal repetition. He was going to offer the "lines" to Fiddler's Monthly, when completed, but they were still in the singular number. That "balmy breath" termination of the initial line had smothered the poem before it was born. Darcy politely addressed a few sentences to Mrs. Camp, and then drew a chair to the opposite window, where Helen was standing.

"Take this seat," he said; "I will not detain you long. The questions I ask are for the purpose of—of unravelling some legal matters. Did Colonel Ruthven ever say anything to you about some New York property in which he was interested?"

Helen started. "Who told you about it?" she asked.

"No one."

"How came you to know of any such property?"

"By accident. Do not ask me. And do not answer any question that I should not ask. I have seen certain papers, but not all that I need. If you do not object to the question ——"

"Father told me once, I don't know how long ago, that he would have inherited some valuable property in New York, but for some fraudulent transaction of which he was the victim. It was at the beginning of the war, and I remember he said he would perhaps have the pleasure of applying the torch to the property wrested from him."

"Did he say his rights were entirely gone?" asked Darcy.

"Yes. And yet he said the present owners were willing to pay him something, if he would accept it."

"And he would not?"

"Oh, no! I think there was an offer made to him by a lawyer. But there were some conditions annexed which he rejected. Will you tell me how you happen to know——"

"I cannot tell you. I am bound to secresy. Hereafter I will tell you all I know, probably, as the injunction will be removed by and by."

"Then I will tell you," said Helen, rising. "You have received these papers from one who is intent upon the attainment of a solitary object?"

Darcy, stricken dumb, looked at her in amazement.

"And that object is to secure possession of property held by kindred, and to secure it either by some legal trick or by the practice of actual deceit."

The blood mounted up to Darcy's temples, as he noted the tokens of hot indignation in her voice and manner. A dozen speeches rushed to his lips, but remembering Nina's charge, he maintained silence.

"And you," continued Helen, in low, distinct tones, scarcely above a whisper, "and you! Darcy Ruthven Gaston! Can it be possible that *you* are aiding in this villainous scheme? Oh! what would your father say if he were alive? What would my father say? What will Henry Gaston say when he hears of your first exploit in this wicked city? Oh! you make me more thoroughly wretched than ever."

And sweeping by him, she passed out, and while he still stood stupefied by her dreadful words, he heard her close the door up stairs with a crash.

CHAPTER XXII.

The Wanderer's Return.

WHEN Dutchy and his *compagnon de voyage* reached the hut on the river bank, they were both pretty well exhausted by their tramp through the deep snow. A fire was soon crackling in the little stove, and the shanty reeking with unaccustomed perfume from the Partagas. Dutchy, squatted in a corner, with his cap pulled down over his eyes, was blinking at the other, wondering whether he had really come down the cliff, or had suddenly risen out of the ground, under the High Bend. In either case he was a mysterious personage. If he had come over the cliff he must be akin to the angelic host, as no mortal could possibly take such a slide and escape death! And if he had risen from beneath, there was some dim apprehension in Dutchy's mind that good people did not inhabit the locality known as "down below."

Seated upon a block, and propped up against the wall of the cabin, Mr. Grey meditated. He did not know exactly what to do with Dutchy. If any special rascality, requiring brute force and bull-dog courage in its performance, were to be done, he knew instinctively that Dutchy would prove an efficient agent. But he was restive under restraint, and possibly not trustworthy. Grey did not indulge in any sentimental dreams about gratitude or disinterested attachment, even if he had any claims upon the uncouth mortal in the corner.

"Not many travellers upon this road, I presume?" said he at last.

"Nary road," answered Dutchy, sententiously, "nary travellers."

"How shall we go to get out of this happy valley?" asked Grey, after another pause.

"Can git on the track, just up yonder," replied Dutchy, jerking his thumb over his shoulder. "Or can git a boat, pole across the river, and git into Pikeville. Railroad bridge over the river; station at Pikeville. 'Commodation trains all stop."

"Pikeville!" said Grey. "Yes, I remember. Suppose we visit Pikeville after resting awhile here? Then we can take the first train in the morning."

"Fust train which way?" said Dutchy, cautiously.

"East, of course! New York! Does anybody want *you* in New York?"

"Shouldn't wonder," responded Dutchy, with a grin.

"Well, then, New York is your safest locality. Nobody will dream of looking for you there, and if they do——"

"Well?"

"Then we could try a little bail, or a little grease. I think I can promise you safety there. I may want you to attend to some business for me. It is getting quite comfortable here! I believe the stove gives light enough to distinguish the pictures! Do you understand these?"

"Keards!" said Dutchy. "I'm in! Euchre or poker! Who'd a thought of playin' keards in this hole! I haven't touched a keard for a spell! What is it? Euchre deck?"

"Yes," answered Grey, laughing; "draw up a block and we'll see what you know. Cut! By-the-by, my friend, suppose you wash your hands a little! You have gotten some smut on your fingers, and will mark the backs of the cards. I forget what you said your name was?"

"Bloke!" answered Dutchy, promptly.

"Ah, Bloke; and where from?"

"Pittsburgh," replied Dutchy, who had never visited that populous city.

"And how came you in New York? First Jack. Your deal."

"Went to New York to get my brother out of a diff'kilty. He was a Gov'ment contractor, and had to give security. I went security and——"

"Spades! I pass. Well? You went security——?"

"And he busted, cuss him! And I had to skedaddle."

Mr. Grey regarded the capitalist with undisguised admiration. The probabilities in the case did not disturb him in the least; but the readiness with which Dutchy conveyed the information charmed him.

"And you have been living in this neighbourhood since?" said he.

"No. Went to Californy; got back last week. Been speculatin' in town lots. What are we bettin' on this game?"

"Five dollars," answered Grey, laying a greenback on the block that served for a table. "My deal."

"Pass!" said Dutchy. "You take it up? Both bowers and ace; that makes four. My deal."

"You have better luck with me than you had with your security business—pass! Ah, you win! Game number one. Here is another five."

At the end of an hour their second cigars were smoked out and Dutchy was twenty-five dollars richer. Mr. Grey put the cards in his pocket and proposed walking. They found the boat, which Dutchy borrowed, by pulling out the staple, leaving the chain and lock upon the bank. There was some ice in the river, but they had little difficulty in reaching the opposite shore. Leaving the boat to drift with the current, they plodded through the snow, and reached Pikeville before the dawn.

"Mr. Bloke," said Grey, as they entered the village, "I have decided upon my course. I fell over that cliff back yonder, and it will be unanimously decided that I am dead. Now, I think of remaining dead for a time. What will be said when they look for my body and fail to find it?"

"Fell in the river and swept away," answered Dutchy. "If you hadn't fell on my back, and broke it, you would have gone into the river at the next bounce!"

"And our foot prints in the snow?" said Grey.

"Foot prints! Look back over the road; the wind is blowing the snow every which way! It will all be smooth in five minutes. When you came down the rock was bare one minute and covered with a drift the next; no foot prints there now."

"And the cabin?"

"Same thing. Fire will be out, and cabin snowed under, just as like as not."

"Well," said Grey, thoughtfully, "we will try that plan. Your name is Bloke—mine is Blake."

"Werry good name, Blake," said Dutchy, gravely; "I know'd a gent of that name in Pittsburgh. Any relation o' yourn?"

"Possibly," said Grey; "we are a numerous family. Here is the station. Hillo! It is open. We can go in and get thawed before train time."

There were two or three officials in the waiting room. Dutchy slunk behind the stove. Mr. Blake accosted them with easy grace.

"Good morning, gentlemen! When will we get a train east?"

"Fifteen minutes. Express went down an hour ago. Road clear, but all trains late. Runnin' wildcat."

"What train will we take?"

"Ten forty accommodation. That is, ten forty last night. Left Scrabbletown twenty minutes ago. Better get your tickets."

Grey invested the necessary amount, tearing the ticket he had bought at the beginning of his journey into small pieces. Observing Mr. Bloke's anxiety to keep hidden, he obligingly moved between him and the light. Nobody seemed to notice them particularly. Bloke recognized all the men as acquaintances when his name was Smelzer. When the belated train arrived he entered the smoking car, followed by Grey, found a vacant seat, and the worthy pair indulged in refreshing sleep, while the train gradually worked eastward. At one of the stopping places ten minutes were allowed for "breakfast." Hot coffee and sandwiches were to be had at the bar counter. Mr. Bloke had a raging tooth, and his face was enveloped in a red handkerchief, but he took enough nutriment to last him the day, while Mr. Blake nibbled a cracker and imbibed a bottle of Scotch ale. Once more gliding along, their train switching off every hour or two, to allow the passage of down trains, waiting sometimes an hour or more, as they were "accommodation," and therefore bound to keep out of the way, but gradually approaching the great city.

"Mr. Bloke," said Grey, "I am going to Brooklyn, when we arrive. That is, after dark. Suppose we get a room apiece, in Jersey City, and try for a little sleep—say, till eight o'clock? Then we can make some changes in our habiliments, and go to Brooklyn by gaslight. What say you?"

"All right, boss!" answered Dutchy; "am I agoin' to Brooklyn with you?"

"Certainly. I cannot tell yet what amusement I can provide for you, but you will have enough to eat, and shelter, and will be out of reach of any Government officials who may be hunting for that security money. I suppose you have no suspicion that *I* am looking for you."

"No," answered Dutchy, slowly; "you aint nary cop, and you aint nary Gov'ment officer. You are up to some game, but I can't guess wot it is. I'm not afeard of you, 'cause you want me for somethin' or other. Don't know wot, and don't care!"

"You are partly right, Mr. Bloke," said Grey, coolly; "I think I can find occupation for you. Meantime, let us have a little gush of confidence. I have reasons for hiding at present, though nobody is looking for me. You have a similar desire, because several persons are looking for you."

Dutchy grinned and nodded.

"Well," continued Grey, "I suppose your searchers are chiefly cops?"

"Werry likely," replied Dutchy.

"Now, nothing can be more simple than to beguile the average cop. You have only to squat down under his nose and you are safe. I will arrange your attire to-morrow in such a fashion as to defy scrutiny. Let me see? Have you had any military experience?"

Dutchy winced. He remembered how he had "shouldered arms" with a log baby. This Mr. Blake might be a cussed leftenant, after all.

"Don't know what you mean," he grunted surlily; "I belonged to a wolunteer company in Pittsburgh, some years back, but I had enough of sogerin'!"

"Have you speculated in bounties, for example?" said the other, with a quiet laugh. "Ah! Mr. Bloke, I am afraid you have defrauded your bleeding country! Never mind, man! she is able to stand a large amount of bleeding, and in the near future the most successful citizens will be those who bleed her most lavishly. You have only anticipated a little. Some geniuses are born too soon."

"Don't know nothin' about it," responded Dutchy. "What kind o' sogerin' do you want?"

"Oh! nothing of importance. A certain familiarity with

soldier phrases, and some slight knowledge of camp life; drill, sentry duty, guard house, and the like."

"I could larn all them," said Dutchy.

"Very well. I will unfold my plan to-night. And now I am going to try for a nap. Waken me when we reach Jersey City."

When these companions crossed the river that night, Mr. Grey wore a second hand white overcoat and a felt hat with a wide brim. His trim, black moustache was concealed under a fiery red one, with side whiskers to match. Dutchy had on a suit of half-worn soldier clothes, with the inevitable blue overcoat and cape. His left arm was gone, and the empty sleeve was pinned gracefully across his breast. His right foot was encased in enormous bandages, and he hobbled along in ungainly fashion, on a crutch. If the bandaged foot happened to touch the ground he groaned dismally.

"Piece o' howitzer shell in the ancle jint," he observed to a sympathizing old gentleman in the cabin; "got it at Gettysburgh."

The old gentleman slipped a ten cent note in his ready hand, sighing over the ingratitude of a country that made no better provision for its martyrs.

They stopped in Brooklyn at a house in a quiet street not very distant from the ferry. Dutchy was able to read the inscription on the door plate while they waited for the response to their ring. It was, "Doctor Lamis, Test Medium. Seances, Wednesdays and Saturdays, at 8 P. M."

CHAPTER XXIII.

WATCHED.

AFTER his brief interview with Helen, Darcy returned to his room feeling very much like the man who was shot out of a coal car into a huge hopper, and who found himself in a heap of the black diamonds at the bottom, after sundry revolutions, and read the inscription over his resting place—"Screened, riddled and broken." He mechanically took out the title deeds again, and set to work anew. Once and again he took up the sealed envelope, but remembering Nina's injunction to reserve it for the last work, and being a true gentleman, he was compelled to lay it aside without investigation. He felt that he had not yet mastered the details in the other papers. The night was clear and cold, and he suddenly resolved to walk out to the locality described as Ruthven's Folly, and examine it by moonlight. The streets were named in the deed, and he could easily get information as to the exact site from policemen.

The cold air revived him, and the blessed elasticity of youth enabled him to throw off the numbness induced by Helen's heavy blows. He was conscious of pure integrity of purpose, but felt his cheek grow hot at the thought of aiding in fraud, however innocently. And the suspicion that he was led into evil by Nina, who seemed so open and ingenuous, stung him to the quick. You cannot put a worse affront upon a youth of generous impulses than beguile him by a woman's agency, especially if she be young and attractive.

"She thinks I will be so impressed by the tokens of wealth around her," he thought, "and by the details in these papers, that I will not dare resist her. So obstinate and wilful! And she has mistaken the natural sympathy enkindled by her sad face and wearied manner for a softer emotion. Perhaps yonder hint of hers, to avoid her for a week, was to warn me against too much presumption! And yet she is willing to exert whatever influence she has gained over me to make me help her in her mysterious scheming! What devil's work can she purpose? What can Helen know about it? How could Helen learn as much as she evidently knows? By George! How lovely she looked when she was belabouring me so cruelly! It would be profitable to get her into a good rage every day and so wear away her melancholy. She looked exactly like her father looked that morning when he plucked out his sabre and rode down upon the enemy! 'Villainous scheme!' she said. And she politely referred me to Tige Gaston. Oh! if I only had Tige Gaston here! But I could not tell him a word, as that she-angel has bound me up as tightly as I would be under oath! I'll go mad if I think any more about it! I'll dismiss the topic and look at the sights in the streets, and tackle it afresh to-morrow night."

He was walking up Broadway, several squares above the Fifth Avenue Hotel, and there were not many unusual sights to attract his attention. He paused at a window to look at some water-colour views, and, while thus engaged, he heard the dismal wail of a hand organ near the picture shop.

A one armed man, turning the crank, grinding out an asthmatic polka. He was clad in a blue military overcoat, rather the worse for wear. One foot was swathed in bandages, and a crutch lay beside him on the pavement. He looked forlorn enough, and Darcy's sympathies were excited. He approached the man and accosted him:

"Cold weather, my friend!" he said. "You look like a soldier. Have you been in the army?"

"Cold enough, sir!" answered the organ-grinder. "Army? I should think I had! One arm gone and t'other pretty nigh worked off turnin' this cussed crank! I fit for the country though!"

"So did I—a little. Where have you left your arm!"

"Gettysburg," answered the other, promptly. "Them rebs guv us fits there! Thankee, sir! This is the first shin-plaster I've got to-day. Most people drop a penny, when they drop anythink. Most of all don't drop nothink!"

"What corps were you in?" asked Darcy, glancing at the man's cap.

"The cavaltry," replied the soldier; "hoss killed by a shell. Was taking the saddle to the rear, when another shell took my arm. Don't remember nothink else, 'cept the horspittle. Laid up four weeks."

"Who commanded your corps?" persisted Darcy.

"Don't remember his name. He was a wolunteer gineral. He got hurted too. Disremember his name; think it was Jones."

"What ails your foot?" said Darcy.

"Minnie ball in it. The doctor rammed and poked about for it half a day; couldn't find it. Anyhow, I was done up, and they sent me on to New York."

A tall, slender man stopped to listen to the last remark. He had keen, almond-shaped black eyes, and a profusion of red beard covering his mouth and chin, and flowing over his breast. There was a jaunty air about him, in spite of his dilapidated appearance, in a white, seedy overcoat and a broad brimmed felt hat. He looked fixedly at Darcy a moment and then addressed the soldier.

"Well, comrade!" he said, "you have selected a cool evening for your promenade! Had any luck to-day?"

"Got about two shillin' in pennies, and this gentleman gave me a dime note. I'm goin' further down town;" and he gathered up his crutch, swung his organ on his back and stumped away, down the street, followed by the last comer. Darcy resumed his brisk walk up Broadway and was soon lost to view.

" Did you notice that man ?" asked the gentleman with the red beard, as he walked slowly by the side of the soldier.

" Yes."

" Would you know him again ?" said the other, eagerly.

"Certainly. Not many men like him. He would be an ugly cuss to tackle in a scuffle. Do *you* know him ?"

" I think I do. He would not be apt to recognize you, if you were fixed up a little. I shall want you to watch him."

" What fur ?" said the lame man, gruffly.

" No matter. To see that he don't take cold. You get along pretty well with your crutch. He will be likely to come back this way. Give me your organ, and keep your eyes open. If he should return, follow him and see where he goes. Thunder ! Why this thing weighs half a ton. I can't carry it."

"Better leave it with me," replied the soldier. "I can get rid of it, not fur off. I'll put it away, and come back here. How long must I wait ?"

" An hour or so," said the other ; " say until ten o'clock. I'll walk a little way after him now. Maybe I can overtake him."

But he underrated Darcy's pedestrian powers. The night was cold, and he walked the more briskly on that account. When the stranger had passed five or six squares, he gave up the chase in disgust. He was wise, as Darcy was moving about five feet to his four.

The number of a cross street was painted on the lamp at the corner, and Darcy found himself in the vicinity of the property he was looking for. The houses were new, and many of them unoccupied, and the street had a generally new appearance. Here and there he saw vacant lots, with masses of rock cropping out of the ground, in sharp contrast with the trim, new houses in the neighborhood. The cross-streets were not curbed, and he was somewhat bewildered, as he was beyond the region of brilliantly lighted shops. But a few questions to a stately policeman gained him the requisite information, and he was able to identify the tract with tolerable accuracy.

The most of it was vacant land, though there were two unfinished houses with brown-stone fronts on one of the corners. The doors and windows were boarded up, and little snow heaps lay on the sills. Darcy stepped the boundaries, and estimated the area, remembering the general descriptions in the deed, and then turned his face towards his lodgings.

"This property is or will be very valuable," he thought, as he approached the more populous part of the city; "and it will not be easy to ascertain the value. I must get acquainted with some real estate broker. When I get to Camden street, I'll go to bed, and quit thinking about things. And to-morrow night I'll take another careful survey of those papers, and perhaps get to the sealed envelope."

Passing the Fifth Avenue Hotel, he thought he would walk through the passages once or twice, and get thawed. The house was warm, and the bar-room was full. He strolled about aimlessly a few minutes, and then pushing the swing door back, he brushed past the red whiskered man in the white overcoat. He was just conscious that he had seen him before, and did not look directly at him, but he thought the other drew back rather more than was needful to give him egress. A minute later he was on the street, and there, standing by the lamp-post, was the lame warrior, leaning on his crutch, but without his organ. As Darcy passed him, he heard the clump of the crutch, following.

"That fellow wants another ten cent note," said the youth to himself, "but won't get it. I must husband my resources, and not duplicate my charities. Besides, I have an uncomfortable suspicion that he was lying about the 'cavaltry.' He is a good walker, if he has a game leg. I have half a mind to put him on his mettle. I will, by George? Let us see what he can do!"

And stretching his long legs to their best stride, he walked straight down Broadway, darting out of the way of passengers who were going in the opposite direction. Fifteen minutes brought him to the Saint Nicholas Hotel, and without pausing, he entered the passage. As he let the door swing back, he distinctly heard the clump of the crutch behind him. He walked through the long passage, into the billiard-room, and getting a seat in a remote corner, watched the door. In two minutes after his arrival, he saw the almond shaped eyes and red beard.

"This is not accident," thought he; "these rascals are following me for some purpose. And now to baffle them."

He walked quietly out, passing the stranger, who was absorbed in a game at a near table, and apparently unconscious of Darcy's existence. He waited at the entrance to the elevator a moment and then entered, and ascended to the third floor. Coming immediately down the side staircase, he gained the parlor floor, and walked gingerly out at the ladies' entrance. The lame soldier was at the main door, watching, and Darcy sped down the street at a great pace. And when he let himself in at Camden street, with his night key, there was no other passenger visible in the quiet street. And the red whiskered man was inquiring at the office desk, if Mr. Gaston, of Lexington, Kentucky, was a guest at the house, and seemed incredulous when answered in the negative.

CHAPTER XXIV.

A New Departure.

DARCY did not regret the absence of fire in his room, as he disrobed and prepared for bed. His race had set the vital current in rapid motion, and he was aglow when he slipped in between the cold sheets.

"Now, then," he thought, "the plot begins to thicken. Let me think the matter over. That whiskered chap knew the soldier. It struck me, when he first accosted him, that they were acquaintances. Then they were together at the Fifth Avenue Hotel; then at the Saint Nicholas. It was a sharp dodge, as Mr. Skillet would say, to go up three floors, and then out at the side door. I have certainly baffled them for the nonce. Now, the question! Who are they? what are they after?

"That one-armed rascal is certainly a stranger; but whenever I think of the black-eyed one, it seems to me that we have met before. I must track back, and see if I can recall him. He was smoking; and while I watched him in the billiard-room, I noticed a peculiarity, when he took his cigar out of his mouth and when he replaced it. That is, he poked out his arm as though his coat sleeve cramped his motions, and then slowly bent his elbow until he reached his ugly mug. There was an air of importance and of perfect self satisfaction about him that was aggravated by that peculiarity. But, pshaw! I have seen over a dozen jackasses do the very same thing. There was that first-class jackass, Spooner, at college, who entered the Soph. class with a plug hat. He used to crook his arm in precisely the same fashion, and he thought he was the biggest man in the class. When the fellows wished to make an extravagant bet, they used to say 'Spooner's estimate of his own value.' And Squizzem, too; he poked his arms out in just the same style when he was giving me that second hand lecture. I cannot identify the black-eyed scamp on this track; he has too many congeners.

"Black-eyed! bold, bad eyes; insolent! I felt my temper rising when he looked so steadily at me. If we meet again, I'll try the strength of his eyes. Pooh! I am not foolish enough to get up a quarrel for nothing. I cannot identify the man. He is just the embodiment of cold-blooded effrontery.

"Next. What was he after? Me! Well, what did he want? Did he intend to pick my pocket? Do I look like a green countryman, I wonder? It could not be that. While I do not seem particularly impecunious, I do not carry any tokens of affluence about me. He was after something else. Ah! I have a clue.

"Miss Norman's affairs. This fellow has been put on my track by some one interested in the settlement of the estate. Let me fix that idea clearly in my mind, and then I'll go to sleep.

"She is intent upon one scheme. And this scheme in some way runs counter to other interests. By George! I'll go see her to-morrow, and tell her I must know more, or quit her service. But I cannot do that, poor girl. I cannot be so rude. Ah! How could Helen say such cruel things about her?

"Have these two women met? Impossible. Yet, how could Helen know of Nina's desire to gain possession of certain property? And this very Ruthven's Folly probably is the property in question. Has Helen any interest, real or imaginary, in it? Impossible. The deeds are in perfect order, and the transfer of title is complete and final. Indeed, the transfer of Darcy Ruthven and his mother was an unnecessary addendum to the original document. I will see Miss Ruthven in the morning, and get more light. And now for sleep."

The morning sun wakened Darcy by shining on his face. He rose and, dressing rapidly, descended the stairs, and met Helen in the hall. She was just leaving the house.

"Allow me to walk a little way with you," he said, with grave politeness; "your parting words last night demand some explanation—from me, at least, and perhaps from you also."

"I spoke hastily," she answered, coldly, "but I meant no offence."

"I think there is a mistake somewhere," said Darcy; "do you know that I have been a law student? Well, I have, and probably would be admitted to practice with some slight formalities if

I should make the effort. The matters I have in hand are, therefore, entrusted to me by one whom I may call my client——"

"Did your client mention me?" said Helen, abruptly.

"No; certainly not."

"Are you at liberty to tell me your client's name?"

"I think not," answered Darcy, after a pause; "may I ask you if there is a name by which you can identify the property you spoke of?"

"Yes," said she, promptly, "it is called Ruthven's Folly."

"Ah! And you thought I was working against your interests——"

"I have no interests," she answered, vehemently. "I will never have an interest in this land. Certainly not by the means you will probably employ. I will not be a party to a scheme that is essentially fraudulent, and I have already announced that determination as emphatically as possible. Please say to your client that my first act, if the property were forced upon me, would be to donate it to a hospital."

Darcy walked by her side, silently meditating. In due time they reached Broadway, and Helen stopped at the door of Mr. Tilter's establishment. Darcy glanced at the sign, "J. Tilter. Hoop Skirts."

"You stop here," he said. "Listen to a word more. Do you think I could take part in a fraudulent scheme?"

"The law," murmured Helen, "the law may be clear, when the equity is doubtful. My father has often told me that a lawyer was bound by every consideration of honour to stand by his client."

"But your father would never have a rogue for a client. And if I ever practice law, which is not probable, I will never let the law excuse me for advocating injustice or fraud. I would starve sooner. And I am perfectly sure that my client would not swerve one hair's breadth from the path of rectitude to obtain possession of ten times the value of Ruthven's Folly. If I am mistaken in this," he continued, noticing her gesture of dissent, "I am surely not mistaken in counting myself incapable of such baseness. I would not dishonour my name, even to regain your good opinion. Good morning."

She stood in the doorway watching him as he strode down the street. He was evidently wounded, and she had been harsh and petulant! Could she be mistaken, or was he misled by one wiser and unscrupulous? Filled with doubts, she began to climb the steps, and was overtaken at the second landing by Mr. Donis, coming up three steps at a time.

"Aha! Miss Harding," he said, with a grin, "you have been taking a mornin' walk with a feller, after all!"

"I do not understand you!" said Helen, haughtily.

"Oh! we need not put on any airs!" replied Mr. Donis, taking off his glove. "Bless you, I've met a many of your sort! Shy as a kitten and skittish as a colt 'till the right feller comes. I think you might be a little more friendly with me, though! Come! I'll say nothin' about your mornin' walk; let me help you up stairs," and he passed his arm around her waist with a chuckle.

Helen dashed his arm down very much as she would have shaken off a snake, and, after a momentary hesitation, turned and went down stairs.

"Time's up!" said Mr. Donis, gayly, as she reached the door. "If you arn't at your machine in five minutes you will be docked two shillin'! He, he! How spunky we are, to be sure!" and he continued the ascent, humming "Tramp, tramp! the boys are marching!"

"This cannot be endured!" said Helen to herself, when she regained the street. "He was insolent enough before, but to *touch* me! I'll go back and tell Mrs. Camp! No, I won't. I'll go tell Mr. Skillet; but it is too early to find him. I will wait until noon."

A troop of girls came thronging in the doorway, and, joining them, Helen went up the steps once more, and entered upon her regular duties. Mr. Donis, in no wise abashed, passed her twice or thrice during the morning with a pleasant smirk on his face. He was too noble minded to harbour resentment, and, in fact, considered the little rebuff he had met on the stairs as the inevitable preliminary to a better acquaintance. It was a little curious that Helen's meditations at the same time were upon the question as to the relative degree of cruelty involved in burning him at a slow fire, or drowning him in a shallow pond; and upon the problem: if five grains of strychnine would kill a big dog, how many grains would kill a puppy. If the puppy had been endowed with the ordinary instinct of his kind, he would have discovered her repugnance. But he was clad in the triple armour of conceit, and happily unconscious.

At noon Helen extravagantly spent ten cents in omnibus fare, and rode down to Wall street. She had learned Mr. Skillet's address from Mrs. Camp a day or two before. The old gentleman had been so kind to her that she felt no sort of hesitation in applying to him, but when she reached his office, she found a sudden fit of shyness taking possession of her. She would probably see Mr. Gaston if she went in! she had not thought of that. While she doubted, the omnibus rolled on, and before she had decided what to do it had reached the ferry, and she got out with the other passengers.

"This is mere weakness!" she murmured. "I must get away from that horrible den. Mrs. Camp was talking last night about the high prices paid to house servants. I will certainly hire myself as seamstress or nurse in some decent family, if I cannot otherwise get away from that odious brute! After all, it would only be a renewal of my Cincinnati life, where I was veritable nurse and seamstress, though I was called a 'governess.' I'll go to Mr. Skillet at once!"

She stood aside to give passage to a troop of men pouring out of the ferry gates. After the first burst passed, the ladies began to appear, and among them a prim-looking damsel, escorted by Mr. Skillet himself. The old gentleman was all politeness and attention, and Helen saw him assisting the lady into an omnibus, shaking hands at parting, and bowing to her as the vehicle drove off. As he replaced his hat Helen touched his arm.

"Oh, Mr. Skillet," she began, "I am so glad to meet you here!"

"And I am glad to see you," he responded, shaking hands cordially. "Why, I was thinkin' of you this very minute! Been to Brooklyn?"

"No, sir; I came down here to see you, and when I reached your office—I—I thought I could not go in."

"It's no consequence!" replied Mr. Skillet, "that is, I told 'em I should not be back. I expected to stay longer to Brooklyn, but I got through sooner than I expected. What's up?"

"I want to get away from Mr. Tilter's, sir, please," said Helen, half crying; "I think I would like to sew in some private family, or teach children."

"Has that jackass been impudent to you? I mean that young whelp."

"Yes, sir."

"I'll put a head onto him!" said Mr. Skillet, in wrath; "or I'll tell Dassy! Yes, yes! I'll tell Dassy. And if he don't have on a two-story Mansard before night I'm a Dutchman! that's all!"

"Please don't tell anybody, Mr. Skillet," said Helen, "but just find me some hiding place where nobody can find me——"

"Except me and Dassy ?"

"Except you, sir. I don't want Mr. Gaston to know where I am either," continued Helen, blushing. "I don't want even Mrs. Camp to know. Oh! if I could only get back to Cincinnati!"

"Well, well!" ejaculated Mr. Skillet, "this bangs the witches! I think the devil has broke loose! But it's no consequence! Why, my child, I have already arranged for a hiding place for you, where nobody will find you, and I was going up to old Tilter this very afternoon to tell you about it! Git in this 'bus and go home. Git your satchel and come right back to this ferry. I'll meet you at three o'clock, right in there at the ferry house, and you will be as snug as a thief in a mill before dark. Don't cry now! I tell you it is all right. Jest keep your mouth shet, and be punctual. I'll say nauthin', and if you would rather not, I won't put a head on that little whelp either. Cuss his impudence! Here we are! Good mornin'! Three o'clock, sharp!"

CHAPTER XXV.

MR. DONIS.

BY an odd coincidence, it happened that Darcy Gaston was engaged in pleasant conference with Mr. Donis at the very moment that Mr. Skillet employed in delivering objurgatory remarks to Helen concerning the same attractive individual. Mr. Tilter had sent the young gentleman to Wall street to purchase exchange for remittance by the next day's steamer. As Mr. Tilter was an "associate member" of the Gold Exchange, Mr. Donis had the *entrée* to that quiet resort, and while the very pillars shook with the shouts of the operators, Darcy was introduced by a fellow clerk, with whom he had some slight acquaintance. This last mentioned youth was also an occasional "operator," on his own account, and he had just "made a turn," that is, he had bought ten thousand dollars and sold it again at one-eighth advance. His name was Jackson, and he represented an extensive firm in unlimited credit, that has since retired from business, after paying ten cents in the dollar of an indebtedness counted by millions.

"Come, Mr. Gaston," he said, flourishing some greenbacks in his hand; "come, Donis! Let us go to Delmonico's and lunch. I've got the money for that turn. Twelve fifty. Let's get outside of it."

Darcy hesitated. He did not like to be "treated" to lunch. His habit was to dine at four or five o'clock, at a quiet restaurant, where the roast beef was exceptionally good and the prices moderate. Yet he had some curiosity to see the interior of Delmonico's, and the thought passed through his mind that Mr. Jackson's money had been easily made and would be readily spent anyhow.

"Come along!" continued Mr. Jackson, "Delmonico will give us some stuffed tommartisses."

"I want a filly!" observed Mr. Donis.

"All right! Come on! Come, Mr. Gaston, I want you to try the tommartisses."

Darcy followed, registering a vow that he would return the treat to-morrow. The waiter, selected by Mr. Jackson, led the way to a private room on the third floor.

"Stuffed tommartisses for two, Augooste, and a bottle of the Widdy Cliquot. Give your order, Donis."

"Filly de boof, ox champingons!" said Mr. Donis, in choice French.

"Oui, monsieur!" said the waiter, and vanished.

While they waited, Mr. Donis twisted his waxed moustache and studied Darcy's plain exterior. It was at a time when young men indulged in large plaids and monkey jackets, and Darcy had not adopted the fashion.

"What are you after to-day, Donis?" said Jackson, while the waiter arranged their repast.

"A little sterling," replied the other; "Tilter wants to remit by to-morrow's steamer."

"Tilter?" said Darcy; "up Broadway, hoop skirts?"

"Exactly!" answered Mr. Jackson. "Donis has a soft thing. About forty girls rattling sewing machines."

"It's a plaguey noosance!" said Mr. Donis. "You have to keep 'em at work, and a feller don't like to order girls about."

"But you have lots of chances to court 'em," observed Mr. Jackson, with a grin; "nobody to interfere with you."

"Don't know about that," said Mr. Donis. "I've been a little sweet on one of 'em, and this morning I saw her walk up to the door with another feller!"

"Why didn't you put a head on him? Come! Set up! Augooste, draw the cork."

"No wine for me, thank you," said Darcy.

"What! You are not temperance, are you?"

"Yes," said Darcy, decidedly.

"Well, that's a pity. But Donis and I can dispose of this bottle. Say! Donis, why didn't you put a head on that feller! He was a poachin' on your property."

"I was a block off when Mary left him, or when he left her. But I caught her on the steps and told her I had seen her beau. Bless you, she was as spunky as a cat! But I just gave her a little hug and let her go."

"Are you going to leave it so," said Mr. Jackson.

"Not much; I'll be all right in a week! Wish I could see that feller, though."

"What's name?" said Mr. Jackson.

"Dunno. She was not disposed to communicate any information. But I'll find out."

"How did the young lady receive your caress?" said Darcy, with his mouth full of "tommartiss."

"Oh! just like 'em all; pretended to be very indignant, of course, and knocked my arm off. Young lady! He! he! She is only a sewing girl!"

"Has she been long with you," continued Darcy, his voice still affected by his efforts at deglutition.

"Only a few days. Old Skillet brought her; picked her up somewhere. Quare old chap! Augooste, give me another drop of the creamy. You had better take the rest, Jackson. I've had mor'n my share."

This was a very true remark.

Darcy had but little appetite. He sat quietly munching a crust, and trying to decide whether he would be justified in throwing Mr. Donis out of the window, or not. But he reflected that it was three stories from the pavement, and concluded that it would be unsafe, as he might fall on the head of some innocent pedestrian and possibly hurt him.

They walked down stairs. Mr. Jackson paid the bill, and hurried back to the gold room. Mr. Donis turned down into Pearl street, Darcy following, until they reached the front of the Cotton Exchange. There had been an auction sale that morning, and the street was filled with bales of cotton, and they had to thread their way between tiers of bales, piled near the sidewalk. Mr. Donis had imbibed about two-thirds of the champagne and saw more bales than the auctioneer had sold.

"Excuse me", said Darcy, "if I transgress in asking, but I have a curiosity to know the name of the sewing girl you mentioned."

"Humph!" said the other, gruffly. "I don't know as it is any of your business."

"Certainly not," replied Darcy, with increasing politeness; "but it occurred to me that it was something unusual among gentlemen, first to insult an unprotected girl, and then to boast of it."

There was such a marked disparity between his tones and his words, that Mr. Donis was sobered a little. He leaned on his cane and reflected, putting his hand up to his moustache. Darcy noticed that he tossed his arm forward, and gradually brought his fingers to his mouth, very much like his pursuer of the previous night. There was something about the motion that increased Darcy's ire.

"A man with human instincts," continued Darcy, after waiting in vain for a response, "could hardly do what you say you did. The fact that the girl was poor enough to be obliged to work for her living, would be a shield of adamant to a gentleman."

"Do you mean to say I'm no gentleman?" said Mr. Donis, fiercely. "Look here! You can take yourself off if you like, or you can have your head knocked off! Whichever you please."

"Stop!" said Darcy, catching his arm, as he raised it threateningly. "You have had too much wine to-day. Wait until to-morrow, and I will call at your place, and repeat my remarks."

"You will, will you?" said Mr. Donis, furiously. "Well, I'll put a mark on you, so that I'll know you again;" and he raised his cane suddenly, and aimed a terrific blow at Darcy's head.

That amiable young gentleman heaved a sigh, partly of regret, and partly of heavenly relief. He had been burning to throttle Mr. Donis for half an hour, and now it was a clear case of self-defence. They were standing in a little area, surrounded by cotton bales, part on the sidewalk and part on the street, and were therefore hidden from the passengers on either side. Darcy started forward, caught the descending cane on his left arm, and disarranged Mr. Donis's necktie with his other hand. The cane dropped in the scuffle, and so did Mr. Donis. Darcy rolled him over into the gutter, which was full of slush, and spoiled the appearance of his hat and monkey jacket. Then he caught his collar again, and bobbed him up and down in the water eighteen times, spoiling all the exhilarating effect of the champagne. He did not strike him at all. At last he drew him out upon the curb, and propped him up against a cotton bale, limp and exhausted.

"My name is Darcy Gaston," he said, as he released him. "I may be found at number fifty-five, Wall street. I am disengaged generally until noon, and will be at your service whenever you may want me. Good morning!" and he walked gingerly out of the area, leaving Mr. Donis in doubt as to the reality of his surroundings, or as to the present money vaue of his attire.

"What ails your arm?" said Mr. Skillet, suddenly pouncing upon Darcy, as he was wrapping the injured member in a wet towel.

"Oh!" said Darcy, "excuse me, sir! I did not know you were in. My arm? Oh! I struck it against something, down in Pearl street."

"You did?" responded Mr. Skillet; "and your face and hair, too? It's no consequence; but it looks as if you had struck agin a streak o' lightning!"

"Yes, sir!" replied Darcy, in some confusion, glancing at the reflection of his scratched countenance, and tumbled hair, in a mirror on the opposite wall.

"I was going to ask you to go up Broadway, with a message to old Tilter. Verbal. Talkin' is safer than writin' sometimes. Can't sue you for damages or nauthin!"

"Tilter!" said Darcy, in dismay. The poor youth thought Helen would see him, scratched and disfigured.

"Ya-as! I want you to give him my compliments; blast his picter! and tell him that whelp of hisen, Donis, that he sent down here after exchange——. What's the matter?"

"Oh, Mr. Skillet, pray don't send me; Mr. Donis is not very well. In fact, he was with me, when I got my arm hurt."

"The dickens he was!" said Mr. Skillet, eyeing Darcy keenly; "and did he git *his* arm hurt?"

"Yes, sir—at least he got somewhat damaged—chiefly in his habiliments. You see, sir," he continued, humbly, "he was telling of his exploits among the sewing girls—and—you know Miss Harding is there, sir, and I ventured to expostulate—and he struck me with a stick—and——"

"Proceed!" said Mr. Skillet.

"Well, I rolled him in the gutter, sir. I did not notice the water in it until it was too late. I see it splashed on me also. But I don't like to take any message that will add to his trouble. I think he will do for a day or two."

"All right!" said Mr. Skillet, "it's no consequence;" and he retired into the back office, where he rolled over on the lounge in security, while the tears rolled down his rosy cheeks.

"Gosh and Gemini!" he said, when he regained his voice; "a nice, quiet, sweet tempered Dassy I've got, I don't think! The pesky young cuss! The unreconstructed young rebbil! Bully for Dassy!"

CHAPTER XXVI.

BAFFLED.

MR. DONIS, who was greatly discouraged by the little skrimmage at which he had assisted, sat leaning against the cotton bale, looking at his soiled garments, and mopping his dishevelled tresses with his handkerchief. There was a brisk air stirring, and as he sat in a draught, the evaporation made him feel cool and collected. Something had to be done, however, and he scrambled to his feet, picked up his hat, late so trim and glossy, and tried to twirl his moustache and look fierce. But it was a failure, as the wax had been washed off by his numerous submersions. He thought he would like to swear, but could not think of any customary expletives that would do justice to the circumstances. Darcy had knelt on his slender legs, and Donis thought they were broken, but they were only damp and decidedly cold.

"Ruined!" he muttered; "sixty-five dollar suit, not to mention the hat. I want a gallon of that fellow's gore."

He picked up his cane, and began to thread his way out of the area. At the entrance he met a stranger, who looked at his splashed attire, and drew aside to give him passage.

"Had a fall, sir?" said he. "Ah! I see; you slipped on the curb. There ought to be a law against blocking up the street in this way. Not hurt, are you?"

"Not much," answered Mr. Donis; "it was not exactly a fall. That is, I had a tussle with a blackguard, and he tripped me up, and then run. I'll be even with him yet."

"Better call a policeman in such cases," observed the stranger "Would you know him again ?"

"Know him ! I should think so, confound him ! I don't know how I am going up Broadway in these clothes, though."

"Why didn't you give him a taste of your stick?" said the other. "It is a good tough stick."

"I gave him one wipe, curse him ! But he tripped me up the next minnit."

"What did you quarrel about?" Donis looked more intently at the questioner before he answered. He wore a seedy white overcoat and a felt hat, but he had nicely fitting kid gloves on his hands, and had a thoroughbred air that impressed his interlocutor. He had almond shaped, black eyes, a hooked nose, and under it, a volume of red beard.

"About a woman," replied Mr. Donis, reluctantly. "I saw him walkin' with her this mornin'; but I didn't know him 'till we had the tussle. She didn't mention his name, neither. But while he was aggravatin' me in there, it just flashed on my mind that he was the same feller. And when he told me he was at 55 Wall street—that's old Skillet's—I knowed I was right, because old Skillet brought the gal to our place."

"Skillet!" said the other; "the stock and gold broker?"

"Yes. This Gaston stays with him. I met him in the gold room. What can I do with these clothes?"

"Come with me," said the stranger, courteously. "I know a place where you can get dried, anyhow. It is close by. Here in Pearl street."

It was a dingy looking cellar, where lager beer was dispensed. But there was a great red stove in the centre. They drew their chairs up, and the stranger called for two glasses of beer. Drink never came amiss to Mr. Donis, and although he had so recently imbibed two-thirds of a bottle of Cliquot, he accepted the lager. The wine had probably got somewhat diluted in his tussle.

"Now take off your coat, and hang it on the chair back. Hans, bring another chair. So ! You might take off your pantaloons, if you like. Nobody here, but beer-swilling Dutchmen."

"I'll lend ter shentlemans a pair of overhalls," said Hans, obligingly; "dey are cleans. Schlippers too." Hans thought they would drink the more lager, the longer they staid, and had some visions of a possible quarter, also. He produced the articles in a moment.

"That is sensible," observed the stranger, approvingly. "Now Hans, see if you can't brush up this hat. We shall want two more lagers presently. Mr.—— I beg your pardon, but I have forgotten your name."

"Donis."

"And mine is Blake. It is rather odd, but I have a little business with your friend. What did you call him? Gaston?"

"No friend of mine," said Mr. Donis, roughly.

"Quite as much yours as mine," replied the other, showing his white teeth; "it is quite likely that we may be too much for him hereafter. He has—well—he has tripped me up, metaphorically, also. And when he tripped me, he ran, as he did from you."

"Give us your hand, Mr. Blake!" said Donis, eagerly. "I'll join in any arrangement to put a head on that Gaston. Did he interfere with any woman of yours?"

"Well, yes. But not seriously. My complaint against him is more on account of his leading me a fool's chase, about two miles, and then slipping out of my very fingers. I tracked him to Skillet's this morning. Two more, Hans! What sort of girl is yours?"

"Big grey eyes. Very stiff and proud. One of our sewing girls in fact. Name of Harding—Mary. She beats the witches with the Singers. I believe she could take one to pieces, and put it together again inside of ten minutes."

"Don't you know where she lives?" said Mr. Blake, carelessly.

"Oh, yes. I followed her home last night."

"Near your place?"

"No. Down in Camden street, Number ninety-six."

"And your place—"

"Tilter's. Hoop skirts. Broadway."

"Oh, yes; I know the locality." He took out his watch and started up. "Bless me! It is nearly three o'clock! I have an appointment at three. Will you excuse me, if I leave you? Your clothes will be dry in half an hour, and Hans will brush the stains off. Give him a quarter, and it will be all right. I'll see you again; good day!"

Mr. Tilter was at the top of the seventy-two steps, when Mr. Blake presented himself, at three, fifteen. Mr. Blake begged permission to say a word to Miss Harding.

"Harding?" said Mr. Tilter, with the quill in his mouth. "Let me see," and he consulted a memorandum book; "Oh, yes. Not in; sick, I suppose. Not been back since noon."

Mr. Blake walked down to Camden street. Number 96 was a cosy little brick house, three stories. Very respectable neighbourhood, certainly, but no brownstone fronts. After some hesitation, he rang the bell.

"Is Miss Harding in?" he asked, when the door opened.

"No, sir," replied the girl.

"Are you sure?"

"I am, thin," responded the girl. "I put her in a 'bus wid her satchel an hour ago."

"Is Mrs. Camp disengaged?" said Mr. Blake, his black eyes snapping with rage; "Please ask her if I can see her a moment."

"Sure you can, sir. Walk into the parlour, plaze."

When Mrs. Camp appeared, Mr. Blake had regained his composure. He had rapidly made up the outlines of a story, while he waited.

"I am sorry to disturb you, Mrs. Camp," he said, politely; "but I had an urgent message for Miss Harding."

"Oh, from Mr. Tilter? Yes, sir, she said he might want to know——But how did you find her address? She told me Mr. Tilter would not know where to send. Take a seat, sir."

Mr. Blake resumed his seat. It would not do to come from Mr. Tilter, evidently.

"Mr. Tilter? Oh, no, madam. My message is from Kentucky.

"Your servant said Miss Harding was out."

"Sarvent!" muttered Bridget, who was listening in the hall. "The divil take his impudence, thin! To call a dacent girl a sarvent, when she is only a help."

"Yes, sir," replied Mrs. Camp; "she has been gone since half-past two."

"Do you know when she will return? I must deliver my message this afternoon, if possible."

"Well, sir," said Mrs. Camp, "I am sorry I cannot give her address. She has left for good, and I have no idea where she has gone."

There was an unmistakable air of truthfulness about Mrs. Camp, and Mr. Blake dismissed the first suggestion—to wit: that she was deceiving him—without hesitation. He was greatly disturbed, evidently.

"It is highly important that I should see Miss Harding," he said; "can you suggest any one to me, who would probably know where to find her?"

"Indeed, I cannot, sir. I have not the most remote idea."

"Would you object to telling me what she said, when she left you?" said Mr. Blake; "perhaps she may have left some clue that I can follow up."

"She just came to my door, and said 'Mrs. Camp, I am obliged to leave you for the present. It is like leaving my home again, and I am sorry;' and she put some money in my hand, for her board, and kissed me. I asked her where she was going——"

"Well, madam," said Mr. Blake, anxiously.

"I can't understand her answer, at all, sir! She looked so quiet and cheerful, and good, that I was not able to question her. She said she would write to me soon, but at present she could not say where she was going! And ever since she left—more than an hour ago—I have felt like blaming myself for not locking her up in her room! I don't know what to think!"

"Will you allow me to call again, Mrs. Camp, some days hence?" said Mr. Blake, rising. "Perhaps she may give an address in her note to you."

"Certainly, sir. But I don't expect a note."

"Did she say she would write?"

"Yes. But she may forget that."

"Never! She would keep her word, if death were the penalty."

"I am greatly distressed. But, patience! We must wait. Good afternoon, madam."

Mr. Blake made a very indifferent pantomime of patience as he left Camden street. His eyes glittered, he ground his teeth, and stamped with fiendish rage upon the stones he traversed.

"Baffled again!" he whispered to himself; "baffled, and by a slip of a girl, and this miserable little Kentucky ignoramus! Baffled by a hair's breadth! Ten thousand million devils! Is the very best and most promising scheme of my entire life to be thwarted by such as these! Is Rupert Grey to be the laughing stock of the civilized world! I am beside myself with rage and disappointment. And to make the humiliation complete, there is the consciousness that I was within one hour of success; only sixty minutes! Ten thousand million billion devils!"

And in this pleasant frame of mind, Mr. Blake, or Mr. Grey, walked down Broadway. Arrived at the Saint Nicholas hotel, he went into the billiard room, and, lighting a cigar, sat apart in a corner, revolving new schemes, and tossing his arm out in the old conceited fashion, as he gradually regained his equanimity.

CHAPTER XXVII.
Nell Gaston.

"NELL!" said Tige Gaston, as he and his wife sat at their glorious hickory wood fire one evening; "Nell, my darling, my mind is ill at ease. I am like old Pegtop."

"Who is Pegtop, Tige?" responded Mrs. Gaston, drawing her chair nearer to him, and leaning her head upon his sturdy arm. These weak-minded people had been married a dozen years, but they still hugged the delusion that they were lovers. Each thought the other a thousand fold more beautiful and good than their most extravagant estimates were when they were only lovers. There had been a time since their marriage when a rosy, rollicking boy had drawn from them a new set of emotions, all flowing with accurate regularity from the parental relation wherein man attains the fullness of godliness—attainable no otherwise beneath the stars. And when the little mound in the churchyard was all that was left to them in the world's estimation, each secretly clung with ineffable comfort to the conviction that the relation was only modified, not changed; and each waited with calm confidence for the time, sure to come, when the boy—still Little Hal—should welcome them to that Land where he waited for them. And while there was but little converse betwixt them upon the topic, each knew the other's thought; and so they drew closer, each to the other, while the flowers bloomed and faded on the mound.

"Pegtop," said Tige, slipping his arm under her head, and so bringing her soft eyes nearer to his own ; " Pegtop was a gentleman, whose short biography may be found somewhere in Marryatt. I cannot tell the story in his expressive language, but the facts are as follows: Pegtop had a son. The son embarked upon the treacherous ocean——"

"He couldn't embark anywhere else, Tige," observed Mrs. Gaston.

"Don't interrupt me, wife! Yes, he could. He might have embarked on a pond. But it was the ocean, and neither young Pegtop nor young Pegtop's bark were ever heard from. So old Pegtop was wont to say his mind was ill at ease, because he did not know his son's fate. But one day a shark was captured somewhere in the tropics, and being cut up, a silver watch was found in his stomach. And the watch was identified as young Pegtop's watch. Then old Pegtop said his mind was at ease, because he now knew exactly what had become of his son."

"Well," said Nell, knitting her brows, "whose shark, or whose watch do you want, Tige? It's a horrid story, though."

"There, now," replied her husband, "you are off again with your literal interpretation. I only said I resembled old Pegtop, because my mind was ill at ease. I don't want any watch."

"Is it Darcy?"

"Of course, it is Darcy. Nobody else has a watch, but Darcy. Ah, Nell! You gave your watch to Darcy, and thought I would not find you out."

"But I had two watches, Tige," answered his wife; "you gave me this on my last birthday. I could not wear two watches, you know. Darcy lost his watch when he was captured over there." Tige and his wife always referred to one of the bloodiest battles of the war as "over there."

"Oh, it's all right," said Mr. Gaston; "but let us return to the original topic. I am anxious about that boy."

"What makes you anxious?"

"His letters," and he produced a small packet. "Here they are, you have read them all. Now, what do you think?"

"I think Darcy is not telling us *everything*," answered Mrs. Gaston, positively. "He don't say one word about his occupations of an evening. Does he go to theatres and balls? Has he female acquaintances? A young man cannot be satisfied without some sort of society. Why don't he describe his evenings?"

"Why, Nell," said Tige, "you forget. Here is to-day's letter. Listen! 'I was up quite late last night. After I posted yesterday's letter, I had some papers to examine, as I have a case in hand, partly legal and partly financial. I find my legal lore very valuable, brother, in many ways. I think of getting some books, and reading up o' nights. If I study the New York Code a little, I can get into a law office here, work up cases, and finally obtain admittance into the profession. After I had worked on the papers a while, I walked out to the Park. It is going to be a great park, Sister Nell, one of these days. Well, after I got back as far as Twenty-third street, I stopped in the Fifth Avenue Hotel. I noticed an ugly rascal there, and he seemed to notice me. Then I walked down to the St. Nicholas, and there was my red whiskered beauty again. So I just got into the elevator, went up two or three floors, got out, tripped down the side stairs and into the street by the ladies' door. Then I made tracks. If the fellow followed me, he must have had wings to his boots, like Mercury. By the bye, Mercury is the god of thieves!"

"The boy will get murdered in that dreadful city!" ejaculated Nell.

"Murdered! Pooh! No danger of that. The fellow saw that watch chain of yours, no doubt, and was after that. What the dickens did the boy go poking about the hotels for? Then he goes on: 'I was all aglow when I reached my room, and was mindful of my promise to Sister Nell to take care of my health, so I tumbled into bed while the circulation was rapid. I write this by the grey light of dawn, as it is too early to go down town, and I am too wide awake to go back to bed.'"

"It is not natural, Tige," observed Mrs. Gaston, "for a healthy young man to object to bed. I am sure you would lie abed half the day if you could get breakfast."

"But I am not a healthy young man, Nell," said Tige; "I feel quite feeble. I was thinking to-day that I ought to take a little trip somewhere."

"Little trip?"

"Yes. With you, of course. How would you like to travel a little?"

"To Omaha, Tige?" said Mrs. Gaston, deceitfully.

"No, I thought we might go to Cincinnati, and perhaps to Pittsburgh; and if I could stand the fatigue——"

"Go on, you old hypocrite!" said Nell. "You want to go to New York!"

"Well, of all the women I have ever met you take the lead!" said Mr. Gaston, in a burst of genuine admiration. "Here I have been blundering along, trying to find out your sentiments, and you just pounce upon mine upon the slightest hint! Now, I will make a clean breast of it! I met Mr. Burton in Lexington to-day——"

"Yes!" said Mrs. Gaston, sarcastically, "I remember Mr. Burton. You undertook his case without a retainer, fought it through a whole term, gained it at last, and then sent him a check for his claim without deducting a fee!"

"Exactly!" said her husband, "so to-day he gave me a thousand dollars; and it is in bank this minute! And I thought you and I could indulge ourselves with a peep at Darcy. Oh, Nell, I am so hungry for a sight of the boy!"

"Me, too, Mars'r Tige! as Nanny says!" rejoined Mrs. Gaston. "Let us go without notifying him, and maybe we'll catch him unawares! *You* talk about being hungry! Why, I am aching all over to see him! When can you go, dear?".

"To-night!" said Tige, starting up. "Why not? Can't you put a few things into a trunk and drive to Lexington in forty minutes? Certainly! I have enough money in my pocket for the trip, and my check book is in my desk. Here, put it in. I don't want anything but two or three shirts. You may fill up the trunk with your own furbelows! Women can't travel without a trunk any more than an elephant! But you are such a darling little woman, that you shall have ten trunks if you like! Kiss me, and go pack up!"

"There are those hams!" said Mrs. Gaston, reflectively. "They ought to come out of pickle on Friday; they will be ruined. Sixteen of them, and perfect beauties!"

"I'll give you a check, Nell, for their full value; will you be gone!"

"No, sir!" she answered, with dignity. "If you have gone stark crazy, I have not! Nanny *might* remember to take the hams out, but——"

"Nell!" said Tige, imploringly, "it is ten o'clock! The train leaves at eleven thirty!"

"Well, sir?"

"And you will require at least an hour to pack that trunk!"

"Don't bother me, Mr. Gaston. Nanny! Do you think you can remember to take the hams out on Friday?"

"You done tole me about de hams, Miss Nell," answered Nanny. "You tole me dis mornin! And I knows about 'em anyhow. Take 'em out in de full ob de moon, wid de sign in de heart. And de middlins gwine to lay in pickle two days longer. De moon fulls on Friday. Can't forget dat, 'kase my rheumatiz allers comes on reg'lar when she fulls."

"Never mind about the moon, Nanny——"

"Werry well, den! You jist hang dat bacon, wid de moon on de wane—you'll see!"

"Well, then," said Mrs. Gaston, "Friday will be all right. And, Nanny, take care of the eggs. If you can keep that speckled hen's eggs separate, I should like to have a setting——"

"Settin'! La! Miss Nelly, wid snow on de ground! 'Taint no good time, nohow; wouldn't have no luck wid chickens. Massy! You done tried dat oncet. Pickin' out eggs is jist temptin' Providence. You seems to be forcin' on de hen chickens she had no right to raise. What right has she to sot on other hens' eggs! Den she don't have no motherly feelin' for de chickens, and don't half huddle 'em. Besides, Miss Nelly, you done tole me about de chickens dis mornin' !"

"It seems to me," quoth Tige, "that you have made all and sundry arrangements this morning, Nell!"

"Don't bother me, Mr. Gaston!" replied Nell. "And Nanny, you can send the last churning to Lexington. Send two pounds to Mrs. Graves, with my compliments, and send the rest to Millikin's."

"Must I send your compl'ments to Mr. Millikin, wid de butter!"

"Certainly not! The old skinflint!"

"Well, den, Miss Nelly, you done tole me about dat dis mornin', when you was packin' de trunk——"

"There! Get out Nanny! Tell John to drive up! You see, Tige, I knew your heart was set on this journey, so I made all needful preparations this morning. You old goose! I knew you would want to rush off by the first train. Really, Tige, at your age, you should be more sober and less impulsive. Why couldn't you wait until to-morrow?"

"True enough, Nell!" replied Tige, deceitfully. "We can wait. I'll tell John to put up the horses. It is a cold night, anyhow."

"Cold! What an absurdity! No, sir! I am not going to do all my packing over again! If you are really bent on this trip, the sooner it is over the better. Besides, you have made me thoroughly uneasy about that boy! I want to see that Skillet man, too. Ah! that boy would make friends anywhere! I want to see if Mr. Skillet keeps him bent double over a desk. Darcy has a weak chest, anyhow. Put on your overcoat! It would be a nice business to miss the train, after all your preparations. And I should have my hands pretty full, keeping you quiet another twenty-four hours! Oh, Tige! if you would only learn to be less headlong you would be perfect! What in the world are you laughing about?"

"Nothing, Nell; only at the idea of my perfection. All ready! How bright the stars are! Good bye, Nanny! Don't forget the full of the moon! And, Nanny, discriminate between the eggs! All right, John!"

"'Scriminate eggs! Mars' Tige 'll be a boy ef he lives till he's a hundred! Dere dey go! Moon on right shoulder! Good luck, anyhow!"

CHAPTER XXVIII.
Cross Purposes.

ON the morning succeeding Mr. Darcy Gaston's flight from the threatening arm of Mr. Donis, Mr. Skillet was late at the office. He found Darcy at his desk, and the youth started up as soon as he entered, and followed him into the back room. Mr. Skillet proceeded to open the morning letters, with his usual composure, and was entirely unconscious of Darcy's high excitement —apparently.

"Mr. Skillet," he began, "I am terribly distressed! Miss Harding has disappeared."

"Miss Harding!" said Mr. Skillet; "Oh! ah! Ya-as. You mean the young lady at Camp's? Well, ask Camp——"

"No use to ask Mr. Camp, sir. She left yesterday, a little after noon, and I am sure she purposely concealed her intentions and destination from Mrs. Camp."

"Changed her boardin' heouse!" said Mr. Skillet. "Well, I s'pose the cookin' didn't suit her. It's no consequence! She'll come out all right. She's true grit! Here's a remittance from Scraggs, at last! the pesky whelp! I guess this will be margin enough."

"She has left the hoop-skirt place, sir," continued Darcy; "I called there this morning. I did not sleep all night. I am filled with a horrible dread, to which I can give no name. I would give one of my arms to know that she was safe."

"Whew!" whistled Mr. Skillet; "Jerusalem! Did she owe you anything."

"No, sir," answered Darcy, indignantly; "but I owed her a great deal. I owed her protection and defence, and I parted from her yesterday morning in ill temper. And now she is gone, gone!"

"And you are a goner!" said Mr. Skillet. "It's no consequence; that is, it's no business of mine. But I crave to know if you have been kind o' flirtin' like with her?"

"Oh! Mr. Skillet."

"Exactly. She's an el'gant gal! Very natural for a young man to be sparkin' a little. I used to be a fool myself, when I was abeout your age. But you'll live to outgrow it. 'Taint half as bad as measles. Now, here's another letter from that hound, Brown.

He says we threw his gold overboard, and he'll sue us for the margin. I think he must be of the Hebrew persuasion. By the bye, a chap was here yesterday evening that must be of the same persuasion. Black eyes, a hook nose; English Jew, I guess. *He* wanted to know about Miss Harding, too. Said he was from Lexington. He came in while you were in Broad street. *He* had been to Mrs. Camp's, too. I heard him talking to Camp, and pumpin' him tremendous! It was a dry suck, though. Camp didn't know no mor'n you do. What do you propose?"

"To find her, sir. I thought you might advise me."

"Advise you? Ya-as! But I crave to know what you propose to do with the young woman, if you find her."

"Do with her," said Darcy, startled. "I don't know, Mr. Skillet. I had not thought of that. But surely, it will be time enough to debate that point when I find her."

"It seems to me," continued Mr. Skillet, "that you will hardly have enough sewing to keep her employed. It seems to me that she has taken some pains to git out of reach. And it seems to me you are undertaking a considerable job in hunting for a young woman in a city like N'Yauk!"

"That is all true, sir," replied Darcy; "but no such arguments weigh a feather! You know that it is impossible to relinquish the search for this lady. You know that every consideration of manhood—of common humanity, will compel me to hunt until I find her. How *could* I rest while uncertain of her fate?"

"Tell me what you propose, then," said Mr. Skillet; "sometimes you can learn suthin', if you listen, even from a fool! I don't mean *you're* a fool. I'ts no consequence."

"I thought of applying to the police——"

"Oh, Gemini!" said Mr. Skillet, in high derision. "I take that back. You mayn't be a right down fool, but if there's a fool killer anywhere around, you'd better git your life insured. Police! Great Cæsar! Where was you raised?"

There was something so stunning in Mr. Skillet's contempt that Darcy was silenced. He sat down, leaned his head on his hand, and reflected. Mr. Skillet watched his changing countenance with great interest. He was studying the habits of a new animal, and each new trait of character appeared to entertain him. At last, Darcy rose and moved to the door.

"Wa-al," said Mr. Skillet, "what's up now? I see you have some new project."

"I thought I would go up to that hoop-skirt place, sir," said Darcy.

"Indeed! And what do you propose to do there?"

"I thought that little devil, Donis, might be there, and I could, perhaps, cut his throat! I am certain she left the place to escape his insolent attentions."

"That would be sensible," observed Mr. Skillet, sarcastically. "Now, you came in here for advice, and you go out without gitten a word. That shows how much advice is worth in this world! Young men think they have forgot more than old men ever knew. Suppose I should tell you what *I* propose? It's cur'ous, now; but you have jest concluded that Miss Harding has no friend in the world but you."

"Ah! Mr. Skillet," said Darcy, returning, "I beg your pardon! I might have known that your kind heart would prompt you to do all that could be done. Advice! I promise to do exactly what you think best."

"You do! Well, then, let her set."

"Let her set?" said Darcy, aghast. "I don't understand you."

"I s'pose not, but it's no consequence. I say, let her set! That is; keep your mouth shet, and listen to all you hear. Be as ignorant as a mule, when another fellow is talkin' and let *him* know everything. Maybe you can learn suthin' from him. He'll think he knows everything, if you just let him set, and he'll think you are next door to a fool if you only keep quiet. Then he won't be in competition, and suthin' will leak out that may be useful. Now I propose to find out exactly where Miss Harding is, and what she is doing. She hadn't ought to bolt off without tellin' a soul where she's gone, and she is not the sort of gal to do it. And she is not the sort of gal to do any rash thing either. She is all right! I'll engage to have a satisfactory account of her within twenty-four hours. My advice is jest to keep quiet, go about your business, and wait. Will you take it?"

"Yes, sir," said Darcy, with alacrity. "I will not stir hand or foot for twenty-four hours, or twenty-four days, if you think it best. My mind is entirely relieved."

"Take old Brown's letter then, and answer it. I'm going down to Cunard's to select a state-room for Miss Norman and Miss Keith. I'm coming back in an hour with the ticket. And she requests you to take the ticket to her at noon to-day. Here's her note. 'Miss Norman's compliments, and will Mr. Skillet please select a state-room for her and Miss Keith, by the *China*, and will Mr. Gaston please bring the ticket to-morrow at noon.' That's all. I 'spose she don't propose takin' *you* to Europe, or she would order another state-room! Git out, please! I must write a note!"

When Darcy closed the door behind him, Mr. Skillet indulged himself in a noiseless laugh.

"The pesky young cuss!" he muttered; "he looked so blamed sorrowful and anxious, that I pooty nigh let the cat out of the bag. I have been thinkin' all along that he was swallered up in Miss Norman, and that she kind o' leaned towards him. But he is sweet on the Harding gal, by Gosh! And no wonder. I fooled him nicely though, sharp as he is."

Darcy's cotemporaneous meditations, on the other side of the door, ran in this wise:

"The blessed old brick! He knows where she is. She is safe! She is safe! He has taken her to his own house! I saw it in his eyes. And now I must be cautious, and not let him discover how much I know. It would spoil all his arrangements. But I'll go up there to-night and may get a peep at her through the window. I *know* she is there, but it would be a comfort just to see her, if only for one moment."

Mr. Darcy Gaston prowled around Mr. Timothy Skillet's residence that night for a full hour. But he got no glimpse of Helen. Indeed, he would have needed visual organs equal to the double million magnifying glasses of Mr. Samuel Weller, to have seen through the blocks of houses on Manhattan Island, across the East River, and through the walls of the highly respectable boarding-house on Jerryboblum street, Brooklyn, where Helen sat demure and placid, annotating compositions that had been presented by the pupils of the Jerryboblum Institute at the end of the last session.

But Darcy had a little adventure during the day. At noon he visited the Fifth Avenue mansion, in obedience to Miss Norman's mandate, taking the steamer ticket with him. He was shown into the drawing-room, where he found Mr. Squizzem and Mrs. Bragdon. They merely acknowledged his polite salutation with the customary society nod, and then resumed their colloquy, totally ignoring his existence. He withdrew to the front window so as to be out of earshot, and they immediately began to discuss him. Mrs. Bragdon learned that he was a "friend of Nina's," and an unbeliever in the progress of the age, and probably a sympathizer with the accursed rebellion. Nina delayed her coming, and while he still waited, Mr. Bragdon also came in, and honoured Darcy with a very searching stare. Then Mr. Squizzem took his leave, and Mr. and Mrs. Bragdon sat idly waiting for Nina, intending to discover what possible business the handsome young stranger could have to transact. Then Nina came, and with the swift perception of her sex, read the thoughts of her sister and brother-in-law, and with equally swift perversity postponed her intended interview with Darcy. She took the steamer ticket, thanked him for his "trouble," and requested him to inform Mr. Skillet that she would decide about the amount of British gold she would require, and communicate with him. And so she dismissed him.

As he went down the steps, when the door closed behind him, he was somewhat surprised to see a black eyed and red-whiskered man on the corner, tossing his arm out from the shoulder, as he placed his cigar between his white teeth, and staring at Darcy with an expression of countenance that was partly astonished, partly indignant, and wholly insolent.

CHAPTER XXIX.

An Angry Household.

"UPON my word, Nina!" said Mr. Bragdon, "I think you might treat us with some small show of consideration, in our own house!"

"What do you mean by consideration?" said Nina, composedly.

"I mean that it is due to Mary and to me, to present your visitors, when we happen to be in the room!"

"And what do you mean by your own house?" continued Nina.

Mr. Bragdon's face became crimson, and Mrs. Bragdon held up her hands.

"Until the estate is settled, the ownership in property inherited by Mary and me, jointly, cannot be determined positively;" observed Nina, after a short pause.

"Exactly!" replied Mr. Bragdon; "when do you propose to arrange for the division?"

"I am waiting for a proposition from you," replied Nina, cautiously.

"I suppose the courts will arrange all that. But this has nothing to do with your visitor. My idea is, that some slight respect is due to the head of a household, from all the members of it. This —person—whoever he is, may be an improper person, and we are bound to maintain appearances. Nobody knows his rank in society!"

"He is probably quite equal to Mr. Squizzem," retorted Nina. "In all that constitutes a gentleman, I think he is far superior."

"Squizzem is a fraud!" said Mr. Bragdon, violently; "if I had my way, he would never show his smooth face in this house again! But he says this Gaskins is a mere Western bumpkin, an adventurer, without any sort of position, except that of a broker's clerk!"

"I have procured a ticket for Liverpool," said Nina, "and shall sail on Wednesday next. In the meantime, I shall see any visitors I please, either here or at the Fifth Avenue Hotel; and I shall not be at home to Mr. Squizzem, either here or there. *His* rank in society is not mine!"

"I am sure, Nina," put in Mrs. Bragdon, "that Mr. Squizzem is admitted everywhere. He is somewhat eccentric, perhaps, but I believe he is generally considered the foremost man of this age."

"Foremost Fiddlestick!" said Mr. Bragdon, irreverently; "he is the most stuck up, conceited old fraud in New York or Brooklyn. Nothing keeps him afloat, but his unlimited cheek!" Mr. Bragdon had caught some of the slang phrases of the age, which he employed when he lost his temper. At other times he rather prided himself upon his general elegance of demeanour and language. Mr. Squizzem was the champion kisser of the age, and Mr. Bragdon had an uncomfortable suspicion that he had kissed his wife, though he did not know it, and was afraid to ask. Mrs. Bragdon had her little tempers too, and her fortune was in her own right. And she believed in Squizzem, and always made Mr. Bragdon escort her to his lectures, when they were delivered in New York.

"I think," continued Mr. Bragdon, "that a fellow that goes about town, kissing all the women he knows, and calling them by their Christian names, ought to be put down!"

"Really, John!" said his wife, tartly; "you allow your prejudices to overcome your reason. Mr. Squizzem does not take any improper liberties with ladies, except where he is very intimate.

AN ANGRY HOUSEHOLD. 141

Mr. Dragger kisses all the members of his congregation, I am told; Miss Keith says so."

Miss Keith quietly glided into the room at this juncture.

"Miss Abby," continued Mrs. Bragdon; "did you not say that Mr. Slam Dragger kissed all the female members of his church?"

"My remark was scarcely so sweeping!" replied Miss Abby. "I don't think he kisses Mrs. Grizzly; she is about ninety. I think he rather regards her with reverence. But he is superior to the bondage of custom or conventional rules. He kisses his children, and the members of his congregation are in one sense his children, and doubtless he feels a Father's affection for them."

"Excepting Mrs. Grizzly!" observed Nina.

"Yes. Probably he would not object to Mrs. Grizzly kissing him. But a man of such purity of mind might do many things that would not be proper or becoming in others. He is so entirely above the ordinary class, that his peculiarities cannot be measured by ordinary rules. The true soul-hunger for sympathy, and for the spiritualistic communings of the higher life, must be estimated by something higher and grander than the obsolete laws of society. In some parts of the world, this soul-intercourse is beautifully indicated, among the untutored inhabitants, by rubbing their noses together. In England and America, the inhabitants usually shake hands, except where the soul-throbs pant for more expressive signs. If you can rise above the prejudices of education and custom, you will readily admit that the contact of noses is as innocent as the contact of hands, and kissing is only the contact of lips. So long as one can rise and soar into those unfathomable depths of the spirit-life, all of these outward manifestations sink into insignificance. You are not shocked when you see a brother kiss his sister. Now, consider all men and women, as the brothers and sisters of one great family, and the objections all disappear!"

"I look forward," said Nina, while Miss Abby recovered breath, "to a sojourn in Europe with more pleasure, because I shall be out of reach of this uncertain state of morals!"

"Do you intend Mr. Gaskins to be your escort?" said Mr. Bragdon, sarcastically.

"Perhaps. I have not met Mr. Gaskins yet, and, therefore, cannot decide. But, if so, you will not be required to disburse any money for his expenses; and, I suppose this point being settled, you will not think it necessary to interfere with my plans. Mr. Coke tells me that I can immediately have all the money I need."

"It is a strange freak, Nina!" said Mr. Bragdon, "and your relations and friends will not know what to think—starting off to Europe in this way, in winter, alone——"

"I beg your pardon," said Nina; "Miss Abby kindly consents to accompany me."

"Well, that does not change the case materially; the world will say that you have quarrelled with us. If you wait until spring Mary and I will probably accompany you."

"Many thanks," replied Nina, coldly; "but I prefer my present plans."

"And how long shall you remain abroad?"

"A year; several years, perhaps. I shall be governed in that matter only by my own inclinations."

"Of all the cases of moon-struck madness!" said Mr. Bragdon, in a towering rage, "this is the worst. I really think I would be justified in putting you under restraint!"

"You could not get possession of my inheritance if you did," replied Nina, contemptuously; "and it is very doubtful whether any court would give you control of my person. The law allows you to tyrannize over your wife, but not your sister-in-law; and, if it did, I would go to some country beyond the reach of the law."

"Nina!" said Mrs. Bragdon, "I am ashamed of you!"

"And I am sorry for you, Mary," replied Nina, moving to the door. "Come, Miss Abby! we will go to the hotel before dinner, and will have to do a little packing. Mr. Bragdon, I will instruct my legal adviser to see you, in relation to a partition of the personal property, at least. This is imperatively necessary. Excuse me, please!" she continued, as he started forward with inflamed visage, "excuse me; I am not well enough to contend with you to-day, and I must really decline a renewal of this discussion. Lawyers can arrange everything between us, without insulting each other. Come, Miss Abby!"

"John!" said Mrs. Bragdon, "you have really gone too far! I am positively shocked! Nina! if you leave this house this afternoon I'll never speak to you again! Never!"

Nina crossed the room and kissed her sister.

"I do not expect to speak to you again, Mary," she said, gently; "you are bound to stand by your husband, and I do not intend to allow him to speak to me henceforth. I forgive his insolence for your sake, but we are strangers from this hour. Good bye! Come, Miss Abby! The atmosphere of this house maddens me!" And she swept out of the room.

"Well!" said Mr. Bragdon, his thin lips quivering, "well! of all the she-devils I ever saw or heard of, Miss Norman is the most pronounced! It will avail nothing to cry, Mary! This had to come, sooner or later! I hear a squall in the nursery. You had better run up. Very likely your amiable sister is strangling the baby! And I'll go see Mr. Coke."

Mrs. Bragdon, catching at the suggestion, rushed up the broad stairs. The infant Bragdon was bawling himself black in the face, because he could not swallow his fist. He inherited temper. Nurse was offering him a libation of catnip tea, dashed with paregoric, and he had just knocked the spoon out of her hand, and was yelling with impotent rage, because he could not knock off nurse's head. Nina had locked herself in her own apartment, and was indulging in the luxury of a quiet flood of tears. Miss Keith was packing a trunk in business-like fashion, and enlivening Miss Norman with Dragger quotations.

"The infelicities of life, my dear," (she said "my dear," instead of "my brethren") "are so many stepping-stones to the higher spiritual state. Theology is always lamentably pugnacious; and nearly all the disputes in the world have their origin in diversity of creeds. All creeds are shackles. The economies of this present life all tend to freedom; and from the rich, warm soil of human consciousness, spring up the flowers that refuse to bloom in the arid desert of creeds. It may be that creeds have their uses, just as the murky vapours of the storm-cloud, charged with devastating forces that threaten destruction to all beneath their dismal canopy, really purify the circumambient fluid, and——"

"If I only knew!" said Nina, suddenly starting up, "if I only knew, positively, what my grandmother would have me do, all would be easy and plain!"

Miss Abby regarded her intently.

"Is there no way to decide the question?" continued Nina. "Can I find out possibly what she would do with that— Miss Abby, how can I extricate myself from these toils?"

"What do you wish to know?" said Miss Abby.

"I wish to have some clear announcement of—I cannot tell you! My grandmother gave me certain directions which I desire to fulfill. But obstacles have arisen, and I cannot do *exactly* what she required me to do; and now I am tormented because I cannot decide what is nearest to her wish that is still possible. Can I find out, by any means, what her wish would be under these changed circumstances?"

"Nothing easier!" said Miss Abby, in a half whisper. "Let us finish packing, and get away. You can have your doubts resolved before you sleep! Don't ask me now, I will tell you at the hotel, after dinner. Set your mind at rest."

CHAPTER XXX.

FOUND.

AFTER Darcy's fruitless promenade in the neighbourhood of Mr. Skillet's residence, walking up on one side of the street, crossing, and then down on the opposite side, he went back to Camden street. A watchful policeman, who had followed his monotonous march with sleepless vigilance, trying to discover which house in the block Darcy intended to enter burglariously, was totally discomfited when the youth turned out of the street. He was hopelessly lost in the throng of passengers when the officer reached the corner.

Arrived at Mr. Camp's quiet fireside, which consisted of a register in the wall of the living room, Darcy watched Mr. Camp as he struggled with his ode to Gentle Spring. The appalling fact that death was the only known rhyme for balmy breath remained, and tortured Mr. Camp's soul.

"What rhymes with breath, Mr. Gaston?" asked Mr. Camp.

"Death."

"That's it!" replied Mr. Camp, grinding his teeth; "it seems to me the words were invented just to torment a fellow."

"What is the trouble?" said Darcy, kindly.

"Why, I have got the first line all right," said Mr. Camp. "'Hail, gentle spring! whose balmy breath——'"

"Why don't you change it?" said Darcy. "Suppose you say, 'Hail, gentle spring! whose breath of balm.'"

"Um! Yes; that might do. I have a word that will rhyme with balm; and I've had it in my mind forty times to-night. But I guess it won't do. Have you seen the paper? there it is. Not much news. Dragger is going to make a speech, over to Brooklyn to-night, on 'Spondoolicks.' If it wasn't so cold, and if I had this thing in shape, I'd go."

"I've never been in Brooklyn," observed Darcy. "Half past

six. Plenty of time. I believe I'll go. I should like to hear Mr. Dragger, and I can't spare Sunday for that sort of amusement."

"Great man, sir!" said Mr. Camp. "Foremost man of the age! Great treat to hear him."

"Well, I'll go, then. What is the route?"

"Fulton street stage. Take the horse-car on t'other side. Conductor can tell you. Got your night-key? All right. Good night!"

Instead of the Fulton street stage, Darcy took his own elongated extremities, and strode down Broadway at a good pace. A passenger on the ferry boat, of whom he made inquiry, was going to hear Dragger, too, and would show him the way. Fine night to walk, and abundant time, so they declined the horse-car. On a corner, half a mile from the river, Darcy paused to admire the exterior of a church. The congregation was gathering, going in the side door by twos and threes.

"Doctor Sturdy's church," observed the stranger; " he is a good preacher, but s'uthin' of a Copperhead. Never would histe the flag onto his steeple."

"Why, he is the very man I have been desiring to hear," said Darcy; "and if you will excuse me, I think I will go in here, and postpone Mr. Dragger."

"Jest as you please," said the other, "but Doctor Sturdy don't preach politics. Good night."

The service was in the lecture room, in the basement. Darcy took a seat near the door. The room filled rapidly, and he moved up in the corner to make room for two ladies, who arrived rather late, escorted by an elderly gentleman. Thick veils hid their faces —as the night was cold—but before she threw her's back, Darcy knew that he was sitting beside Helen Ruthven. She had not seen him, and he drew farther back, and shaded his face with his hand, while his heart struggled to get out of his body.

Doctor Sturdy might as well have preached to a stone as to Darcy. He did not see him, did not hear the sound of his voice. When the hymns were sung, he heard Helen's voice, and nothing else. And while the discourse was being delivered, Darcy was investigating the emotions that are popularly supposed to belong to the hydraulic organ that was thumping against his ribs.

He was conscious of a blissful feeling of contentment. The mere fact that he was near her again was enough. But why did this fact make him oblivious to all other facts? Was it because he was now assured of her safety? No. An hour ago he was perfectly certain that she was under Mr. Skillet's roof. It was not that. How came she there? How did it chance that he was there to find her? He had no faith in chance. It was an omen full of glorious promise. Did Mr. Skillet know where she was? Beyond a doubt he did. Had he placed her in Brooklyn to hide her from him? Impossible! And he revolved these and kindred questions in his mind during the forty minutes which Doctor Sturdy consumed in his discourse. Then another hymn, a plaintive minor, and Helen's voice again, and suddenly he discovered that he loved her.

Loved her! of course, with every drop of his blood! How blind he had been! He had been loving her ever since that night on the train. The first glance of her great eyes had enslaved him for life. Now, he could recall the thrill that passed through his frame as he discovered that she was not a child, but a woman. And he gave full play to the tumultuous thoughts and memories crowding upon his mind, and rose mechanically with the rest when the benediction was pronounced. As she passed out, he leaned forward and whispered,

"Allow me to escort you."

She started at the sound of his voice, and turned, facing him.

"Oh, Mr. Gaston!" she said, "I did not expect to see you here."

"Heaven is kinder than we think," he replied. "I have been very unhappy about you, and now—may I walk with you?"

"Mrs. Bruce, this is Mr. Gaston, a friend of my father's. He came with me from Kentucky."

"Happy to see you, Mr. Gaston," said the elder lady; "will you walk round with Miss Harding? We will follow in a short time. There is a meeting of the session, and I will wait for Mr. Bruce, and you will wait at home for us."

Darcy bowed, offered his arm to Helen, and passed out, under the stars. There were several millions of them, and he thought they were all winking at him. He winked back.

"Did Mr. Skillet tell you—anything?" said Helen, when they were in the street.

"Nothing. I did not know you were in Brooklyn, until you sat down by me. Ah! then I knew."

She looked at him inquiringly, but said nothing.

"Last night, when I learned from Mrs. Camp that you were gone, and that she did not know where you went, I was filled with apprehensions. I spent the night in the streets."

"In the streets!" said Helen.

"Yes. I wandered about, aimlessly, hoping some fortunate chance would reveal your whereabouts to me. Chance! How dare I say chance! I mean, I hoped for Heavenly guidance. I dreaded a thousand evils, to all of which I thought you might be exposed! I prayed as I never prayed before, only asking that I might get where my arm would reach you. I thought, in all that vast multitude in the great city, I alone could defend you, and that I would gladly peril my life, if need be, to place you in safety once more. Look you! If you had known that a dog was suffering the tortures I endured through the long hours of darkness you would have pitied him!"

"I did not think—" said Helen, overcome by his tremulous accents, "I did not know you would——"

"No matter, now," said he, "my prayers are all answered now! I have found you again."

"I was obliged to come away from that place in Broadway. I could not stay longer, and Mr. Skillet brought me here. I have a school, and am so thankful for the occupation. If I had been allowed to select for myself, I could not have asked for circumstances so favorable. Mr. Bruce has three daughters at my school, and I board at his house."

"May I come here sometimes?" said Darcy, timidly; "pray do not say no. I will only come at such intervals as you please to appoint. But if you deny me! Alas! You are angry because I have been working with some law papers——"

"I have no interest in the law papers," said she, firmly; "I am resolved to repudiate all connection with them."

"I will abandon the matter at once," said Darcy, "if you will only look kindly upon me once more. I do not know of any possible interest you can have in the property. But I will quit the search if you wish me to do so. It is all mysterious to me, and I am sick of it, anyhow."

"You say you do not know of any interest I can have," said Helen, doubtfully; "why did you ask me about the property, a few days ago?"

"I cannot tell you," answered Darcy, in some confusion, "because my duty to my client keeps me silent."

"If you relinquish the case?" said she.

"Even then," replied Darcy, "I should be bound to remain silent. I am so much mortified to find that you think me capable of fraud——"

"I never said that," objected Helen; "I said your client proposed fraud. I am sure of that at least. Here is the house. I cannot decide at once about your visits. But I think you——"

"Please allow that point to remain unsettled," said Darcy, earnestly. "I will not come for a long, long time. But let me come again, if it is only to learn that I must come no more."

"You will have to come in now," answered Helen; "Mrs. Bruce told you to wait for her. It would be rude to refuse. And about the property, I think you had better ascertain what the legal rights are; and I rely upon you to tell me exactly my position with reference to it, or to any part of it. Can you engage to do this?"

"Certainly. If I find you have any interest, or are in any way concerned in the distribution, I will tell you first."

"Before you tell your client?"

"You are my first client!" answered Darcy, passionately. "Your claims upon me override all other claims. Oh, Helen! if I dared——, but I do not dare! I may come, then—when I finish my investigation?"

"Yes." She looked at him, astonished at his excitement, as he caught her hand and pressed it against his breast.

"Then I will come to-morrow evening," said Darcy, triumphantly; "I will open the sealed envelope this blessed night. What street is this?"

"Jeryboblum."

"Four doors from the corner. I feel like making poetry—

"'Hail! gentle Spring, whose balmy breath——'"

Helen led the way into the house, feeling her heart sink, as she recognised the evident tokens of inebriation. So young a man, and so short a time in that wicked city, and already a victim to the prevalent vice of the age! Would it be *very* improper if she should write to Henry Gaston, Esq., begging him to use his influence with his young brother, and warn him against the horrid demon of drink!

Meantime, Darcy, in the pangs of delirium that Helen's eyes had created, sat quiet in the handsome parlour, while Mr. and Mrs. Bruce put him through a polite catechism, touching the main points in Doctor Sturdy's excellent discourse. It was a tough ordeal, but he passed it safely, chiefly because the old couple were won by his handsome countenance and sparkling eyes. When he arose to depart, they cordially invited him to repeat his visit. He shook hands with them, and with Helen, who went to her room immediately, mourning that this promising youth should put a thief into his mouth to steal away his brains. Darcy walked back to Camden street, audibly invoking " Gentle Spring," at every step, while the frosty air made his ears tingle.

CHAPTER XXXI.

MEDIUMS.

THERE had been some "business" relations, of a questionable character, betwixt Mr. Rupert Grey and Doctor Lamis. The latter had been regimental surgeon early in the war, and Mr. Grey was commissary. The accounts which were rendered, certified " upon honor," and supported by vouchers in duplicate, were according to the regulations, but it was said by some ill-natured copperheads, that they had been "cooked," and both officers resigned in indignant haste, after a short service. As Mr. Grey had no experience in culinary matters, whatever cooking was done, was done by Doctor Lamis, who got a portion of broth for his pains. He had been quite impecunious before the war, but he had bought the residence in Brooklyn since his retirement from the army, which he had paid for, opened a spiritualistic medium shop, and joined Mr. Dragger's church. That is, he took a pew. When Mr. Grey blossomed into Mr. Blake, he went directly to the Brooklyn residence for two reasons: First, because it was in a retired street, and he had reasons for keeping out of view; and second, because, being dead, he thought some one might desire to commune with his spirit, and he desired to be on hand when the occasion arrived.

Doctor Lamis had a seance on each Wednesday night, and when Darcy, as recorded in the previous chapter, was giving undivided attention to Doctor Sturdy's Wednesday evening lecture, Doctor Lamis was stirring up the ghosts in a neighbouring street. There were two ladies, closely veiled, who had come in a carriage, and they sat apart from the rest, while the first relay of spirits were being interrogated. The "test medium" was a slender, hollow-eyed woman, twenty-five probably, who seemed to be on tolerably intimate terms with spirits that had shuffled off their mortal coils at periods more or less remote, as well as with those whose departures from the present sphere had been recent.

With the questions and responses that occupied the earlier part of the seance, the present story has nothing to do. The hollow-eyed young woman was evidently out of health, and at nine o'clock Doctor Lamis announced that she was too much indisposed to continue her mediation. The larger part of the company retired, leaving the two veiled ladies, who had thus far received no benefit from their attendance. There was a fee always paid at the door on entrance, and Doctor Lamis approached them to give them some small return for their outlay, in the form of spiritual lore.

"There was some obstacle to-night, ladies," he said, bowing, "that prevented as clear manifestations as usual. You did not take part?"

"No," answered the shorter lady; "we wished to wait until we could have a more private seance. My friend thought you could perhaps furnish another medium——"

"It is not customary to renew the seances. The spirits do not respond so readily. You should have joined the circle when you arrived."

"We understand," responded the taller lady, "that the seance is over. We would, if convenient, renew the sitting," and she held out her hand with a crisp, new ten dollar note in her gloved fingers. The Doctor instinctively took the money.

"It is irregular," he muttered; "but if you will excuse me for a few minutes, I will see what can be done," and he left the room.

The Doctor was absent a full half-hour. Just before his reappearance, the ladies noticed the solitary burner that was lighted, gradually growing dim. They both manifested some uneasiness, and were about to retire from the gloomy room, when he re-entered, followed by a tall old gentleman, perfectly bald, but adorned with a silvery beard flowing down upon his breast. He wore a black robe, with loose sleeves, something like the gown of a priest. A pair of spectacles with side shades concealed his eyes. He supported his steps with a long staff, though he exhibited no signs of feebleness, as he crossed the room, and took the seat lately occupied by the test medium. The light grew dimmer.

"I cannot promise success, ladies," said the Doctor gravely, in a low tone; "but my venerable preceptor consents to make the effort. Will you please sit at the table, and remove your veils?"

"Is that imperatively necessary?" said the taller lady, as she took the seat indicated.

"No!" replied the old man, in a husky voice; "it will make no difference. Place your hands on the table, thus! Now remain quiet."

After five or ten minutes of silence, there was a ticking sound on the table, like the click of a telegraphic instrument.

"Proceed!" said the old man; "mention no names, but state your wishes. With whom do you wish to commune?"

"With him I sent on a mission recently, from whom I received one message."

The ticking sound on the table continued, while the old man sat mute, his white beard floating over his breast, his head bowed down.

"I found not that for which you sent me, but I found the next," he muttered. "What do you desire?"

"The next!" said the tall lady, in visible excitement. "Where is the next?"

"In due time you shall know fully. You know much already."

"Then I am right," said the lady. "When shall I know?"

"It depends upon yourself," replied the medium, huskily. "When your purpose is distinct and positive, summon me again."

"One word more," said the lady; "is the person I seek in New York?"

"You know!" was the response; "violate not the truth, even in your thought. Ask me only that which you do not know."

The lady was silent. There was a crash on the table, that sounded like the blow of an open palm. The ticking sound ceased.

"Gone!" said the old man. "What more?"

"I should like to ask a question of—of—a relation who was dear to me. But I shrink from the thought."

"Courage and truth need know no fear," replied the man.

"One question only," said the lady, hurriedly; "if I may."

There was a longer silence. Then a little musical box standing on the mantel began to play. It was a plaintive air, and when it was finished the click of the spring that stopped the machinery was distinctly heard.

Another brief interval of silence, and then there were light ticks heard on the table. All the surroundings were impressive. The darkened room, the quiet so profound that the occupants heard each other breathe. The veiled women bending over the table with white hands outspread upon its polished surface. The old medium, with snowy beard, his head bent down, waiting.

"Reluctant!" he murmured; "nevertheless, ask your question."

"I cannot do exactly what was required of me," said the lady slowly, "and I am doubtful about my duty!"

"Fulfil the will!" answered the medium. There was another blow upon the table, and the ticking ceased. "We are alone," he continued, pushing his chair back from the table. They all arose, and the old man, with stately dignity, walked out of the room. The gas gradually grew more brilliant, and the two ladies, bidding the Doctor good night, departed. As they passed through the hall, the taller lady was several steps in advance. Doctor Lamis held the outer door open for her egress. A side door in the hall swung back, as the shorter lady passed, and she saw the old man, standing within the dark room. He arrested her steps an instant, beckoning her nearer.

"Come alone to-morrow night," he whispered, and immediately retired, closing the door noiselessly. The carriage was at the curb, and the ladies entered and drove off.

"Now, Nina," said Miss Keith, "tell me just what you think about all this!"

"Wait a little, Miss Abby," replied Nina; "everything is so strange! I cannot make up my mind. I am not sure that I have done right to come. Yet I feel better satisfied, too. I must sleep upon it. To-morrow I will tell you."

When Doctor Lamis closed the door, he went back to the side room, and found the venerable medium divesting himself of spectacles and beard. He turned up the gas, drew a comfortable arm-chair to the register, and lighted his cigar. The Doctor watched his proceedings in silence.

"Well, Lamis," said the medium, "you have had a tolerably successful night. Those last goers appeared to be liberal."

"They did not pay enough to compensate me for the fright," answered the Doctor; "you are certainly the most brazen man of my acquaintance. Did you know them?"

The other straightened out his arm, and bringing his fingers to his mouth with elegant deliberation, removed his cigar, and blew out a succession of smoke rings. Replacing the weed, with the same elaborate precision, he shook his head, negatively.

"Then what the deuce did you mean by 'fulfilling the will?' The first thing I thought when you began, was, that you knew the parties."

"Through their veils?" said Rupert; "pooh! You don't make any allowance for a fellow's discernment. When you get two women together, all you have to do, is to let them contradict each other a short time, to find out whatever you want to know."

"But they didn't talk at all. One of them never said a word," persisted Doctor Lamis; "what did you mean by the will?"

Another pause, while Rupert went through his graceful performance with his cigar, and blew off another series of rings. There was an air of cold-blooded insolence in all that he did, that was highly attractive.

"Hum!" he said, thoughtfully; "the will? Well, I know very little about the will, and I have been meditating upon that very topic since the ladies left. If you will wait twenty-four hours I may be able to tell you more. As for the existence of a will, that was clearly revealed by the tall lady's questions. I intend to know more about the will to-morrow; and, in fact, I invited the other one to return to-morrow night alone."

"You did!" said the other, aghast; "when did you give the invitation?"

"While you were doing the polite at the door. Bless you, she'll come! Curiosity will bring her, if nothing else; and whatever she knows, I shall know, I presume."

"You are mighty close and mysterious, Grey," said the Doctor, irritably: "I believe there is some trick about this business."

"Well," responded Grey, coolly; "suppose there is? It seems to me that you have not lost much thus far. You said they gave you a new fee before I went in. How much?"

"Five dollars," said Doctor Lamis, keeping back a part of the price. Rupert had an easy habit of borrowing, and no sort of a habit of paying.

"I don't want any," observed Rupert; "you may collar all the dollars, and I will take my share in information. Don't be so suspicious! I am telling you the exact truth. There is some sort of a will, and if judiciously managed, there may be some profit in it. But I don't know its provisions," and here he removed his cigar, ground his teeth savagely, and replaced it. "I have a suspicion that I know some things about it; but I don't know enough. Ah!" he concluded, with a gentle sigh, "let us be patient. Patience always conquers."

"Perhaps you can explain what you meant by 'not finding that for which you were sent, and finding the next.' There must have been something in that, for the young woman was impressed."

Rupert leaned back, and laughed.

"My dear Lamis," he said; "you do not discriminate! You saw me before I put on these," and he touched the beard and glasses, and you knew who was behind them. But these ladies had no reason to suspect anything unreal. They were already somewhat awed by your former operations, and when I came in, they were prepared for some stunning revelations. All I had to do was to keep solemn, and say nothing. All that tomfoolery about "the next" was just as good as any other humbug. When I found I was getting out of my depth, I dismissed the spirit, and broke up the seance. What the deuce! Do you wish to monopolize *all* the humbug! Let's go to bed!"

CHAPTER XXXII.

THE SEALED ENVELOPE.

DARCY reached Camden street in due time, that is, an hour before midnight. Mr. Camp had been floored by the balmy breath of gentle spring, and was dreaming of stocks and bonds. It is a remarkable fact in psychology that poets never dream poetry, but invariably fall back upon the prosaic events of daily life and occupation when they get into dreamland. So Mr. Camp bothered his restless brains, even while he slept, in calculating safe margins on stock operations, and the shrill whistle of the winter blast that shook his windows suggested no thought of the rhymeless breath of the coming season. Anyhow, it was far more satisfactory to make furtive dives after the missing or reluctant syllable during business hours, as there was always present to Mr. Camp's mind the conviction that Mr. Skillet would put him in a lunatic asylum if he ever caught him in the fine frenzy of poetic composition.

Mr. Gaston locked the street door, and, taking off his boots, ascended the stairs in his stocking-feet. He was tired, and, like all heedless boys, he threw off his overcoat, and stretched himself

THE SEALED ENVELOPE. 155

at full length on the lounge to rest. The register in his room was open, fortunately, but as he fell asleep in two minutes, and slept profoundly three hours, he contracted a very respectable cold. There was an alarm of fire in the neighborhood, and the rattle of the engines under his window aroused him, and consulting his watch, he found it was two o'clock. Starting up, he got out Nina's packet, and selecting the sealed envelope, he opened it, and took out the documents it contained.

There were several papers, all written in Nina's hand. He took up the first, which was endorsed "Extracts from the will." As he glanced over this paper, he noticed the absence of names, and the substitution of initials wherever the description of persons was necessary.

"I give and bequeath to A. B. all that parcel of land known as Number One, with all the improvements thereon, and I direct my executors to give a clear title to this property, free of all charge for taxes, assessments or commissions, to the said A. B. And if from any cause this transfer shall be delayed, either by reason of any difficulty in finding the said A. B., or by reason of his refusal to accept the same, or on any other account, I direct my executors to fulfil these instructions at date of transfer, whenever that may be. And if the growth of the city in that direction shall enhance the value of this parcel of ground a hundred fold before the date of this transfer, I charge my executors to disregard this fact. And I expressly forbid any compromise or composition, such as the substitution of other property for this parcel Number One, or the assessment of money value, with or without the knowledge and concurrence of said A. B., or any other settlement than the transfer of the ground itself, every acre, rood, perch or square inch, as fully described in the mortgage from the father of said A. B. to me, and also in the formal release of title, signed by the said A. B. and his mother, then a widow."

"Ruthven's Folly!" said Darcy; "we are getting along. Number One is identified, anyhow. And now to pin Mr. A. B."

He took up the old deeds, and looking through them, found the release of title.

"Darcy Ruthven! A. B. Ah! I begin to see light," said Darcy. "Now, I wonder if I am justified in going any further? She has substituted these initials for the very purpose of concealing from me the true names, not knowing that the deeds would reveal them to me. Oh, Helen! it is really in your interest that I am working now! If this will is valid—then Helen is an heiress and I shall be stricken dumb. I must read to the end now."

The next extract from the will contained a description of the house erected upon the property, and a memorandum of the cost of building, which amounted to forty thousand dollars. Then followed memoranda relating to the removal of various liens, some held by bankers, and some imposed by the builders in default of payment. All of these were recorded as against " C. D., his heirs, executors, administrators or assigns." It appeared from one of the other papers that the whole property, Number One, had finally been sold under process of law, by the sheriff, to satisfy these numerous claims, and "bought by me at said Sheriff's sale, as recorded in a certain Court, and by me transferred to said A. B.'s father for the consideration named in a mortgage executed on the same date, with bond attached, &c."

"This costly house," continued the record, "gave the name to this estate."

"Ruthven's Folly! Built by the elder Ruthven," said Darcy to himself, "and thereby involving the estate, and creating these various liens. It seems that this testator either stepped in to save the builder from ruin, or—to get a valuable property at a nominal price."

"Although the title to this property, Number One," continued the record, "is legally in me, yet the present value is so far beyond all my outlays, that a large sum is due, in equity, to the former owner. It was also agreed between the father of A. B. and myself, that my apparent ownership should remain until his son was of age; and to reimburse me for all my expenditures, certain other parcels of ground were transferred to me. But when A. B. attained his majority, I refused to execute the deed for prudential reasons, and A. B. and his mother united in a formal relinquishment of all claims upon Number One, after prolonged discussion, conducted in very bad temper on both sides.

"But my purpose has always been fixed to restore this property whenever it could be safely done. A. B. removed to Cincinnati, and is now practising law in that city. The final altercation between us was of so serious a nature as to preclude the possibility of friendly conference on either side. And this tardy justice is done to A. B. in the hope that death will have softened all asperities between us.

"And if it should happen that A. B. also has departed this

life, when the provisions of this will are to be carried out, then I hereby direct my executors to see that his heir, or whosoever shall bear his name, shall be placed in peaceable possession of Number One, according to the instructions hereinbefore given.

"And failing this—that is to say, if no heir or representative of the said A. B. can be found, I then direct my executors to pay to Rupert Grey, during his life, a sum equal to the annual interest (at seven per centum) on the assessed value of said property, in quarterly payments year by year, while the property itself shall remain in possession of my natural heirs."

There was a note appended in parenthesis.

("This last provision is expressly revoked in a codicil.")

The paper ended here. Darcy read it all over again, and tried to recall the explanations that Helen gave. Colonel Ruthven had died in the assurance that this property was wrongfully wrested from him, and in undoubted enmity against the testator. Darcy remembered a dozen stories, told him by his own father, of Ruthven's haughty refusal to receive fees, honestly earned, when his clients intimated that they were excessive. He was morbidly sensitive upon all topics in which money was involved; and it is probable that the dispute with Mr. Norman over this identical property had heightened this sensibility. The reader will remember that Mr. Coke held a note from him, rejecting with disdain a *quasi* proposal to restore Ruthven's Folly, which was made by Mrs. Norman, recently deceased; but neither Colonel Ruthven nor Darcy had the slightest idea of the present value of the property, which had enhanced enormously since the war began. And in the first flush of his military ardour, Colonel Ruthven was more earnestly set upon the destrution of this special house, where his school days were spent, because it was now in possession of those who were doubly his enemies, who insulted him with suggestions of an "amicable settlement" at the very beginning of hostilities.

But what was Nina's design? So far as the will went, there was no need of anything beyond ordinary formalities, to give the property into Helen's possession. She seemed to dread some interference, but certainly no claim could be set up that could overthrow the will.

There was a second paper, however. Darcy took it from the envelope, and, unfolding it, found it was a note addressed to himself.

"Mr. Gaston will have discovered," it ran, "from the extracts given, that some irregularity must have attended the transfer of Number One; but I have learned that the title is undoubtedly in the estate not yet divided. The will has no value, as a legal document, as a later will was made, giving sole possession of all the estate to my grandmother. I have given Mr. Gaston all these extracts, and have specially followed the references to property Number One, because I wish him to devise some method whereby I can have certain special parcels of property conveyed to me, so that I may be able to sell or otherwise dispose of them, without consulting the desires of other heirs to the same property. And if Mr. Gaston will prepare such documents as may be needed to effect this, I shall be greatly obliged to him. Take Number One as an illustration, and perfect the papers that will convey to me, in my sole right, the ownership to that, and by this means the transfers of other parcels will readily follow.

"And Mr. Gaston will doubtless understand that I desire to obtain exclusive possession of this or any other property belonging to the estate, at the proper value, and not otherwise. In fact, the only obstacle to be feared is the possibility that others who have a joint interest with me, may *also* desire special portions—for example: Number One. In which event, it is my earnest desire to pay out of my own inheritance as much more than the actual value, as may compensate the other parties in interest for their relinquishment of a similar preference. But I—for special reasons—object to a partition of certain parcels—Number One, for example. And Mr. Gaston will render me the greatest service, if he can arrange matters so that I can attain my object without contention. The question of price to be paid is entirely secondary. The main point is to get sole possession of such parcels as I may designate—Number One, for illustration—by any legal means, and by the payment of any sum, just or exorbitant.

"Mr. Gaston will now perceive the necessity for the secrecy that has hitherto been observed in the initial steps. If the other parties in interest should discover my preference for special portions of the inheritance, it is highly probable that they would interpose serious obstacles to the accomplishment of my designs. It is not necessary to explain the reasons that would actuate them; nor is it at all necessary to acquaint them with my purposes. Without accurate knowledge of the law, I am still persuaded that I could attain my object by legal proceedings, which would, however, be very objectionable and very distasteful to me; and I can only say, in conclusion, that I rely entirely upon Mr. Gaston's discretion and judgment, and confidently expect him to devise a plan whereby the partition of the estate can be amicably arranged, not only in the way that I desire, but also in such a manner as will be perfectly equitable, or, rather, far more *profitable* to the other heirs than to me. Only, I *must* have at least one choice.

"*Monday night.* "N. N."

"This is a stunner!" said Darcy, as he undressed and prepared himself for his peaceful couch. "This Miss Norman has a mind of her own! She talks about law-points, as if they were the obstacles to be overcome, whereas the real task is to circumvent that sharp looking fellow, Mr. Bragdon, who stared so insolently at me. One thing is clear. Helen has no interest under that old will. Shall I tell her about its provisions? Ah! here is a nice question! If I could only get at Brother Tige!"

Darcy would not have slept so quietly if he had known that Brother Tige was at that moment approaching New York at the rate of thirty miles to the hour, rolling from side to side in a sleeping car, and dreaming about him, and Helen, with occasional dips into the private history of Mr. Rupert Grey, some of whose later exploits Tige had investigated while he waited in Cincinnati for the eastern bound train.

CHAPTER XXXIII.

Mr. Skillet's Sympathy.

MR. SKILLET was an early riser. His bachelor household was a model of punctuality and order. His breakfast was always ready at seven o'clock, at all seasons of the year, and while he discussed this meal, he usually gave orders for his dinner at six. On the morning succeeding the events last recorded, he was crossing Fulton Ferry at about eight.

Arriving at Jeryboblum street, he found Helen in the parlour, still wading through the rhetorical flourishes in the pile of "compositions" that had been presented by her pupils on the previous day. There had been a holiday of two weeks, between sessions, and Miss Keith always improved these shining hours, by giving the young ladies some abstruse topic to write upon, requiring them to present four pages each at the re-opening of the Institute. It is to be regretted that these specimens of light literature never got into print; not so much on account of the substantial loss incurred by the reading public, as because their publication would have revealed a startling similarity in logic and rhetoric, to the discourses and lectures of the renowned first men of the age. Those of the girls who were deeply pious, fell into the same strain as that adopted by the Reverend Dragger. Those who were not troubled with piety, but took philosophy as a substitute, employed the more felicitous expressions of the other first man, Mr. Squizzem. In the main, and viewing the matter in its moral aspect, there was no material difference between the philosophy and the piety,—as the first contradicted all established laws of logic, and the second scouted all popular creeds. Both classes were composed in the gush dialect, which had this advantage: The meaning of the words employed was transitive, and the same words and sentences would serve to indicate a strictly original postulate in social economy, (that had been exploded for twenty centuries), or to illustrate a novel proposition in Theology, which had been propounded to Eve by her interlocutor nearly six thousand years ago. This peculiarity of the gush tongue was one proof of the progress of the age, as the sense of the passages depended entirely upon the tones or expression of countenance, on the part of the reader. A solemn air indicated theology; an air of suppressed wisdom indicated philosophy.

Helen would have been overwhelmed, if it had not been for her previous training in Cincinnati, where Mrs. Crowder had indoctrinated her in the philosophy and religion of Professor Hang, who also dealt exclusively in gush. She had been required to read "Lies for To-morrow" in her daily instructions to Mrs. Crowder's daughters, and she had only the grammatical construction of the sentences to bother her, as the sentiments of the Essays, being in gush, made no impression upon her mind.

"I am so glad to see you, Mr. Skillet," said Helen, "I have been reading these compositions, and I really don't know what I ought to do about them."

"Exactly!" said Mr. Skillet, "I see! Ya-as! How are you to-day?"

"Quite well, sir. And I can never tell you how deep my debt of gratitude to you——"

"Oh! it's no consequence," said Mr. Skillet; "I'll send in my bill. Let it set, please."

"The change from that horrid place, to this! Oh dear! How could I live as long as I did, where that wretched man was! Mrs. Bruce is so kind, and her daughters are charming! And I heard a real de-light-ful discourse last night from Doctor Sturdy: almost equal to Kentucky!"

"Well," said Mr. Skillet, "you kicked up quite a considerable rumpus, yesterday! The whole of N'Yauk was in an uproar. There was Dassy—sot up all night, and then whaled your man at Tilter's."

"My man at Tilter's?" said Helen, astonished.

"Ya-as! I mean that slick young whelp, Donis. He came down town and made some brags about courtin' you, and Dassy heard him. He put a head onto him in about two minits! I seed the chap afterwards, a comin' out of a beer cellar, lookin' quite seedy. His hat was stove in, and all the tar was washed outen his mustash. Bully for Dassy! I was a goin' to old Tilter to enter a complaint, but I thought after I seed him—I mean Donis—that I could let him set! I guess the young cuss won't bother any other gal this week!"

"I am very sorry," said Helen, piously repressing and trampling upon her first feeling of delight; "I hope Mr. Gaston did not hurt him seriously."

"Oh, it's no consequence!" replied Mr. Skillet; "when I see Tilter, I'll tell him to swop that whelp off for a kitten, and then drown the kitten to keep t'other feller from swopping back! But what am I to tell Dassy?"

"I don't understand, sir."

"Why, he was half demented! He wanted to hire the police force to look for you! He kinder feels like he had a lien on you, since you come on the same train with him. He said he would give one of his arms or legs to know you were safe! I promised him to find out by to-day, and now I crave to know what I'm to tell him?"

"Suppose he does not ask you?" said Helen, demurely.

"Oh! he'll ask fast enough. I shall find him at the office when I go back waitin' for me."

"If he asks, you may tell him I am quite safe and well. You might say I am teaching school."

"And shall I tell him where the school is?" asked Mr. Skillet, shutting one eye; "he might want to put in some compositions himself."

"I don't think it will be necessary," answered Helen, blushing a little; "don't you think it will be better to make no exceptions?"

"It's no consequence," said Mr. Skillet, somewhat disappointed; "but I may tell him I know where you are, and have seen you! It will be quite like a cold bath to the boy, too! And now I must go. What is the matter with the compositions?"

"Oh! I had forgotten. Miss Keith gave the young ladies a topic to write upon during the vacation. It is "The Cognition of the Inner Life," and I don't know what she meant, and am afraid none of the young ladies knew either. I have read them all, and I cannot find one word of sense in any! I did not know such—stuff—I was going to say, could be written. May I read one to to you?"

Mr. Skillet started to his feet and seized his hat.

"Jerusalem!" he ejaculated; "five minits of nine. I must git across. That boy will hang himself on a hat peg in the back office. Good mornin', Miss Harding."

"That was a narrow escape!" he muttered, as he raced down to the ferry; "if I had stayed there another minit, she'd a read that pile of she-literatoor to me. What in the dickins can I tell Dassy? He'll put me through as soon as I tell him I know where she is. She is pooty and slick as molasses candy, by Gemini! But she don't care no more for Dassy than for old Camp! Wimmen is mighty tickelish securities to invest in, anyhow! You can never tell how much margin to ask. Dassy may as well hang up his fiddle!"

As he predicted, Mr. Skillet found Darcy at the office. The young gentleman was poring over a complicated account, and was apparently far more interested in the figures which related to investments in sundry stocks than to any investments in the securities that Mr. Skillet had just apostrophized. The old gentleman slipped into the back office, and busied himself with the morning letters, dreading the interview that he was sure was impending.

In due time, Darcy came in for the letters. Mr. Skillet had made pencil memoranda upon them, which he explained volubly.

"This cheque is from Scoop," he said, "and you must write polite to him. He wants gold for sterling, and not for speculation. Tell Camp to charge him a naith commission. That's regular, anyway, and he won't think he's cheated if we charge full commission. He has not sent quite enough for the ten thousand, but it's no consequence. Buy it for him regular, as soon as the Board opens, and send him statements. This is Brittle's letter. He says, sell out and close his account. All right! Charge him a sixteenth both ways. Camp will tell you his balance. I think we are carrying Fifty for him."

"Can't we take ten of it for Mr. Scoop?" said Darcy.

"No! Let every tub set on its own bottom. My rule has always been to keep each transaction separate. Don't mix things. If you once learn to stick to your commissions, through thick and thin, you'll come out all right. That's the first principle. The other is: keep your margins up. It's no consequence who your customer is. If it's your father or your mother-in-law, always git your margin. If you want to turn plaguey fool and squander your earnin's, you can always give them to a hospital! But don't give 'em away while you are playing at business. Hadn't you better git out now, and go round to the gold room? I'd like to git Scoop's ten at the opening."

"Fifteen minutes of ten, sir," said Darcy; "I wanted to ask you about——"

"All right!" said Mr. Skillet; "when you come back."

"Only one word, sir——"

"You can't say nauthin' in one word!" objected Mr. Skillet, testily. "Oh! about the gal? Wa-al, she is all right, safe and sound!"

"Yes, sir," replied Darcy indifferently; "thank you, sir. But I desired to ask you what I ought to do if I *knew* that a man was following me and watching all my movements."

"Following you?"

"Yes, sir. There is a great red whiskered rascal that I have found two or three times dogging my footsteps. There is no doubt about it."

"Dogging your footsteps! Wa-al! I've got an English mastiff to my heouse. I'll lend him to you, and then you can dog *his* footsteps, and mebbe a small slice of one of his legs. You'd better come round to-night and git a little acquainted with 'Towzer.' He is not much friendly at first, but you can git him to know you. Have you spoke to the man?"

"No, sir."

"Why not?"

"Because I—I thought I might get into a quarrel. These New

York policemen are so thick that one can't knock a fellow down without being caught."

"It seems to me," quoth Mr. Skillet, "that you knocked that Donis cuss around quite considerable, yesterday, without gitten caught!"

"Yes, sir; but that was in Pearl street, and we were behind the cotton bales. Ah! if I could only get the other fellow there!"

"Wa-al! S'pose you did—what then?"

"Then I could—speak to him, sir. You don't know how annoying it is to be followed and watched. Three minutes of ten—I'm off, sir."

"Wa-al!" said Mr. Skillet, solus, "this bangs the witches. I can't understand these young whelps any more than the wimmen. He cares no more for Miss Harding than she does for him. I s'pose it's all right. Here I sot, getting ready to bust into tears of sympathy, and he just nods his head and goes about his business. I can't understand it! Yesterday he was all afire, and ready to engage the mayor and aldermen in a hunt for my little school-marm. To-day, he only wants to go for some red whiskered chap and put a head onto him. It's a clean waste of raw material to be gettin' up sympathy, and I'll quit that line of business. Hello! What is it, Jim?"

The office Mercury presented a neat little note, written on mourning paper.

"Miss Norman presents her compliments to Mr. Skillet, and will thank him to call some time this morning, at the Fifth Avenue Hotel."

"Fifth Avenoo Hotel!" said Mr. Skillet. "Some fine mornin' I'll get a note from Rome or Jerusalem, asking me to step across and have a talk. Fifth Avenoo; two miles, good. But it's no consequence. I'll have to go. What the dickens is she doin' at the Fifth Avenoo Hotel?"

CHAPTER XXXIV.

Miss Abby's Visit.

THE mysterious invitation which Miss Abby received from the venerable medium, possessed her mind the whole succeeding day. She felt that it was private and confidential, though she did not precisely understand whether the message was from the spirit world, or from the medium on his own account. During the day, which was ostensibly occupied in preparation for the coming voyage, she studiously avoided conversation with Nina, who, in turn, was preoccupied and silent. The sober light of day dispelled some of the mists of the previous night, and the realities of living interests around her displaced the unnatural excitement that attended the seance. Still, Nina was not able to shake off the influence entirely, especially as the mysterious injunctions she had apparently received, chimed with tolerable accuracy with her previous purposes. She finally decided to send for Mr. Skillet, and resolved to be guided by his advice, in the matter that most specially interested her.

It was about noon, when Nina announced to Miss Abby that she expected Mr. Skillet, who would probably accept an invitation to lunch with them.

"Then I will go to Brooklyn after lunch," said Miss Abby, "as you will want to talk business; and I have to arrange finally for the conduct of the Institute during my absence. Mr. Skillet assures me that the young lady he recommended is eminently qualified, but I should like to see her myself."

When Mr. Skillet arrived, Miss Keith metaphorically collared him on the threshold.

"Excuse me a moment, Nina," said she; "but I will not have another favourable opportunity to consult Mr. Skillet about the Institute. What is the lady's name?"

"Oh! Ah! You mean the school-marm? Miss Harding."

"Miss Harding. Yes. Do you happen to know anything of her inner life? I mean her spiritual perceptions?"

"Exactly!" said Mr. Skillet. "I don't think she has any. She goes to hear Dr. Sturdy preach, over to Brooklyn. I recommended Dragger, but——"

"She did not accept your advice?"

"Wa-al, it warn't exactly advice. I only told her it was a good place to hear first-class hifalootin. Great Cæsar! Nobody can come up to Dragger in hifalootin. Miss Harding had a lot of writing about the 'inner life,' which the scholars brought in yesterday."

"Yes," said Miss Abby, complacently; "I gave them that topic at the end of last session."

"Wa-al, that's jest in Dragger's line, you know."

Miss Abby winced. The model essay upon the topic was one

of the Reverend Dragger's sermons. She thought Mr. Skillet a disagreeable old heretic.

"Dragger preached last Sunday," continued Mr. Skillet, "about the imaginations of men's hearts, and he proved that all religion consisted in the imagination. The *Herald* says it was a masterly effort."

"Yes," answered Miss Keith; "I heard him. But Miss Harding went to Dr. Sturdy's, because the Bruces go there. You said she lived at Mr. Bruce's?"

"I wanted she should go to your old boardin' house," said Mr. Skillet, "but Mrs. Bruce kind o' took to her."

"It would have been more judicious to have gone to Mrs. Smith's," observed Miss Abby. "Mrs. Bruce always pays her bills, and Mrs. Smith don't. However, you have arranged it all, and I shall not object. I have not met Miss Harding, though, and I am going over to Brooklyn to-day to ascertain the extent of her scholastic attainments."

"Do as you please," replied Mr. Skillet; "but I advise you to let her set! If you put her through Dragger, she won't go up head. But as for regular schoolin', I guess she can stand. But if she don't seem to suit, you can git another, and I'll take her for governess to my nieces. Miss Norman, what are your orders?"

"First, to take off your overcoat, and join us at lunch," replied Nina," and afterwards to advise me about a personal matter. Miss Abby is going to Brooklyn, presently. You had better take the carriage, Miss Abby."

"I shall not return until late, probably," said Miss Keith.

"Then it is more important to have the carriage. We are ready, Mr. Skillet."

When Mr. Skillet left the hotel, early in the afternoon, he was in a very confused mental state. Miss Norman had, to use his own words, knocked the spots out of him.

"It's no consequence!" he cogitated; "but she is dead set in her intentions. It is the quarest business I ever mixed in. But she is dead set! She wouldn't listen to any objections. And I happen to know that Bragdon is jest as dead set on the same property. I can't see my way out, and I mustn't ask Dassy. It won't do for him to be mixed."

Miss Keith had sundry things to do in Brooklyn. She called at the Institute, introduced herself to Helen, and then sat by, observant, while she heard recitations. It was history day, and

MISS ABBY'S VISIT. 167

the classes were not as well prepared as was desirable, being the second day of the session. But the new teacher was patient and sympathizing, and the pupils got through the trial without serious failures. Miss Harding complimented them upon their previous training, very justly, for Miss Keith was a highly accomplished instructress. And the latter was duly impressed with the Kentucky girl's readiness, in helping the stumbling pupils through or over the hard places. Helen did not know she was being investigated, and therefore felt no trepidation, and made no failures. Miss Abby left the Institute at five o'clock highly pleased with her successor. Somehow she did not get her own consent to discuss the relative merits of the two schools of theology represented by Dragger and Sturdy. There was a certain air about Helen that restrained her. The carriage had been dismissed, with instructions to the coachman to present himself at Doctor Lamis's at eight o'clock.

Miss Abby dined with Mrs. Smith. It was a farewell visit, as she would sail the next week. Mrs. Smith, by an effort of will that made her feel quite limp afterwards, took twenty dollars out of her pocket-book, and paid it to Miss Keith "on account." She had two girls at the Institute.

It was seven o'clock when Miss Keith arrived at the spiritual mansion. She was shown into the side room, now brilliantly lighted, and was courteously received by the venerable medium himself.

"Did you come alone?" he asked, standing behind her chair, which he had wheeled up to the grate.

"Yes; you said come alone."

"True; there are so many scoffers in the world that I always feel doubtful. Are you convinced of the reality of spiritual manifestations?"

"Undoubtedly," answered Miss Abby.

"Well, did you think all the responses last night were from the spirit world?"

"Yes; I had no reason to doubt it."

"Ah! you were mistaken! There is such a thing in psychological science as the domination of living souls, by mere force of will. I was under such domination last night. One of the responses was from a living man! Do not move! Wait while you count fifty, and he will present himself."

Miss Keith was strong minded. But while she counted fifty

silently, she thought she could hear her own heart beat. A step on the soft carpet, barely audible, and Rupert Grey stood before her, with the same bold eyes, the same dressy exterior, the same smooth moustache, with the even white teeth glistening under it. She glanced around the room. The medium had vanished, leaving no trace behind.

"I am charmed to see you, Miss Keith," said Rupert, holding out his white hand. "Pray do not be shocked by my sudden appearance! I am quite full of vital energy, I assure you."

"I thought you were killed!" faltered Miss Abby. "The *Herald*, to-day, said no traces of your body could be found!"

"Precisely," replied Rupert, with easy indifference; "I do not intend it to be found at present—except by my friends. I hope I may count Miss Keith among them?"

"I am entirely bewildered!" said Miss Abby. "Does Nina know?"

"I trust not, answered Rupert; "my chief motive for remaining dead is to mislead Nina. And next to the pleasure of seeing you again, the most agreeable part of the present interview will be the formation of an alliance between us."

"An alliance against Nina!" said Miss Keith. "I cannot take part in any scheme against her."

"Certainly not!" replied Rupert, drawing a chair up and seating himself beside her. "I purpose no harm to Nina. On the contrary, I hope to aid her in some pet schemes of hers; but, to succeed, she must remain ignorant of my existence, while you must enlighten me upon two or three points. First: what business has Mr. Gaston in charge for her?"

"I don't know," said Miss Abby, shortly.

"Positively?" said Grey, eyeing her keenly.

"Positively! He has seen her several times, but I have no idea of the nature of their conferences. Something relating to the estate, I presume, but this is mere surmise. He was sent at first by Mr. Skillet."

"And the lady? Mr. Gaston has taken a lady to Nina's house, certainly. Where is she, and who is she?"

"No lady ever came with Mr. Gaston. Nina has no house; she is at the Fifth Avenue Hotel. We are going to Europe by the 'China' next week."

"We?"

"Yes; Nina and I."

" And no one else?"

" No one else, excepting Nina's maid."

Mr. Grey pushed back his chair, muttering something very like an oath. He was so positively assured that Nina was harbouring Helen that he found himself repeating the fact to his own mind, while he reflected upon Miss Abby's denial. He strode about the room, pulling his black moustache, and labouring to devise a new plan. His effort with Miss Keith was an evident failure. At last he pushed his chair nearer the grate, and once more sat down beside her.

" Part of my plan," he said—" indeed, the culmination of it—related to you! After I accomplish my purpose, which is merely the enforcement of a legal claim against the Norman estate, I intend to win your confidence and your regard. I trust you to remain silent about me until the time arrives for me to see Nina and the Bragdons. There is your carriage, I presume; it has stopped at the door." He took her hand, pressed it gently, and before she knew it, he had leaned forward and kissed her. She was rather shocked, but, as they were alone, she speedily recovered her composure.

" If I take him," she murmured, when the carriage arrived at the hotel, " I'll stop his smoke! And I don't see as I have to tell Nina anything about him at present."

CHAPTER XXXV.

Nina's Dilemma.

THE more Miss Keith thought about her interview with Rupert the more dissatisfied she felt. And while she was in a little flutter of pleasant excitement whenever she thought of his concluding remarks, she still resented the cool impudence of his "approaches." He seemed to take for granted that he had only his own consent to gain. This is a very comfortable frame of mind at the beginning of a courtship, but it is not lasting if the feminine part of the courting is thoroughly done. The natural law, which requires a certain amount of wooing from the dominant power, is inexorable. If Mr. Grey, who could simulate all the virtues, had manifested some timidity, or distrust of his own fascinations, he would have accomplished more. But the unfortunate conceit, that ruins so many of the stronger sex, could not be hidden, and it happened to spoil all his plans in this instance.

"Nina," said Miss Abby, "I suppose you made an attempt to confer with the spirit of Mr. Grey, last night?"

"Yes," replied Nina, starting. "I was thinking of him this minute."

"What were you thinking, dear?"

"It seems a shocking thing to say, Miss Abby," replied Nina, "but I was asking myself if it was probable that dead people ever told lies. What is the doctrine of the Spiritualists upon that point?"

"Spirits," said Miss Abby, "that is, *real* spirits, always tell the truth. The revelations from the spirit spheres would be infallible if we could always have a reliable medium. I suppose all the cases of false teaching or false revelation may be attributed to the fault or incompetency of the medium. What is it that you doubt?"

"I hardly know," answered Nina, wearily; "I am so tired of distrust! And I had so firmly decided that I had found one man of unswerving integrity. But I have been all day asking myself if Mr. Gaston *could* be misled by Rupert?"

Miss Keith devoured Nina with her eyes.

"You know, Miss Abby," she continued, "that I am the seventh child of my father, who was the seventh of his. I cannot shake off the superstition that this gives me peculiar insight into the thoughts and motives of people. And I have always felt, when conversing with Mr. Gaston, that he was dealing with perfect candour. But there was some concealment of his thoughts, I remember, when I asked him about Rupert. Can it be possible that these two have formed a compact to deceive me?"

Miss Keith reflected. Rupert was a nice man, and wore such elegant gloves! But he was impecunious at present, and Nina was rich. And, then, that septenary arrangement made her shiver in spite of her good sense. Moreover, she was passably honest, and candour was her favourite weakness.

"Nina," she said, oracularly, "I don't like Mr. Gaston. He is a rebel, and he is as full of conceit as he can be. But he don't tell lies. I am sure of that. *You* might be deceived, but no man could deceive me."

"Conceit?" said Nina. "That sounds like a harsh judgment,

Miss Abby. I have seen no evidence of it. But it was a strange coincidence that he should have been on the train with Rupert, and yet not know him——"

"But Mr. Grey knows him," replied Miss Keith.

"Knows him? You mean he knew him."

"No, I don't. I mean to say Mr. Grey knows him, and knows he has been visiting you."

"Oh!" said Nina, "I understand. You refer to Rupert's spiritual state. I was speaking of Mr. Gaston's knowledge. He said he met Rupert on the train, but did not even know his name until after his arrival in New York. The papers described the fatal accident, and announced that Mr. Rupert Grey was the victim."

"I don't refer to the spiritual state," said Miss Abby, positively; "I don't think Mr. Grey has any spiritual state. I don't believe there was any fatal accident. I believe Mr. Grey is alive, and as well as you are. And I think he has some designs against your estate, and does not show himself, because he expects to succeed better by employing other agencies. There! I have cleared my conscience now, and you can draw your own conclusions."

Nina regarded Miss Abby with wondering eyes. She spoke positively, snapping out her sentences with emphatic precision; and Nina began to recall her first interview with Darcy, and tried to remember his exact words.

"Miss Abby," she said, after a brief silence, "you have said too little or too much. Do you think Mr. Gaston is aware of Rupert's existence, if he is indeed alive?"

"I don't know," replied Miss Keith.

"But you have just said that Rupert knows him."

"Yes. I cannot say whether Mr. Gaston knows Mr. Grey, or not. You ought to be able to use that peculiar insight of yours, and decide that point for yourself."

"But, Miss Abby," persisted Nina, "you were present last night, and heard the responses——"

"You did not call Mr. Grey by name," said Miss Abby; "I am not at all sure—indeed, I am quite sure Mr. Grey's disembodied spirit did not answer you. There!"

"And the other?" said Nina, tremulously; "if I were sure the whole thing was a deception! But it would make no difference. My course is perfectly plain. Miss Abby, was the whole affair a sham?"

"I don't know!" snapped Miss Abby. "The medium you had was a sham, I really believe."

"Then!" said Nina, starting to her feet, "then it was Rupert Grey! Nobody else could know how to answer. Ah! I see now. But how did it happen that he was there? Oh! dear. Shall I never get out of these toils? If I live another day I will terminate these doubts. And if Mr. Gaston has deceived me I will never trust mortal man again!"

Miss Abby cogitated. Darcy had offended her mortally, more by his disdainful manner than by his words. Her confidence in the native intelligence of the black race, founded upon the rhapsodies of Squizzem and Dragger, had been rudely shaken by Darcy's cold assertion of its essential inferiority, and his simple analysis of some of the gush lingo had displeased her also. But there was a streak of honesty in her character that perpetually asserted itself, and she could not even remain silent and allow Nina to suppose she shared her doubts.

"I am sure I don't know what is the extent of your confidence," she said, at last; "but I have no reason to think Mr. Gaston insincere. Indeed, I think he is entirely truthful and ingenuous. He looks like a man who says just what he thinks. But I do think he is a very dangerous man! And I am not willing for you to repose unlimited confidence in him."

Nina crossed the room and kissed her.

"Now, Nina," said Miss Abby, tossing her head petulantly, "I don't wish you to misunderstand me. These Kentucky people are perfectly hateful."

"Why, you never saw any Kentucky people, excepting Mr. Gaston."

"Yes, I have!" replied Miss Keith; "that teacher Mr. Skillet found is from Kentucky. She is thoroughly educated, no doubt, and I leave the Institute in her hands without the slightest apprehension. But——"

"But what?"

"But she has that same abominable air of self-satisfaction. I was positively afraid to ask her a dozen questions, all of which I had arranged in my mind——what is it?"

A servant had brought in a couple of cards.

"Mr. Timothy Skillet," said Nina, reading the cards, "and Henry Gaston, Esq. Request the gentlemen to walk in."

Mr. Skillet was in a high state of excitement. His companion was a large, well-formed man in the prime of life, sedate in demeanour, with honest eyes that roved around the spacious apartment, even while he made his polite salutations.

"I hope you will pardon this unseasonable intrusion," he said; "but Mr. Skillet told me I should find my brother here. I have just arrived and cannot sleep until I see him."

"Mr. Darcy Gaston ?" said Nina.

"Yes, Madam."

"He has not been here to-day."

Tige was discomfited. He had just told his wife that she should see the boy in five minutes. Nina noticed his disappointment.

"He is quite well," she continued, kindly; "though Mr. Skillet can give you more recent intelligence about him."

"It's no consequence," said Mr. Skillet; "but I was sure he was here. He left the office at five. He was perfectly well, except a kind o' sneezin'. Caught cold, I guess. Let's go to Camp's, Mr. Gaston."

Tige followed him to the door and then turned back and stood a moment before Nina, reading her countenance with sober anxiety.

"I am afraid I transgress," he said, with a deprecating gesture; "but my poor wife is devoured with anxiety—I don't know why. Mr. Skillet has assured her that Darcy is safe and well, but she refuses to believe him. She has no one but Darcy in the world; and after two days of tiresome travel she insists upon finding him to-night. And I thought if I might bring her to you—only for a moment—and let you tell her that he was well."

"I will go to her," said Nina, promptly.

"Nay. Let me bring her to you. She is in the parlour, close at hand. How kind you are. Darcy's letters about you have seemed to me extravagant until now."

"Bring Mrs. Gaston," replied Nina, a rosy hue overspreading her forehead and cheeks. "We will try to entertain her while you are gone."

"And you jest stay, too, Mr. Gaston," said Mr. Skillet. "I will go to Camp's and bring Dassy. No earthly use for you to go. If he is not there I'll find out where he is, and come back for you. He was as lively as a cricket only four hours ago. Anyhow, the whelp is big enough to take care of himself. And Miss Norman can give you the information you want about t'other one, too."

And Mr. Skillet bustled out without waiting for a reply.

Tige brought his wife, who was courteously received by Nina. It only requires fifteen seconds for two truthful women to become intimate. Nell was drinking in the refreshing streams of information that Nina was able to supply, touching Darcy's appearance, seasoned with bits of conversation of no importance, but invaluable to Nell, who could recognize " her boy" in phrases and sentiments that Nina remembered.

Mr. Gaston, like a true gentleman, took a seat near Miss Keith, who had been rather overlooked in the hurried introduction and interview. He got a gallon of gush in five minutes. But he had heard a hundred addresses to gentlemen of the jury, in cases where an appeal to the tender sensibilities of husbands and fathers was the only leg the orator had to stand upon. So he took the gush without winking, and Miss Abby began to think Kentucky was a good sort of a place, after all. Tige was a born courtier.

CHAPTER XXXVI.

The Outlet.

THE swift interchange of question and answer, all relating to Mr. Darcy Gaston, his looks, his habits and his purposes, occupied the attention of the two ladies, while Tige and Miss Abby vapourized gush in the opposite corner. Mrs. Gaston had been troubled by dreams and presentiments, and she found a ready listener in Miss Norman, who was greatly attracted by the little lady's earnest devotion to the youth. She referred to "Tige," once and again, in her fluent recital, until Miss Norman interrupted her by asking who Tige was.

"Mr. Gaston," answered Nell; "his name is Henry; but at college he got this nickname, because of the invariable sweetness of his temper. No one ever knew him to be angry."

"And his brother resembles him, I suppose?" said Nina.

"Well, not exactly. Darcy is the best boy in the world, but he has a fiery temper. And when his mind is made up, he is adamant! He was at college when the war began. Mr. Gaston had written and spoken a great deal against the whole theory of secession, and he corresponded with Darcy on the same subject, and really thought the boy held his views. But one dreadful day, we got a letter from him, that only contained a few words; it just said: 'Dear brother Tige, I can't stand *everything*. I am off to the army. Captain Ruthven went last night.' And we heard no more of him until the surgeon of the prison wrote to us, saying Darcy would die, if we did not get him out."

"Captain Ruthven," said Nina. "Ah! Was that Mr. Darcy Ruthven?"

"Yes," answered Nell, surprised. "You have heard of him?"

"Oh, yes. I heard that he died or was killed."

"Yes. He died at home. He had been desperately wounded, two or three times, and at last was left at Lexington, when the Confederate forces retired from the town. His wife died soon after."

"And he left no family?"

"One daughter. Helen. The sweetest girl in Kentucky."

"A daughter," said Nina, eagerly. "Oh! Mrs. Gaston, is she still alive?"

"Certainly! That is, I have not heard of her death. But she has disappeared unaccountably. She went to Cincinnati not long ago, to take charge of the education of some children. Tige went there to look for her, very recently, but she was gone."

"Gone!" said Nina, wringing her hands.

"Yes. My husband has sought for her in Chicago, where she was supposed to be. He spent a week there, but found no traces of her. Tige, dear, please come over here. Miss Norman is interested in poor Helen's story."

"Interested!" ejaculated Nina, as Tige came obediently. "Mr. Gaston, if you can bring this girl to me, you will relieve me of the only anxiety that troubles my life. Why have I not heard that Mr. Ruthven had a daughter? Why has your brother never told me?"

"Darcy never saw her, I believe. Nell sent him to Lexington to see her, and convey some message, but she had already gone to Cincinnati. I went there a short time afterwards, and learned that she had mysteriously disappeared. She was governess in the family of Mrs. Crowder. While there she had become acquainted with a man who was supposed to be a gentleman, but who was a great scoundrel, and under his evil influence, she secretly left the city. This man was a friend of Professor Hang, of Chicago—at least, so Mrs. Crowder said—and he had also disappeared, saying he was going there. I went to Chicago a little later, found Professor Haug, and learned that he had never seen or heard of this man."

"And his name?" said Nina, leaning forward, eagerly.

"I think I will not tell his name," replied Tige, slowly. "I am on his track, if I am not greatly mistaken. Everything depends upon the first steps. I dare not whisper his name, lest he should hear, and escape me! He certainly came to New York."

"Have you seen him?" asked Nina.

"No. But I have his photograph." He took out his pocket-book and selected the picture, which he presented to Nina. A deadly pallor overspread her face, as she looked at the bold, black eyes, so resolute and insolent. She returned the picture with a trembling hand.

"And this is the only clue you have?" she said, as Tige replaced the card.

"Not entirely. I found another scoundrel in Cincinnati, who knows this one. He had been a client of mine in a criminal suit, and I got him off. I afterwards learned that he was certainly guilty. Heaven forgive me! He was at the hotel in Cincinnati, drunk, and while he and I sat in the smoking-room, only three nights ago, he revealed two or three important matters to me. I shall find him anon, and then!" He paused, and a ferocious expression crept over his countenance, transforming the gentle Tige into an incarnate fiend. "If he once comes within reach of my arm," he continued, "he may go scot free—if he can."

Nina and Nell looked with apprehension upon the funereal face of the handsome athlete.

"Mr. Gaston," whispered Nina, after a momentary silence; "this man is Rupert Grey."

"Ah!" said Tige; "you know him then?"

"Yes. But he is beyond your reach. He is dead."

"Dead!" said Tige, incredulously.

"He was killed on the railway; he fell over a great precipice, and no vestige of his body has been found. A careful search has been made, and I am assured that he fell into the river, at the foot of the cliff, and was swept away, miles below the scene of the accident."

"Indeed!" said Tige indifferently. "Well, to return to Helen. Can you tell me why he sought her out."

"Yes. I sent him to find Darcy Ruthven or his heirs."

"You!" said Tige, recoiling, "you!"

"Yes, I," responded Nina: "resume your seat, please. I have charge of certain property in which Darcy Ruthven or his heir is interested. And I sent Rupert Grey to find him, and bring him to me. He wrote me from Lexington, I think, or perhaps from Cincinnati, saying Ruthven was dead, but he had found the heir. I thought he meant another. He did not tell me of the daughter. And now I begin to have some glimmering of the truth! Rupert has somehow discovered that Miss Ruthven would inherit property, and has—married her."

"No," answered Tige, slowly; "he has not married her."

"Are you sure?" said Nina, doubtfully.

"Quite sure. Can it be Ruthven's Folly that you mean by the property?"

"Ruthven's Folly!" said Nina.

"I thought it might be that, because I have heard of the Ruthvens' interest in it. But you are mistaken, if that is the land you refer to. I investigated that title ten years ago. The Ruthvens have no more claim than I have. The transfers are all in order."

"Mr. Gaston," said Nina, desperately, "I will tell you everything! That land came into my grandfather's possession wrongfully!"

"Yes," said Tige, "I know that, too."

"Do you? Well, the settled purpose of my heart is to restore that identical property. I could not rest in my grave if I failed to give it back. And I have had your brother investigating deeds, and had almost arranged for the restoration of the land to him——"

"To Darcy?" said Tige, interrupting her.

"To your brother. Because his name is Darcy Ruthven. I thought the proper owner had died childless, and my instructions are explicit, requiring me to give it to 'whoever bears his name.' And the only obstacles now in my way are two. First: the property is the joint inheritance of my married sister and myself. I need to gain a clear title. Second: to find Helen Ruthven, and give her the deed. How can I accomplish this?"

"Is the estate undivided?" said Tige.

"Yes. I am going to Europe within a week, and before I sail I hope to secure this property. If I tell my sister and her husband that I intend to transfer it away from the family, they will leave no means untried to prevent me. I do not know the value of it. But I am resolved to get it, at any cost. And I am resolved to dispose of it as I have said."

"There is another obstacle," said Mr. Gaston, reflecting, "and I am inclined to think it more serious than either you have named. If Colonel Ruthven were alive, no power would be great enough to make him take the property."

"But he is dead."

"True. And his daughter inherits his resentments! She will not touch a penny of it."

"Ah! if I could but see her!" said Nina, plaintively. "Only tell me how to gain exclusive title. I will risk the rest."

"There is no difficulty there," said Tige, composedly; "I will tell your legal adviser how to arrange it."

"But I have no legal adviser. Mr. Coke is the family lawyer, and he has charge of my sister's interests as well as mine. I relied upon your brother to devise the plan. I have placed all the papers in his hands."

"Well, I will tell him the outlet. Dismiss your anxiety. I am sure you can get this identical property without trouble. To find the child is another matter. Ah! here is Mr. Skillet? Alone!"

"Over to Brooklyn!" said Mr. Skillet, "ten o'clock, too. Took his night key. Said he would stay until midnight p'r'aps! I began to think I was a blamed old fool! But it's no consequence. Dassy is too cute for me, and so is the school-marm! Bless 'em, how composed they both looked when I knowed it was jest as natural for them to be bilin' over, as for a kittle on a red hot stove! But they pulled the wool over my eyes, slick! He was there last night, the sly young cuss! Went to hear Dragger, he said. Nary Dragger! It was the school-marm. *Your* school-marm, Miss Keith! She came from Kentucky with him. Same train, I mean. She was with that Mr. Grey that got smashed onto the rocks! Dassy sorter froze to her, when the brakesman came back. It's no consequence! What in thunder are you all starin' at? She is just as pooty as a pink! but she is sly as a weasel! Dassy seed her last night. He up and told Mrs. Camp this evening, because she was a frettin' about the gal. Took me twenty minits to git it out of her. But she didn't know where she was. Dassy wouldn't tell. He just said he was goin' to see her, and he bolted, soon as it was dark. And now, what will you do? Let 'em set or go after Dassy? I'm all ready, Mr. Gaston, if you want to go. I can put my finger onto him in thirty-five minits!"

"Go, Tige!" said Nell.

"Of course. Miss Norman, I will not apologize for asking you to wait also. Look!" and he took another carte from his pocket book. "Who is this, Mr. Skillet?"

"The schoolmarm! Miss Harding. Pooty as a pink, by Gemini!"

"Who is it, Nell?"

"Helen! Oh, Tige, is it indeed Helen?"

"Beyond a doubt! Come, Mr. Skillet, we shall have a jolly supper together before midnight. Miss Norman, will you join us?"

"With great pleasure, and I will keep Mrs. Gaston until you return. *Au revoir!*"

"Here!" said Mr. Skillet to Tige, "you've dropped your picter. No! It's a man! by Gemini! It is that ugly cuss that got smashed out on the railroad. Wa-al! it's no consequence! But I'd as lieve carry a picter of the devil in *my* pocket! Come on!"

CHAPTER XXXVII.

Followed Again.

DARCY counted the hours impatiently as the long day waxed and waned. When Trinity steeple banged out five o'clock, after the usual preliminary chime, he donned his overcoat and hastened to Camden street. He would not have gone, but he was becoming fastidious about his attire. After bestowing unaccustomed labour upon his outward adornments, he read the papers all over again, and, taking compassion upon Mrs. Camp, he told her he had found Helen, and that she was well and happy. He was not at liberty to say where she was, but it was quite possible that he would see her to-night, and he would take Mrs. Camp's love to her with pleasure. His own, too, he added, mentally.

He was going to walk down, so as to give them time to finish dinner at Mr. Bruce's; but he had dallied over the law papers, and it was near seven. So he took a Fulton street omnibus. As he took his seat, after paying his fare, another passenger entered. He had almond-shaped black eyes, and enough red beard to stuff a small mattress. He was totally oblivious of Darcy's existence, though that sweet tempered youth was scowling at him with vengeful brows. The stage rolled down Broadway, and Darcy made up his mind. He would ride down to Fulton street, then get out, walk back to Ann street, race round to Nassau, and back into Fulton. If Mr. Redwhiskers followed he would have an understanding with him. Nassau street would not be infested by cops at that hour, and he would not detain the gentleman long.

Fulton street was reached at last. Darcy had moved near to the door, and he slipped out, darted up Broadway, and down Ann street to Nassau, and then walked quietly down to the corner. Nobody in sight. In fact, the red whiskers had not stirred. Their owner had tried Darcy before, and, with half a minute's start, he knew he could not get up with him. So he kept his seat.

As Darcy passed through the ferry gate he heard the boat's signal of departure, and hastened down the slip. Before he stepped on board he saw the red whiskers just behind him. Darcy decided to wait for another boat, and drew back. So did red whiskers. The boat glided out into the darkness, and Darcy walked back to the waiting-room. Looking through the window, he saw the other lighting a cigar, and apparently waiting composedly for the next boat. There were too many people thronging into the ferry house for a private interview. A scrimmage, which, of course, would follow his address, kept him quiet. He had half made up his mind to step out, knock the cigar out of the fellow's mouth and then walk back. The other boat came into the slip, and he slipped out with the rest. He brushed by the red whiskers just as he straightened out his arm to withdraw the cigar, with the old, insolent air. Darcy thrust his clenched fists deep down in his overcoat pockets, and held them there by main force. There was a fracas between two truck drivers, and a policeman sauntered down the slip, parted them with a word or two, and then marched back with martial step. As he passed, Darcy touched his arm.

"May I say a word to you?" said he, as the officer turned. "This person," and he pointed to the gentleman with the red beard, "has followed me once and again. I think he is a pickpocket. Will you please investigate him?"

"Hi, now!" said the officer, "what game are you up to, Cap? What are you follerin' this gent for?"

"To steal my watch," replied Darcy, confronting the almond eyes; "and, policeman, if you will promise not to arrest me, I will knock his two insolent eyes into one!"

"Hi, now!" repeated the majestic cop, "none o' your foolishness here. Do you make a complaint agin this gent?"

Darcy had a wholesome dread of the station-house. If he

should make formal complaint he might be detained on the New York side. He had been rash! If he had waited until they both reached Brooklyn, he could have led his follower to some quiet spot and settled the business without the aid of law.

"Ask him what he follows me for?" said he at length. "He has not answered you."

"I beg your pardon!" said the stranger. "Are you speaking to me?"

"Come out of the gangway!" said the policeman. "Here, Cap, let's have a look at you by the gaslight."

The stranger followed composedly, and Darcy reluctantly.

"Now," said the officer, as the trio stood under the gas at the door of the waiting-room, "now, Cap, seems to me you've got more red whiskers than ever growed on your own chin. It is pooty nigh as bad as the shignons the wimmen wear!" and he took the flowing beard in his fingers and slipped it off the smooth chin, while the almond eyes snapped viciously. The boat was about to start. Darcy heard the rattle of the chain and the clang of the engineer's bell. He walked swiftly down the slip and leaped on board, when the boat was three feet out. He caught a final glimpse of the baleful eyes as the stranger adjusted his rosy beard. In another minute he was out in the stream, and Mr. Grey was baffled once more.

"Thousand devils!" said that worthy, wrathfully. "Your cursed interference has forced me to lose him again! Could you not see what was the matter? That infernal young cub has carried off my woman! and I have been following him in this disguise a whole week! Can't you tell a gentleman when you see one!"

The masterful air of the man, as he swept his arm round and replaced the cigar in his mouth, awed the policeman. Grey took a bank note carelessly from his waistcoat pocket, and put it into the ready hand of the officer.

"This is all irregular, Cap'n!" he said, apologetically; "it's clean agin the law to go about with false beards, and old white coats. I was obliged to haul you up when he called me."

"Too late to talk about it now," answered Rupert; "I'll find him some other time. Here is the other boat. Ten minutes start of me! It is perfectly hopeless to-night. No matter; I am sure to win at last."

"Well," said the watchful guardian of the peace, as Grey walked quietly down the slip, "he is a cool one—he is! You bet! But t'other feller was quite some savage, too. If them fellers meet in some quiet spot there will be some fur flying. You bet! A woman in the business, of course. And I can't say as I blame her much if she has run off with t'other one. This black-eyed chap is a reg'lar devil. You bet! He'll be took up for murder some day, and git off with justifiable homicide, or by the insanity dodge! There goes that lame soger, again. Some day I'll just tread on that game foot of his'n, and see if he squeals. Lame sogers is pooty nigh played out, anyhow. Hello! he's talking to my Red-whiskers. There they go into the gents' cabin. Some devilment hatching there, you bet!"

"Mr. Bloke!" said Grey, "you are half an hour late. If you had been here on time you might have followed our young friend and found out his hiding place."

"Couldn't help it!" growled the soldier; "had to dodge a cussed cop. I'm gitten werry uncomfortable, anyway. That cop at the ferry looks at me every evenin' as if he'd like to git acquainted with me. I'm goin' to cross at Wall street after this."

"The cops are against us," said Grey. "The youngster we are looking for just handed me over to your ferry cop."

"He did!" said Bloke, aghast.

"He did. He said I wanted his watch."

"Cuss his impudence!" said the soldier. "Why didn't you put a head onto him, boss?"

"The opportunity was not favorable," replied Grey; "but while I was explaining to the policeman, he slipped away and got off on the last boat. I had followed him from Camden street all the way to the ferry. He dodged me once, but I was sure he was coming, so I waited for him. It never occurred to me that he would dart off as he did. He leaped aboard after the boat started. He must have jumped ten feet."

Mr. Grey's estimate was not far wrong. Darcy's first thought, when his feet struck the deck, was that he had pretty nearly jumped across the boat. He scrambled out of the crowd and gained the bow, where he had plenty of room. The night was cold, and the shivering passengers kept the cabins.

"That scowling face," thought Darcy, as he paced the narrow passage between the chains; "surely I have seen it before. The black moustache under the red one! Why cannot I recall that face? It is not possible that I should feel this desperate enmity without cause. Was he one of the officers at the fort, where I was imprisoned? No. I remember every one. Besides, I harbour no resentment against them. They were rough men, but they did not maltreat me. This man has exhibited malice some time, or I could not thus desire to throttle him. Pickpocket! Not he. Why cannot I remember? Is there another man in the world who throws his head back, who swings his arm out in that conceited, insolent way, whenever he fingers his beard?

"Why does he dog me? It is absurd to think that he only wants to rob. He would not select me, certainly. Is he trying to discover any one else, through me? Ah!"

He leaned against the rail and looked up at the sparkling heavens, while a torrent of suggestions swept through his brain, confusing, bewildering, almost stunning him.

"I thought I would wait a little longer," he murmured; "but I should go mad if I did not sift this mystery to the bottom. This night will I know, if ever, what hold that villain has upon Helen. For it is Grey! I remember now. I remember how I shrank from him on the train, and how I dreamed about him afterwards. Grey! Alive and resolute and strong. Oh! miserable civilization. If we had lived a hundred years ago, I could have waited here for his arrival and invited him to retire with me and end this contest with our own hands! It may come to that at last. Somehow, I *know* that he stands between me and Helen. Somehow, he has estranged her and made her repulse me. Somehow, he has poisoned her mind against me. How could she charge me with fraud if this man had not belied me? And his name was in that old will. Is it possible that Helen thought I was working in his interests! Is it possible that Helen knows he is alive! Patience! In a few hours I shall know."

The boat slipped into her dock, and Darcy sprang ashore. Only ten minutes between him and Helen. And he found the time short enough, as he stilled his tumultuous thoughts and smoothed his brow, before he rang the bell in Jeryboblum street.

CHAPTER XXXVIII.

A Declaration.

HELEN was seated under a drop-light, busy with needle-work, when Darcy entered the comfortable "sitting room" in Jeryboblum street. Three young Bruces were on the opposite side of the round table, conning their lessons. Mr. and Mrs. Bruce were out "to spend the evening." Darcy made a polite speech, regretting their absence, but it was a hollow mockery. He would not have wept profusely, if they had taken the three interesting girls with them. They were charming girls, for they gathered up their books, half an hour after he arrived, and retired to an adjoining room where they were in sight, but out of earshot.

"I have some information for you," he said, "and I am happy to think you will be pleased to hear it."

She looked up at him, noticing a certain huskiness in his voice.

"You have a cold?" she said. "Don't talk if it troubles you."

"But I must talk, and you must listen. First: You have no possible interest in the Norman property, at present. There was only one portion of it in question, and that belongs to the estate, beyond a doubt."

"Ruthven's Folly," said Helen, quietly.

"Ah! you have heard of it. Please tell me who enlightened you."

"My father told me some parts of the story," she answered reluctantly.

"And have you learned more, since—since you left Kentucky?"

"Yes."

He waited for more explanation, but she kept her head bent over her work, and added nothing to the monosyllable.

"I will not ask you any questions," said Darcy, "at least not now. Shall I tell you the rest?"

She bowed her head, without looking up.

"Well," said Darcy, slowly, "I think the owner of Ruthven's Folly intends to give you a clean deed——"

"I will never take it!" she said, looking at him with flashing eyes. "I have no claim under the law. My father has told me so many times."

A DECLARATION.

"True," replied he, surprised at her vehemence, "no legal claim. But Miss Norman is intent upon this solitary purpose. To transfer this land to you, and so resolute is she, that she will listen to no opposition. It is some matter of conscience, I think. Perhaps the original transfer was unfair. I do not *know* this, but infer it. The value of the property must be large. I have been over the land. I have learned the price of contiguous property. Ruthven's Folly is worth more than a hundred thousand dollars. I am satisfied that it rightfully belongs to you!"

"One dollar or one hundred millions!" said Helen, resolutely; "I tell you I will not receive a penny of it. If it is forced upon me by law, I will transfer it to a hospital as soon as my ownership is assured. I do not desire the possession. I only ask for permission to earn enough for my needs, and I am doing that now."

"You make me happy," said Darcy, passionately; "if you are resolved to refuse this gift."

"I am resolved!" said Helen, with haughty vehemence; "who dares to offer me a gift!"

Darcy arose, and took the seat nearer to her. There was a little book with a tortoise shell cover on the table. He took it up, and examined it. It was a copy of the New Testament, and bore the marks of use. On the fly leaf was written, "To darling Helen, from Father and Mother; Christmas, 1860." He drew back a little behind her, and furtively kissed the book, while the thought passed through his mind that he was swearing allegiance to something or somebody. She half turned towards him, and he thrust the little book in his breast, under the fold of his waistcoat.

"I dare!" he answered; "but first, I must tell you something more. The man who left you on the train,—the paper said his name was Rupert Grey—the man of whom I dreamed that night—do you remember?"

A pallor spread over her face, but she looked steadily at him without reply.

"The time has come when you must tell me what interest he has in you, or you in him!" continued Darcy. "He is alive! I saw him within the hour. I have seen him repeatedly, disguised under a red beard, but to-night I saw him, with the beard plucked away. He followed me to the ferry, where I accosted him, and finally handed him over to a policeman."

She covered her eyes with her hands for a moment, and when she withdrew them, Darcy was appalled at the expression of anguish and horror upon her countenance.

"Stop a moment," she said; "do you say you have had no intercourse with him hitherto?"

"Not a word since we parted on the train. I have thought the story of his death was true."

"And this investigation,—I mean your search into the legal title to Ruthven's Folly,—did he not instigate that?"

"Certainly not!" replied Darcy; "I have been acting under instructions from Miss Norman. I tell you the man has been dead to me, except for a strange presentiment——"

"And to me also!" she said, wringing her hands. "Oh, wretched woman that I am! I have hoped and prayed for the assurance of his death. And now that I know that he is alive, there is nothing left for me but death! Oh, forgive me!" and she caught his hand which he had stretched out to her—"forgive my cruel words to you, my cruel suspicion! I thought you were aiding him in his wicked designs against me!"

"Oh, Helen!" he murmured.

"All that miserable day on the train, before he disappeared, she continued, "he was unfolding his villainous schemes to me. And when the story came—*you* told me—of his certain death, I felt that Heaven had given me sudden deliverance. And when you came to me the other night—ah! you asked me precisely the same questions he had asked—I thought you and he had concocted a new scheme, and that his pretended death was part of it!"

"How could you think this," whispered Darcy, drawing still nearer to her; "how could you fail to see that I loved you—that my life was bound up in you!——" She held up her hand, repelling him, but he caught it in his, and poured out his soul in a torrent of passionate words—not heeding her dismay. "Nay, listen to me! When I found you might inherit all this money, I drew back, because I am poor. But when you avowed your determination to refuse it, joy came to my heart again, for I can work and earn, and the obstacles that are in my way are but shadows. Oh, Helen! if you will only allow me to love you, I will not come near you again, until I can say I have enough. Enough! I have enough now. My earnings are already far beyond my needs! But you have not known me long enough, though your father and mine were life-long friends. Let me come once a week, if no more,

A DECLARATION.

and just say, 'I love you,' and I will wait for years if you will, for your response!"

"You are mad!" she said, recoiling; "say not another word! I must not listen——"

"To-morrow, then!" he pleaded; "don't answer me now, but tell me I may come to-morrow evening!"

"Never! Never come again! Never say such words to me again!"

"Listen!" said Darcy, seizing her hand again; "you must hear me! I divine that this wretched scoundrel who has dogged me nearly every night for a week, this Rupert Grey, has some strange influence over you! He is between you and me, Helen! I will cut him into a hundred pieces before I will relinquish you. Do not be controlled by so shallow a rascal. Oh, if I dared to plead with you to give me a husband's right to defend you——"

"Be silent!" she said, with white lips; "you are talking to Rupert Grey's wife! Do you hear? His wife!"

Darcy dropped her hand, and turned away. The agony in her tones and manner was as nothing, he thought, compared with that which he endured. Married! And to Rupert Grey!

The three girls in the other room, were reciting their tasks to each other. Darcy listened with dull ears, catching the monotonous sentence a dozen times repeated : "A verb is a word which signifies to be, or to do, or to suffer; as, I am, I love, I am loved."

"I am so stunned by this intelligence," said Darcy, gravely, after a prolonged silence, "that I hardly know what is decorous to say. I have said some things about your—your husband!" and he gasped, "that I should recall. I had not dreamed that such horrors could be in real life. It is not proper to ask you any further questions. And I am torn asunder by two different feelings; joy—a fierce, devilish joy, in the conviction that this horrible marriage is horrible to you; and unfeigned sorrow that the man is so far unworthy of you, and that he gives no token that will warrant a hope for anything better. I will say nothing about the shock to me. I will not apologize for the professions I have made, in happy ignorance of your true relations. And in the midst of the horror of great darkness, that envelopes my life, I can only see one certain ray of light. It would be unbecoming in me to ask—it would be more unbecoming in you to tell—anything that Mr. Grey would keep secret. But I am the son of your Father's trusted friend; a friend who loved your Father so truly, that he gave me his name. And it is plain to my mind that I may ask you to remember this. Think of me only as a man who would worthily bear the name of your Father, and honour me by demanding any service a gentleman could render to a dear sister, whenever the need may arise."

"You are kind, and I thank you," she murmured; "and it is due to you and to me to say a word more. I have been weak and foolish, but I have tried to do right—always. I have been rash, was ignorant, and easily entrapped. But while I remember that you bear the name of Darcy Ruthven, I will also not forget that I am his daughter, and I will never participate in dishonest plans or purposes. I will not have a dollar from the Normans, or from Ruthven's Folly. Alas! The true name of the property is Ruthven's Curse! Are you going? Good night!"

As Darcy passed up through the hall, he heard the old song again. "A verb is a word which signifies to be, or to do, or to suffer; as, I am, I love, I am loved."

"If they would leave off the last three words," thought Darcy, "I think I might pass for a Verb!"

CHAPTER XXXIX.

THE LITTLE GAME.

AFTER dismissing Miss Abby Keith, Rupert ascended to his own chamber, the front room on the second floor. He had a habit of taking the best places in all houses, by the aggressive force of sheer effrontery. He was always well placed in hotels, and when he returned from his Western journey, and decided to favor Dr. Lamis with a visit, he coolly requested his host to give him this chamber, "as he liked to have a view of the street." Dutchy, *alias* Bloke, occupied the little hall-room, on the same floor. Mr. Grey found this worthy waiting for him at the head of the stairs. His lame foot was still in bandages, but he was without his crutch, and he followed Rupert into his comfortable apartment, without limping.

"Take a seat, Mr. Bloke," said he, politely; "I have two pills to take now, and two more at bed time. Lamis says I am threatened with a return of those cursed chills I found in Virginia."

He took a pill-box from a drawer in the bureau, and while Dutchy watched all his proceedings, he cut an apple in half, scraped a portion of it upon the end of a paper knife, imbedded two of the pills in the pulp and swallowed them.

"Nice?" asked Dutchy, with a shudder. "K'neen, I'spose?"

"Yes," replied Rupert; "very nice. Will you have the other two? Quinine, two grains each! About the size of pistol bullets."

"Thankee!" said Mr. Bloke; "I guess I won't take any. What do you want with that young feller we've been follerin'?"

"Well," answered Grey, meditating, "I think you will have to knock him in the head for me. But do not be hasty. I must get some information from him first. He will go back to New York to-night. Say about ten. We will watch the ferry."

"Pooty cold work!" said Bloke; "Boss, I'm gittin' sick of this here business! All the cops in N'Yauk will know me before spring. I think I'll move away somewheres."

"Pooh!" said Rupert, "you are frightened at shadows. I'll get you a place in the Custom House, and you will be perfectly safe. We need not go to the ferry until ten, or thereabouts. How will you amuse yourself?"

"If we had keards," said Bloke, "we might try a little euchre."

"Cards! Of course. Here is a new pack. But I am not going to lose this time. Have you any money?"

"Guess I can cover your bets," said Dutchy, with a grin; "How much will you go?"

"Five dollars a game, and ten on the rub," said Grey, shuffling the cards; "how much can you afford to lose?"

"Much as you can win, I guess," responded Dutchy, drawing up his chair; "Here's my five. Cover it!"

After four or five games, Dutchy being loser in all, he produced a long pocket-book from some unexplored recess of his habiliments, and took out a package of bright new notes.

"Cussed bad luck!" he muttered, "Boss, let's double the bet."

"Agreed," replied Grey, "you will be out of your misery all the sooner. Where did you get this clean money? You must have negotiated a loan at some bank—with a crowbar!"

"Never you mind!" said Bloke; "win it, and then it will be yourn. Spades!"

The little clock on the mantel struck nine, as Dutchy put his empty pocket-book on the glowing coals in the grate. Rupert was putting his in a deep pocket, in the inside of his waistcoat. The fatal cards were still on the table. Dutchy gathered them up, and, slipping half of them in his pocket, threw the remainder in the fire.

"I'll be ready, Boss," he said, as he moved to the door; "you can call for me at ten. Mebbe I'll git a nap." He stood a moment watching Rupert light his cigar, and manipulate it between the first and second fingers of his right hand, as he removed it from under his black moustache, blowing out the rings of smoke. Phrenologists say the organ of self-esteem is situated on the back of the cranium. When it is so well developed as to merge into conceit, its gravity tilts the head back, and the chin up. And as Rupert moved his cigar back and forth, straightening his arm out, and tossing his chin upward, Dutchy appeared to be fascinated. He closed the door after him, and walked softly down the staircase and into the quiet street.

There was an oyster-house on the corner of an alley, and Dutchy dropped in here, ordering a "plate o' fried and a lager." While he waited for the meal, he sat at a corner table, and examined the cards he had slipped into his pocket. They were checker-backed, and Dutchy scrutinized them closely under the flaring gas-light. When the oysters came, he put the cards away again, and fell to.

"All the Jacks have a wide streak in the checker!" he muttered, "and all the aces have a narrer streak. He might as well have stole that money. Must git it back! And I will!"

On the opposite corner was an apothecary shop. Dutchy paid for his feast, and then went across and looked through the window. A smart-looking youth was seated behind the counter, reading the U. S. Pharmacopœia. Dutchy walked in boldly, and addressed the erudite youth:

"Say, Mister!" he began with doleful accents; "I've got a pet dorg. Newfinland. Big as a small hoss. But I've got to kill him, and I want to do it with doctor's stuff."

"All right, sir," said the youth; "what'll you have?"

"Guess you know best," replied Dutchy. "I wan't su'thin that'll kill him quick, without hurtin."

"Strychnine?" said the young man.

"Is that strong stuff?"

"Guess you'd think so," said the apothecary, "if you'd try a grain or two." He took a small bottle from the case, and shook the crystals. "Enough in this bottle to kill a regiment."

"Can't you make it into a pill?" said Dutchy. "You see my dorg has been bit by a mad dorg, and I am afeard o' him. If you can make it in a pill or two, I could put it in a bit of meat."

The young Esculapius was ambitious. He was not often left in charge of the store, and he burned to show his mastery of his dreadful art. However, there were certain formalities.

"It is not regular," he said, "to sell strychnine, without a doctor's prescription. You see it is dangerous stuff."

"Ezackly!" responded Dutchy; "it's dangerous stuff I want. No doctor is goin' to give me a prescription for dorg-pizon. Cuss the dorg! I'd shoot him, and be done with it, only he's a pet. My children would go crazy, if I was to shoot Bull! But if he dies, you know, they can't say nauthin', and they won't git bit neither. Does the stuff cost much?"

"I s'pose a dollar will do. Pills? You can sprinkle the powder on the meat——"

"Pills is the best," said Dutchy, positively; "make me a couple. Here is the dollar. Cuss the dorg! He is as expensive as a human."

The apothecary retired behind the screen over the prescription case, took a little paste on the end of a spatula, and rolled out the pills.

"Mark 'em pizon, please," said Dutchy, as the other rolled the pills in flour; "that is, mark the box."

"Of course, replied the dispenser; "label has skull and crossbones on it. Now just please write your name and address in this book. We always take the names of people who buy poisons."

"Ezackly," said Dutchy, readily; "only I'm done with writin. Been in the war, and got a ball in my right elber. My writin' days are done. You write it down, and I'll make my mark. Cap'n Thomas Smith, N'Yauk Zooaves, two hundred and sixty-nine, Burton street."

"Where the dickens is Burton street?" said the apothecary, writing the address.

"Half a mile off," replied Dutchy, pocketing the pills, "and I've got to walk. Snowin' too! Cuss the luck! Good night."

Dutchy had a latch key. He gained his hall chamber, and threw himself on the bed, not to sleep, but to meditate. He heard a murmur of voices down stairs, and distinguished the tones of his friend, Mr. Blake, in conversation with Doctor Lamis. With the prompt courage that would have been heroic in a better man, engaged in lawful enterprise, he walked into Rupert's room. The gas was burning, and the pill-box was on the mantel. Dutchy took it up, threw the two pills it contained into the grate, replaced them with his recent purchase, and then walked soberly back to his virtuous couch.

Rupert wakened him from a profound slumber, five minutes later.

"Come, Mr. Bloke," he said, gaily; "let us take a promenade."

"Cussed cold," growled Dutchy, sitting up on the bedside.

"Well, the exercise will warm you. Better bring your crutch too. It would be useful, if we have to scuffle."

"Got su'thin better nor that," said Dutchy; "I'm all ready."

He followed Rupert across the hall and into his chamber. The latter took his hirsute adornments from the bureau, and was about to put them on. But after a moment's reflection, he thrust them back in the drawer.

"I think I will dispense with that rosy beard hereafter," he said; "the policeman pulled it off to-night, and it is a nuisance, anyhow. And now I'll take the other pill, and be done with it."

The little clock on the mantel struck ten.

"Too late! Can't stop to scrape apples now. Will do when we return. I say, Bloke! the bank notes I won from you to-night are exactly like those described in the stevedore robbery. Same bank, and all new."

"Cuss the bank," replied Bloke, rudely; "never you mind the bank, boss. Wot you want with that pistol?"

"Ah! I don't know," said Rupert; "but it is handy to have a Derringer. Come on."

As Dutchy limped down stairs behind him, he thought if he should find an opportunity in the street, he would try the thickness of his patron's skull. That Derringer was an insult to him, personally.

CHAPTER XL.

The Old Church.

WHEN Darcy Gaston turned away from Mr. Bruce's door, he was muttering to himself the sing-song repetitions of the girls' lessons, in Lindley Murray: "To be, to do, and to suffer!"

"It is an easy problem to solve," he thought; "to be a man; to do known duty; to suffer such experiences as come providentially. The light has gone out of my life for the present, but I can find duty in the midst of darkness. What inexplicable fate could have given this gentle girl to yonder brute! She shudders at the very mention of his name, and if he should maltreat her, I dare not interfere!"

He walked down the street, while the snow spotted his coat and hat. It was falling in little flakes, and very gently, just whitening the ground. So filled with the memories of the last hour, that he did not notice his route, turning the corners when he came to them, and walking rapidly on. When he looked around him at last, he was at the door-step again. He had gone around the square, unconscious. He felt as a man feels who has taken an over dose of opium.

"This will never do," he murmured; "I am behaving like a school-boy. Now for home, and bed! Home! Ah, what a dull business this life is! Nothing but eating and sleeping. I cannot see before me anything worth striving for. I'll fast all day tomorrow, and see if I can't get hungry. Here is the corner, and the ferry is off here to the left."

He fell into a semi-stupor again, and, gradually slackening his pace, he stopped at last, and leaned idly against an iron railing fencing in an old building. Looking incuriously through the bars, he noticed the outlines of the house. The gable facing the street, and a steeple upon it. Surely he had seen it before! A gray stone was let into the red brick wall, and some sort of inscription upon it, hidden by patches of snow. He tried to read it, but could only make out one word: "Sexton." He looked down the long street, noticing the gas lamps on either side, and noticing also the portentous quiet. Then he heard the thud of a crutch—clamp! clamp!—coming down a side street, and finally saw the cripple turning the corner. He watched him, fascinated, as he limped past the church, clamp, clamp! down to the next corner, around it, and out of sight.

Wide awake now, and alert. The next event would be the appearance of Rupert Grey. He took his revolver from the pocket on his hip, and, with his thumb on the hammer, thrust it into the outside pocket of his overcoat, and waited.

The church was on the corner, surrounded by an iron railing. There was a narrow passage between it and the next house, closed by an iron grating. As the clamp of the crutch died away, this gate was pushed open, and a man stepped out upon the snow-covered pavement. Darcy turned as he approached, and faced him. His pulses were not accelerated, but he gathered up his faculties, feeling that a catastrophe was impending. There flashed across his mind the memory of his only battle-field, and of the supreme moment when an overwhelming force of cavalry galloped down the hillside upon him, surrounding him with a forest of glittering sabres.

"Good evening," said the stranger, courteously. He removed his cigar as he spoke, and, blowing a cloud of smoke into the frosty air, replaced the cigar with elaborate grace, his head thrown back, and his chin upturned.

"Good evening," replied Darcy, with cold composure.

"I have desired an interview with you," said the new comer, "since I left you so abruptly on the train."

"Yes," said Darcy, "you have made several attempts to find out my habitation and habits. I hope you are satisfied with your success."

"Only passably," returned Mr. Grey; "I am afraid you rather shunned me. Once or twice I was quite within reach of you, but you seemed to evade me very adroitly. That was a good dodge to-night, when you handed me over to a policeman. But the contest is unequal, my dear sir. And you are probably aware of the fact that you are cornered, if I may use the expression."

"What do you desire?" said Darcy, calmly; "I thought you meditated robbery, until I saw you with your red beard displaced. Perhaps I have not been mistaken, after all. I have but little worth stealing, and there would be some risk involved in taking that."

"Your candor charms me," responded Grey; "I only desire the return of the property I left in your charge. The young woman."

"Ah!" said Darcy, startled, "I cannot comply with your request. She is not under my charge."

"But you can probably find her?" said Rupert, drawing nearer; "you will perhaps see her again."

"I think not. I do not expect to see her again."

"Well," said Rupert, throwing his cigar at his feet, "you will, perhaps, oblige me by saying when and where you saw her last?"

Darcy meditated. The crisis had arrived. He drew back the hammer of the pistol, still in his hand. At the same moment the thought that he could not kill this particular villain, because of his relationship to Helen, dawned upon his mind. How could he ever go to her again, with bloody hands! And yet if he were only dead!

"I cannot answer your question," he said, at length; "I know nothing that I can reveal. And I must terminate this interview. It is growing late."

Clamp! clamp! The dull thud of the crutch coming around the corner. The cripple appeared, and, painfully limping, approached. Darcy placed his back against the railing.

"Mr. Bloke!" said Grey, "this gentleman is reticent, and all my eloquence is wasted upon him. Mr. Gaston," he continued, suddenly, "you are in peril! Answer my question, or take the consequences! You will not? Then, curse you! I'll see that you do not answer any other! Go for him, Bloke!"

As Dutchy raised his crutch, straightening himself upon his defective leg, Darcy darted forward, and caught Rupert by the throat with his left hand. He drew forth the pistol with his right, and aiming at the repulsive visage of the soldier, fired. Dutchy pushed the muzzle aside, almost as it touched his face, and two of his fingers dropped in the snow. At the same instant Rupert pressed the derringer against Darcy's breast, and pulled the trigger, as Dutchy's heavy crutch descended upon his head. Darcy fell forward, rolled over once, and then lay motionless. The white snow was stained with crimson. The murderers pushed the iron grating open and rushed through the narrow alley, as a carriage turned the church corner.

"Don't run," whispered Rupert, as they emerged upon the next street, "walk quietly. Where is your crutch?"

"Broke it over that feller's head! Was that a kerridge that come round the corner?"

"Yes. But it can't come through the alley. We've killed him, Bloke!"

"You bet," answered Mr. Bloke.

"It is a bad business! Curse his obstinacy! We must get out of this neighbourhood without delay. Are you sure he was dead?"

"I smelt his coat burnin'," replied Dutchy; "your pistol was touchin' his breast; if it shoots strong, he's as dead as a hammer, and if his head arn't made outen iron, it's mashed in two inches deep. Let's go down this street."

"You are mad!" said Rupert, "this street will take us back to the old church."

"Yes. I thought I might find my fingers!" and he held up the bleeding stump. "Don't hurt much! Feels kind o' numb like. But I must wrap it up. Lend us your hankercher!"

Rupert looked at the stolid face of his companion, with undisguised admiration.

"You should have been a soldier, Bloke," he said; "I would give all the money I have to bring that youth to life again!"

"You'll have to give me some of it for helping to kill him!" said Dutchy; "my fingers was worth two hundred dollars apiece, if only for stealin'! What a cussed young wildcat he was! If I hadn't been there, boss, *you* would have been a layin' with your toes turned up!"

They gained the house unmolested. Dutchy followed his patron into his room. Doctor Lamis was summoned, and after copious washings of the wounded hand, he cut away the torn flesh, secured the little arteries, and dressed the wound artistically. "He was foolin' with Mr. Blake's pistol," he said, "and it went off in his hand."

"Now, Boss," said Dutchy, when the Doctor retired, "if you'll give me one of them prime smokers of yourn, I'll take a whiff or two before I go to bed. And you had better settle up with me for all this business, too. I shall move to-morrow pooty early."

"How much do you want?" said Rupert, giving him the cigar.

"Well, say four hundred dollars!"

"Four hundred devils!" replied Rupert; "do you think I have a bush that bears greenbacks?"

"Shouldn't wonder," said Dutchy, gruffly; any way you win'd three hundred clean dollars from me to-night. I want them and another hundred."

"Your demands are too heavy, Mr. Bloke," said Rupert, coolly; "I will give you say fifty dollars. Not a cent more! No use to debate that point!"

He turned his back upon Dutchy, and leaned his head upon the arm of his chair. Dutchy felt in the pocket of his overcoat for the "billy" he habitually carried. His mind was made up. He would tap his patron gently on the temple, and would then "settle" according to his own ideas of justice. Before he drew the deadly little weapon out, Mr. Grey arose.

"I had nearly forgotten the pills," he murmured. Dutchy

dropped the billy, and stretched himself out upon the lounge, smoking vigorously.

Mr. Grey scraped the apple again, dropped the pills into the pulp, covered them up carefully and swallowed them.

Mr. Dutchy, overcome with fatigue, fell asleep, after tossing his cigar into the fire.

CHAPTER XLI.
MR. SKILLET'S PLAN.

AS the carriage rolled down Broadway, conveying Mr. Skillet and Mr. Henry Gaston, the former entertained Tige with voluminous accounts of the doings of "Dassy," from the catastrophe on the snow-bound train down to the present day. He had an attentive listener, and Mr. Skillet, charmed out of his customary bashfulness, " talked right along," to use his own expression.

"I seed that the boy was ra-al grit," he said, "when he first sot himself down by Miss Harding. That Grey chap knowed him. He mentioned his name before he left the car."

"Yes," answered Mr. Gaston; "he met Darcy in Lexington. I heard of it recently. He had noticed him particularly, though Darcy did not remember him when they met."

"It's no consequence!" said Mr. Skillet. "You see, I had proposed the trip to Scrabbletown, and I felt sorter responsible, so I sot down behind him and put in my oar when he got aground. Miss Harding would not tell what relation she was, though I gave her a hint or two. After he got through with his story I took him back to the smoking car and put him through sprouts. I asked what he proposed, and he! he! ho! he didn't understand me. He don't know good English, but he's larnin'! He's awful smart. Won't do to tell him that, though! I haven't summered him and wintered him yet, but there's mighty good stuff in him, by Gemini!"

"You have been very kind to him, Mr. Skillet," said Tige, "and my wife and I have felt very grateful to you. Darcy's letters are full of your praises."

"It's no consequence!" replied Mr. Skillet, visibly gratified. "I jest nat'rally froze to the boy from the fust. Wan't it cur'us now, that I should pick him out of all them passengers to jine me on the committee to interview the conductor? Well! I found out he had no business, and was going to hunt up a place for himself, without references, without any knowledge of business, except Greek and Latin!"

"He would have left no means untried," said Mr. Gaston; "he was resolved to find employment here."

"And he'd a' got it," replied Mr. Skillet; "some feller would have been smart enough to gobble him up. What the dickens do you carry that ugly whelp's picter for? I mean Grey?"

"I discovered that he had some rascally scheme, involving Helen Ruthven, and I wished to study his countenance a little."

"Helen Ruthven?" said Mr. Skillet, confused, "what in thunder does it all mean? You said Miss Harding's picter was Helen."

"Yes. She has changed her name, probably at the instigation of Grey. She is the daughter of my Father's partner. An orphan. with no relation in the world."

"Don't know about that!" said Mr. Skillet; "if she is the darter of that rebbil Colonel Ruthven, she has some relations in N'Yank!"

"Ah, yes!" replied Mr. Gaston; "you mean Miss Norman?"

"No, I don't mean Miss Norman! It's no consequence! Let her set! I must think it over a little. Jerusalem! Who would have thought it!"

Mr. Skillet wriggled about in his seat, venting sundry ejaculations, and evidently much exercised by his reflections. He put up the carriage window, and as the snow blew in he closed it again, apologizing to Mr. Gaston for exposing a Southerner to the wintry blast. When the carriage drove up on the ferry boat Mr. Skillet found his voice again.

"I knowed your brother was named for Colonel Ruthven, for he told me so. But I did not know that he left a family."

"Only this daughter," said Mr. Gaston.

"Did you happen to know his wife?"

"Oh, yes! She was a most excellent lady. She died very soon after her husband."

"You didn't know her maiden name?"

"Certainly. Miss Delancy."

"Oh! Ah! Yes!" said Mr. Skillet; "it's no consequence. Jerusalem! If I hadn't been a blamed old fool I'd a knowed what made me take to the child; of course!"

"I'm afraid I don't understand you, Mr. Skillet," said Gaston.

"No! I s'pose not. Jerusalem! I can tell you the story in few words. Old Rupert Norman, the grandfather of the lady at the Fifth Av'noo, was my fust boss. He raised me, in fact. When I growed up he gave me a hint that he had picked out a wife for me. It's no consequence! but it was a woman I couldn't tackle no way! Jerusalem! she had a chin a mile long! But that was only a part of the trouble; I had picked out another for myself, and her name was Helen Delancy. She was as poor as git out, and so was I. She had nauthin' but her schoolin', and I was gitten eight hundred dollars a year. Mighty big wages for them times, too! There was another fellow after the chin woman, who had beans enough to cover her chin, and she kind o' leaned to him, but her people wouldn't hear of him. He was a raal good fellow, and told me all his troubles, and I lent him a hundred dollars to run away with the chin woman. He was a amiable cuss, and she whaled him like blazes before they had been married a month. Then I persuaded Helen to marry me privately, over to Jersey City. She didn't tell even her sister, who lived with an aunt in Lexington, and she died the very day Mr. Ruthven married his wife. Somehow, I've always hated even to hear his name mentioned. It's no consequence!" and Mr. Skillet wiped away a tear or two—"but I buried her in Greenwood. I wrote to Ruthven, and just said she was dead and buried, but he had gone off to Canada on his wedding trip, and did not git my letter for a month. I never told a soul about my marriage, until to-night, and I'm jest tellin' you to let you see that Helen Ruthven is my niece. Blood is thicker nor water, and that's the reason I took to the child without knowing her!"

"But she is not a blood relation," said Gaston, who was greatly interested; "she is Mrs. Skillet's niece——"

"Well!" responded Mr. Skillet, obstinately, "don't the Scripter say ' bone of your bone, and flesh of your flesh?' She is my bone and flesh relation, and that is good as blood. She's *my* niece, by Gemini! Here we are, in Brooklyn. Driver! turn down to the right! I'm goin' to take you past the boardin'-house where I lived. It's next to an old church, where we both attended. When I got some beans of my own I bought that heouse, and I own it yet. Hello! what's that!"

Two pistol shots, so close together that they almost sounded like one report. The carriage turned the corner.

"Hi, driver!" said Mr. Skillet. "Stop! Su'thin' is up here! There is a man on the sidewalk! Hi! hold up!" and he scrambled out and approached the prostrate body, followed by Tige.

"Blood on the snow!" said Mr. Skillet, as he leaned over the motionless form and peered into the upturned face. "Ah! oh! Mr. Gaston, git into the carriage again, please, and drive to the second corner, and bring the doctor—Doctor Chase! It's no consequence! You needn't stop to look! Git out, please! Don't stand foolin' there! You needn't look!"

"Oh, Darcy!" said Tige, falling on his knees in the trampled snow. "Oh, my poor boy! Have I indeed only found you to see you die! Oh! Mr. Skillet, my place is here; go you for the doctor. He is not dead; I feel a feeble pulse. Oh, my brother!"

Mr. Skillet scrambled into the carriage, while Tige gently raised his brother's head and rested it upon his arm. He tried to take the still smoking pistol from Darcy's hand, but he clutched it with so firm a grip that Tige relinquished it after the first effort. He noticed the broken crutch, and, under the light of the gas lamp, he saw two bloody fingers lying beside the splintered wood. He looked at Darcy's hands and found them both unwounded.

"Oh, yes!" murmured Tige, "he fell with his weapon in his hand, and he has maimed his murderer for life. The boy was surprised, or was overpowered by numbers. I would have ventured him against any solitary assailant. Ah! here is the carriage! How can I ever face Nell with these dreadful tidings!"

The doctor was a deliberate old practitioner, who took all sorts of events with unshaken coolness. He touched Darcy's wrist, lifted one eyelid, felt his face, lifted the pistol arm, and, with expert fingers, twisted the weapon from Darcy's grasp.

"Is he dead?" whispered Mr. Skillet.

"Certainly not! I must get him into the light. Where shall we take him, Mr. Skillet?"

"Right here!" responded Mr. Skillet. "Mrs. Baker; boardin'-heouse; there's a paper on the door: 'Rooms to let'—hold on! I'll ring."

"I am afraid to ask a question, Doctor," said Tige, plaintively; "he is my only brother!"

"I could not answer you, my dear sir, if you did," replied the doctor; "there is a good deal of life in him yet. I can tell you better when we get him into the light."

"My compliments to Mrs. Baker!" said Mr. Skillet, as the door opened—"Mr. Skillet's compliments—and tell her I want the best room in the heouse!"

"Mrs. Baker has gone to bed, sir!" said the frightened servant.

"All right! It's no consequence! Jest go holler at her door that Mr. Skillet wants a room!"

The girl attempted to close the street door, but Mr. Skillet kicked it wide open and entered the hall.

"If you don't go for your missus!" said he to the domestic, who recoiled as he approached, "cuss me, if there won't be a funeral issuing out'n your room to-morrow mornin! d'ye hear! Git out then!"

The servant fled, and Mr. Skillet ran down the steps and assisted Tige and the doctor as they raised Darcy from the pavement. They carried him into the hall, and to the foot of the stair-case. Mrs. Baker appeared at the head at the same moment.

"I've got no rooms!" she screamed, "and I don't know any Mr. Kittle!"

"It's me, Mrs. Baker," said Mr. Skillet, "I've a friend here who has got hurted, and I must have a room."

"Oh! Mr. Skillet! I beg your pardon, sir! Bridget said Mr. Kittle. First floor, sir; front room. Bridget, light the gas!"

While the doctor was examining the wound in Darcy's breast, Mr. Skillet discovered another on his head. The doctor took a small book from Darcy's bosom, bound in tortoise-shell. The bullet had gone through both covers, splintering the shell into a hundred pieces, and had entered his breast. The doctor cut away waistcoat and shirt, turned him half over, and found the bullet under the shoulder blade.

"The book saved him!" said the doctor. "It deflected the ball, which has not entered the ribs. See! It ran round under the muscles, and came out here. And now for the other hurt."

After an examination that lasted five minutes, but which seemed to Tige to be five hours, the doctor arose, went to the basin and washed his hands.

"The hurts are serious, gentlemen, but not necessarily fatal. With youth and a sound constitution on his side, I think good nursing will bring him through!"

"And I'll carry out my plan, by Gemini!" said Mr. Skillet, in a whisper to Tige.

"What plan, Mr. Skillet?"

"None of your business, by Gemini! But keep your mouth shet, please, and leave it to me; I'll manœuvre him!"

CHAPTER XLII.

THE RED SPOTS IN THE SNOW.

THE wounds in Darcy's breast and back were speedily dressed, after Doctor Chase had carefully followed the track of the bullet, and satisfied himself that no serious damage had resulted from the pistol shot. But there were two separate wounds on his head; one over the eye, and the other on the side just above the ear. Mr. Bloke struck him with the top of the crutch, and the transverse piece had evidently inflicted the more serious hurt, which would have been instantly fatal, if the force of the blow had not been divided between the two wounds, and if his hat had not somewhat defended his head. After nearly an hour's skilful manipulation, Doctor Chase announced that he had done all that was possible, and that there was no immediate danger.

"He will be conscious presently," said the Doctor; "his pulses are improving. Keep the room dark, and keep him quiet as possible. I will return at daylight. Good night."

"My dear Mr. Skillet," said Tige, "will you please return to the hotel, and bring Mrs. Gaston?"

"Not much!" replied Mr. Skillet, emphatically. "Do you s'pose I'm made outen stun? It's pooty bad cheese, to see Dassy a layin' there so quiet; but it's a sight wuss to face the women with such a story. Go yourself! You're no use here. I'll stay till you git back."

"But, Mr. Skillet ——"

"Go about your business, please! Don't you see he's goin' to wake presently? Now if he sees you here, he'll git excited, but he won't mind me. You'd better git out."

"That is true," answered Gaston; "you are always right, Mr. Skillet."

"Most gen'rally," acquiesced Mr. Skillet.

"I will go back, then. Eleven o'clock. Oh, Mr. Skillet, I cannot thank you as I ought for your kindness ——"

"It's no consequence! Please to git out! And don't slam the door after you. And if you bring any women back with you, tell 'em to do their howlin' in the carriage! We hadn't ought to have any fuss here. Hist! Git out!"

Mr. Skillet drew his chair to the bedside, and took Darcy's hand in his. The old gentleman had repressed his own feelings while Tige was present; but when left alone with the young man, he quietly let some tears drop out of his blue eyes. There had grown up between these two a far stronger friendship than either of them dreamed of. Darcy was so outspoken and loyal, that his employer believed in him implicitly, and daily studied his straightforward, manly character, with increasing admiration. On the other hand, Darcy had recognized the substratum of genuine kindness, underlying the rough exterior, and admired the shrewd practical wisdom of Mr. Skillet's business maxims, as he saw their application day by day.

"Brother Tige!" murmured Darcy, "I can't see you, but you are here."

"Keep your mouth shet, please," whispered Mr. Skillet, in reply. "It's me. It's no consequence about Brother Tige jest now."

"Yes, sir," said Darcy, obediently; "but Helen! Helen!"

"Ya-as!" said Mr. Skillet, "it's all right. Let her set. I'll attend to her. She's all right. Don't bother your brains about her. The Doctor says you must keep quiet. You've sorter had a fall, but it's no consequence, if you jest keep still."

Darcy lay still, with his eyes closed. The gas was turned down, and Mr. Skillet, who kept his hand, could feel the nervous twitching of his fingers, but could not see his face.

"You may ask me one question," he said, "if you will be still afterwards."

"Helen!"

"She's all right! I'll send for her in the mornin' ——"

"No, no!" replied Darcy; "don't send. But see that he don't find her. I mean the devil."

"He's a tolerably hard customer to stave off!" muttered Mr. Skillet; "but we'll manœuvre him. Don't distress yourself about him."

There was another long silence, and Darcy apparently slept. Mr. Skillet mentally swore at the doctor for leaving the case, but uttered no sound. The street was very quiet, and the watcher could hear the tinkle of the bells, as a horse car passed the corner below. Then he heard midnight announced from a steeple four or five squares distant.

"I say!" whispered Darcy, suddenly; "there were two of them, you know?"

"Oh, ya-as! certainly!" replied Mr. Skillet.

"Two devils."

"Ya-as! I know more 'n two hundred myself. But it's no consequence. We'll manœuvre 'em."

Asleep again. Mr. Skillet felt Darcy's wrist. The blood was bounding through its appointed channels with steady regularity, but Mr. Skillet thought the pulses too strong for the circumstances. Fever coming on, no doubt.

Tige had taken a latchkey with him, and while Mr. Skillet was debating with himself as to the best way to recall that cussed doctor, the door opened gently, and Mr. Gaston and his wife stole softly into the room. Mrs. Gaston deposited her bonnet and wrappings on the lounge, and then motioning Mr. Skillet aside, quietly took possession of his chair. There was a business-like air about all her movements that awed the old gentleman, and he retired into the hall, beckoning Tige after him.

"She's a hull team, she is!" he whispered; "I guess we'd better let her manœuvre him now. He has been talking."

"Has he?" said Tige, excitedly.

"Ya-as! It wan't much, though. He fust called for brother Tige."

"Did he? I'll go to him now."

"Not much!" replied Mr. Skillet; "he is sleeping agin, and anyway he pooty soon quit you, and went for Helen. Didn't stay long there either. Then he went for the devil."

"His mind was wandering," said Tige.

"Mebbe so!" said Mr. Skillet; "but he seemed tolerably level too! He said the devil was after Helen. Then he said there was two devils, and I knowed he was right. Then he dropped off to sleep agin."

"Now, Mr. Skillet," said Tige, "I insist upon one thing! You must have some sleep! Can you sleep here, or will you take the carriage, which waits at the corner, and go back to New York?"

"Will you mind your business, please!" replied Mr. Skillet; "I am not going away from here till Dassy is up! There! You and your wife have been travellin', and you'd better go to bed! I'd rather set up as not!"

"Well, if you won't go, I'll dismiss the carriage. I will return in a minute."

But he was gone several minutes, and when he returned, there was a look of grim ferocity on his amiable visage, that startled Mr. Skillet. Tige beckoned him out in the hall.

"When I had sent away the carriage," said Tige, "I stopped

to look at the bloody snow on the corner. I found some drops on the sidewalk near the church railing. Then I saw the drops following footprints through a narrow alley, between this house and the church. I followed the tracks, finding blood drops occasionally, but footprints in the snow until I reached the house where they ceased. The door plate bears the name of Doctor Lamis."

"Why he's the spiritooal hound," said Mr. Skillet; "plenty of fools in N'Yauk and Brooklyn. He is coining money."

"Yes," replied Tige; "but I happen to know who lives with him."

"Indeed!"

"Yes. It is the present habitation of Mr. Rupert Grey. And Mr. Grey has attempted murder, if he has not succeeded. And I intend to have a settlement!"

"D'ye mean fight?" said Mr. Skillet.

"It depends;" replied Tige; "I intend to see that he does not escape. If the law cannot reach the case, I will take it in hand. The man who harms Darcy Gaston puts his life in peril, if I can reach him."

"Fightin' is a bad business," observed Mr. Skillet, shaking his head; "still, if it must be done, the sooner the better. Let's go round there now, and shake up the heouse! By Gemini! I'll take a hand, if the game ain't full already!"

"We must get policemen," said Tige, "and let them watch the house."

"Policemen!" answered Mr. Skillet, "Oh, Jerusalem!"

"But we *must* keep within the law," insisted Tige; "if we get the police force on the track of this murderer, we can watch also, if necessary."

"Brother Tige," murmured Darcy.

"I am here, Darcy, boy!" answered Tige, rushing to the bedside, and taking Darcy's hand.

"I can't see you, Brother. Sister Nell, you are here also?"

"Yes," whispered Nell; "but you had better keep quiet, Darcy. To-morrow we will talk."

"Helen, brother! Save Helen!"

"She is safe, Darcy. Compose your mind and go to sleep again. I know where to find your assailant. He shall not escape."

"Let him go, Brother! I charge you. If he will go, let him escape. Has he killed me?"

"Not much," said Mr. Skillet; "the Doctor says you are all right. Don't talk any foolishness about killen'!"

"Promise me one thing, Brother," said Darcy, in a tone of entreaty, "Go, find Grey, and tell him to flee. If you will do this, I will be quiet."

"I will do it, Darcy."

"Now, Brother, now!"

"Very well. I will go at once."

"And I'll go with you," said Mr. Skillet, following Tige; "mebbe it will take two of us to persuade him. Put on your overcoat. I'm all ready."

They walked out into the quiet street. Tige, confident in his strength, thought of no weapons. With his naked hands he could tear the wretch to pieces. Mr. Skillet saw Darcy's pistol on the table, and quietly slipped it into his pocket. Did not want to use the thing, but it was convenient to have it about one. Might be mad dogs or something of the sort, in the street.

All was dark and still at the house of Dr. Lamis. Mr. Gaston rang the bell, and the window over the front door was opened and a man looked out.

"Who is there?" he said.

"We want Mr. Grey," replied Tige. "Let him come down for a moment."

"Who are you?" said the man.

"No matter. It is of great importance to Mr. Grey, that we should speak with him instantly. His life may depend upon it."

"Git him out onto the sidewalk," whispered Mr. Skillet. "If you shoot him inside the heouse, he can take the law of you!"

"Mr. Grey cannot come," said the man at the window. "He is dying or dead!"

CHAPTER XLIII.

THE FRIENDS' PARTING.

SOMETHING uncanny about Dutchy's appearance had excited suspicion in the mind of the apothecary, while they were debating over the bottle of strychnine. Suppose this grizzly looking customer should happen to have evil designs against some more important personage than a dorg? And suppose the sale of virulent poison should be hereafter traced to this identical Dispensatory? The young chemist shuddered as he estimated the possible consequences! On the other hand, if by the substitution of some other drug, the dorg should have his life prolonged, and accidentally happen to bite the customer, it was an open question whether or not society would be shaken to its foundations. He would rather take that risk anyhow. So at the last moment, he deftly changed bottles, and made the two pills of Bi-carbonate of soda.

Dutchy waited a full half hour, while he lay so quietly on the lounge, to see the effect of the deadly pills. His knowledge on the general subject was limited, and he expected to see his patron fall suddenly into convulsions, grow black in the face, and then expire.

Instead of meeting these reasonable expectations, Mr. Grey arose with a yawn, and announced his intention of seeking tired Nature's sweet restorer, if Mr. Bloke would have the goodness to retire.

Dutchy arose also, a portentous gloom gathering upon his face.

"Give me what money you're goin' to give, Boss!" said he; "I arn't goin' to risk my neck in this town."

"Where will you go, Bloke?"

"Dunno. Must git up and git outen here, though."

Mr. Grey took out his pocket book, and drawing a chair to the table, sat down, and counted out some money. He was oppressed with a new sensation; a feeling of remorse, tinged with some dread also, and his mind was preoccupied. Dutchy stood near him, a little behind, and watched the counting.

"How much, Boss?" he said, in a husky voice.

"Fifty Dollars."

"Look at them keards, Boss," said Dutchy, suddenly laying a half dozen on the table, face downwards. "I can pick out all the jacks and all the aces."

"Ah!" said Rupert, coolly, "you are a dangerous man to encounter, Mr. Bloke!"

"I guess you're right, Boss," replied Dutchy; "but don't you think you could give me back them three hundred dollars? Them is the same jacks and aces that win'd them offen me!"

"What the devil do you mean!" said Rupert, starting up and facing him.

"This!" replied Dutchy, raising the billy, and striking his patron over his almond shaped eyes.

He caught him, as he fell forward, and laid him gently on the hearth rug. There was an iron stand, holding shovel and poker, near his head, and Dutchy moved the body towards it, so that the round bar at the base of the stand was stained with the blood. He took the pocket-book from the relaxing grasp of his associate, gathered up the notes that were counted out on the table, and then sat down to consider the situation. First: Lock the door.

As he sat there, smoking a cigar, which he had taken from Rupert's case, he recalled the circumstances attending their short acquaintance. Grey had been kind to him, on the whole. The truth was—though Dutchy never dreamed it—that Rupert felt under heavy obligations to this savage brute, because his body had certainly saved him from sudden death, when he fell upon it, at their first encounter. And he had been pleased with the readiness wherewith Dutchy evaded him, with lies of unusual proportions, so grotesque in conception and utterance. And he thought he might be able to utilize Dutchy's genius in carrying out such parts of his plans as might require bull dog ferocity and unblushing effrontery.

"He was werry good to me," thought Dutchy, as he smoked; "and I didn't like to hit him. That cussed pison cost a dollar, and wasn't worth a cent! And now I must git! I'll take nothin' of hisen 'cept this money, and I'd a won it if he hadn't cheated! So it's as good as mine anyway. Guess I'll take his red beard, too. He'll not want it! Cuss me, if I don't dress up in his good clothes!"

He rummaged in the bureau and wardrobe, and selected a suit, which he exchanged for his military rags, very rapidly. He fitted on the red beard and the broad brimmed hat. He took a handful of cigars and thrust them into the pocket of his overcoat, and then burnt up his own attire in the grate, a few rags at a time. When they were all consumed, he stood before the glass, and practised the motions of the arm, in removing the cigar from his lips, in his late patron's elaborate fashion.

"Think I'll do!" muttered Dutchy. "Now for the Bowery! and to-morrow, I'll take the first train; there's a train at two o'clock to-night. What a fool I was to forget it. All right. Good night, Boss."

He turned down the gas, unlocked the door, and passed down stairs. The front door was chained and barred, and he could not open it without dangerous noise. So he went to the parlour, opened the inside shutters, raised the sash, and finding the street quiet, dropped safely down. The policeman who had pulled aside the red beard, early in the evening, nodded civilly to it again, as Trinity steeple announced midnight. The policeman remembered the greenback, that concluded the former interview and gilded it with the hue of romance. The red whiskers passed majestically through Fulton street, up Broadway to Chambers street, and finally disappeared in the cars of the Hudson River Railroad.

Beneath these fictitious adornments Dutchy carried a moustache of his own. It was a fierce collection of bristles, of which he was rather vain. So, when he walked into a barber shop in Albany, and demanded a clean shave, he parted with the last possibility of identification, as he had preserved this pet growth through all his former disguises. He gazed at his image in the glass, trimmed and brushed, his countenance burnished, and his very eyebrows smoothed, and mourned the departure of his old likeness. At a neighbouring shop he bought a hat with a round top; and all his former foes, the cops of New York, would have passed him under review, without recognition. Dutchy was extinct. He bought a hair brush, four paper collars, and a small satchel with a gorgeous strap, all from the same shop, boldly paying with clean five dollar notes. After a comfortable breakfast he took the western bound train, and with twenty-five cheap cigars in his new satchel he disappeared from the surface of the society that had known him hitherto.

But while he was crossing the East River, at the beginning of his journey, Doctor Lamis, who had looked into Grey's room accidentally, was horrified at the appearance of things in that cosy chamber. Rupert was senseless, and apparently dead. The Doctor drew his body under the chandelier, and in the midst of his examinations Mr. Gaston's summons called him to the window. After a brief colloquy he descended the stairs and admitted Mr. Skillet and Tige, who followed him to the room above.

The blow had been delivered with a vigorous hand. The Doctor washed away the blood, and with the assistance of Mr. Gaston, placed Rupert upon the bed. Tige furtively examined the two limp hands and found the usual complement of fingers on each.

"I am at a loss to account for this!" said Doctor Lamis; "I left him only fifteen or twenty minutes ago—no; it must have been near an hour—and he was perfectly well. His head was near the poker stand, and the base of it is bloody. But I cannot conceive how so violent a fall was possible."

14

"Was he alone?" said Tige.

"No. Bloke, that is the lame soldier, was with him. Stay! I will call him up and question him." And he left the room.

"He is gone!" said the Doctor, returning in a minute; "his room is empty. Gentlemen, I fear there has been some foul play here. This soldier came in here only two hours ago with two fingers shot off. I now believe Grey shot him! See, here is his pistol. And after I bound up his wounds I left them here, evidently repressing strong excitement, and the quarrel was, doubtless, renewed, and Bloke inflicted this wound!"

"You say 'his pistol,'" observed Tige, taking up the weapon; "whose pistol? Bloke's?"

"No; Grey's," replied the Doctor. Tige put the pistol in his pocket.

"Did he and this soldier come in together?" asked Mr. Gaston.

"Yes. Grey had a latchkey. They have been together all the evening. This is a horrible calamity. Hist! He is stirring!"

"Go for him, Bloke!" muttered Rupert, staring vacantly at the three men.

"How do you feel, Grey?" said the Doctor, starting forward.

"Shaky! That devil struck me with the poker, I suppose. There is a flask on the mantel. Give me a drop or two."

The Doctor poured out a tablespoonful, diluted it, and raised Rupert's head while he slowly swallowed the liquor.

"Who are these gentlemen, Lamis?" whispered Rupert.

"It's no consequence!" replied Mr. Skillet; "we had a little business with you, but it will keep."

Rupert, still dizzy, felt in his breast pocket. No pocket-book.

"Lamis, please look on the floor and the table," he said; "I had my pocket-book in my hand when the ruffian struck me. Ah! you do not find it. Gone! gone! Robbed and almost murdered here in my own room, by so base a hound! I must get up and hunt for him!"

"No use, Grey!" said the Doctor; "he is out of your reach by this time. You might as well hunt a needle in a haystack. He is across the river, of course. To-morrow we can put detectives on his track. But now you must positively keep quiet. You have a broken head to nurse."

"Pooh!" said Rupert; "it is a hard knock, I know; but I shall be all right in an hour. What time is it? My watch is gone! Ah! Mr. Bloke, you did your business by wholesale." And he sat up on the bedside.

"It is the whisky, Grey," replied the Doctor; "and when the effect of the stimulant wears off, you will be shaky enough. Will you be able to undress, if we leave you? It is midnight."

"To-morrow morning, then, gentlemen," said Rupert, "if you will excuse me till then. Ten thousand devils! How my head aches."

When his visitors retired Mr. Grey locked the door. Then he looked for his Derringer. It was gone. He listened to the departing footsteps of the strangers, and when Lamis came up stairs again, he asked him half a dozen pertinent questions about them and their inquiries. Then, dismissing the Doctor after he had dressed his cracked crown, this iron willed man dressed himself anew, in the best clothes Dutchy had left him, and at two o'clock A. M. Mr. Grey was in the station at Cortlandt street ferry, getting the lost passenger's baggage, for which he produced the check, and having it rechecked for Washington, District of Columbia.

CHAPTER XLIV.

A New Relation.

DARCY was awake and quite composed when his brother returned with Mr. Skillet. Tige, assisted by sundry ejaculatory amendments by Mr. Skillet, recounted the interview with Grey and Doctor Lamis.

"I found two fingers where you had fallen, Darcy," said Tigé; "did you shoot?"

"Yes. I shot the lame soldier; I thought I had certainly killed him. He had his crutch uplifted to strike. That is all I know until I heard your voice."

"And the other—I mean Grey?"

"I had my left hand on his throat; then I fell."

"But what did Grey do?"

"I am not certain," said Darcy, reluctantly; "get him away and I will recall the circumstances to-morrow. Will he be able to travel to-morrow?"

"This murdering villain shot you, Darcy!" said Tige. "You know he did. Why do you try to screen him? You would not be alive now if this little book had not been in your bosom."

"Ha!" said Darcy, "the book! She took away my weapon and shielded me with the Gospel of Peace!"

"It's no consequence!" said Mr. Skillet, fidgeting in his chair, thinking Darcy was becoming incoherent again. "You'd better shet your mouth now, and go to sleep! Come, Mr. Gaston! Mrs. Baker says we can have this next room. Mrs. Gaston won't go, I know!"

"Not I!" said Nell. "I slept three hours in the cars. I am going to stay with Darcy until daylight. Go, Tige! I'll make him go to sleep when you are gone."

"Brother Tige!" said Darcy, "will you see Grey early to-morrow, and send him away? Tell him I will charge him with assault with intent to kill, as soon as I am able to walk! No safety for him on this Continent! And, brother, if he has not enough money to get away, give him what is necessary; everything depends upon his escape!"

"Be content, Darcy," answered Tige, "it shall be as you wish; but if he will not go?"

"Then you won't mind killing him, brother! He ought to die, on many accounts; but I cannot harm him."

"Well," said Mr. Skillet, "it seems to me that you are level at one minnit and mad as a March hare the next. But Gosh and Gemini! you'll talk all night if we stay. Git out, please, Mr. Gaston! Good night, Mrs. Gaston. You can call if you need us; only the next room."

"Now Darcy, boy," said his sister, when the gentlemen retired, "you must go to sleep. I promised for you."

"Sister Nell," answered Darcy, "push the lounge up here. Take one of these pillows and lie down there. As soon as you are quiet, I will go to sleep if I can; there is no need to watch me."

Doctor Chase's examination the next morning resulted in blinding the patient, by covering his eyes with a multitude of bandages. The eye was hurt, and the cautious surgeon feared inflammation. The other wounds were doing well, and if he kept dark and quiet another day, and if no new symptoms appeared, he might sit up the next. Better not talk much, especially upon exciting topics; somebody might read the paper to him. Tea and toast, and, if he desired it, ice cream.

"How much ice cream, doctor?" murmured Darcy.

"How much do you want?"

"A gallon."

A NEW RELATION.

"Very well. You had better take half a pint at a time—say at intervals of three hours. This gentleman is certainly a Southerner," he continued to Mrs. Gaston; "all Southerners are the old boy on ice cream! It is terribly poor stuff, too, but it is harmless! Let him have it. And I think I may say he is doing well. You need not apprehend serious consequences. The eye is the only trouble, and darkness is the best treatment. Good morning!"

When Tige awoke, at eight o'clock, Mr. Skillet informed him that he had already been round "to see that spiritooal cuss," and that Mr. Grey had disappeared during the night. The old gentleman had left Mr. Gaston asleep and greeted him with this intelligence as soon as he opened his eyes.

"He was too smart for us, Mr. Gaston!" said he. "He seed you was a lawyer; could tell you by the cut of your jib! and he concluded it wan't best to stay. And I think his head was level on that p'int. Blast his picter! And now let's git some breakfast. Mrs. Baker has the best coffee in Brooklyn."

After the morning meal, Mr. Skillet watched Darcy fifteen minutes, while Mrs. Gaston fed him on ice cream. Then he went to Mrs. Bruce's, hunting for his niece.

"Put on your overshoes!" he said, as soon as she appeared. "Fine bright mornin', but snow on the ground. Git on your wraps, and come out! I've su'thin to tell you."

"Oh, Mr. Skillet," said Helen, "please excuse me. I don't want to go out; I'm afraid."

"Afraid of that Grey devil!" said Mr. Skillet. "It's no consequence; he'll not trouble you. He's off, with the law after him. Come out, and I'll tell you all about it."

Helen took his arm, as they emerged into the crisp morning air, wondering what strange revelations were coming.

"How much can you stand?" said Mr. Skillet, eyeing her curiously. "You always seemed to have plenty of grit. But I've got two or three things to tell you that will surprise you—mebbe shock you, too! I dunno! It's hard to tell how you'll take it."

"Do not fear for me, Mr. Skillet," answered Helen, "I am so unhappy that no new misfortune can terrify me."

"Indeed!" said Mr. Skillet; "well, one misfortune at a time. Your name is Helen Ruthven, and your mother's name was Delancy."

Helen looked at him in terror.

"Don't be skeart, child! That ain't the wust of it. Your

mother had a sister, Helen Delancy. She was privately married. She died before you was born. But her husband is your uncle, I calkilate."

"Yes, sir."

"And you are holdin' on to that uncle's arm this minnit. There! Now is your time to faint! How do you like findin' an old uncle like me? Tell the truth, child!"

"Oh, uncle!" said Helen, turning swimming eyes upon him.

"Ah, well! Don't turn on the waterspout jest yet. You'll want all the tears you've got direckly. I felt a drawin' to you, child, from the fust. And all I've got to say is, that my heouse is yourn. And you will comfort the few remaining days of your old uncle if you will jest come and live all over it. Three-story brown stone front, English basement, gas and water all over the heouse, and stationary tubs in the basement."

"Dear uncle," said Helen, "I will do whatever you bid me. But tell me how you learned all this. Did Mr. Gaston tell you my real name?"

"Ya-as. Stop here, Helen. I attended church here with your Aunt Helen, twenty years ago; and we lived to that house."

"Uncle, there is blood on the snow!"

"Ya-as! There was a scrimmage here last night. Nobody got killed, though. Remember that. Do you mind hearin' about it?"

"I am anxious to hear. Don't fear to tell me, uncle. I won't faint, or cry out."

"Wa-al, you're true grit, child!" said Mr. Skillet; "I allus said so. It makes me feel warm all over to hear you call me uncle. It's cur'ous now, but my two nieces at the Institoot, who are my own brother's children, don't seem as near to me as you do. But s'pose I was to tell you that somebody—me, for instance, was in that scuffle, and got hurt——"

"But I see you alive and well."

"It's no consequence. I'll break it by degrees. There is a young man that came here to Brooklyn last night, to visit a lady; and he had been followed by an ugly cuss from N'Yauk; and I s'pose the ugly cuss was layin' in wait for him, and found him here. And they had some words——"

"Oh, uncle!" said Helen, clinging to his arm, while the color forsook her cheeks.

"There, there!" said her uncle; "I knowed you would go off. Nobody killed, I tell you. But one of 'em got hurt some; and we took him right in there, to Mrs. Baker's, number twenty-nine, and he's there now. And the doctor says he's all right, if we keep the room dark a day or two. His brother and sister are with him this minnit. Come all the way from Kentucky to see him. There!"

"Was it Mr. Gaston, uncle? Ah! I see it was. He came to see me last night. And Mr. Henry Gaston is here?"

"Right here! We'll go in and see him. There was some shootin' done last night, but nobody killed. Dassy had a little book in his pocket, with a hard back onto it, and it turned the bullet. That's all the story, child, and every word is true."

"Did he know the man?" said Helen, eagerly.

"I guess he did. It was a fellow that was supposed to be dead. Ah, Helen! When I asked you before about that devil, Grey, I did not know I was your uncle. But now you will tell me. Dassy knew, and Dassy said he could not shoot him, because you disarmed him. And when Dassy come to last night, the first words he said were: 'Tige, go tell Grey to escape!' And the next words were: 'Tige, save Helen!' What in the dickens are you crying about? It's no consequence, I tell you. Nobody got killed."

"I will tell you everything, uncle. Oh, wretched woman that I am! How can I ever explain my folly and my wickedness!"

"Never mind, Helen," said Mr. Skillet; "don't tell me a word. I don't crave to know. The devil's gone. Let him set."

"But I must tell you, uncle. Nobody but you can deliver me from that wretch. And you and Mr. Gaston can do it, I am sure. I will endure all the shame and contempt. Oh, how I despise myself! But I will tell the truth, and all of it."

"That's allus safe, child. Come in. We'll find Mr. Gaston in two minnits. There is his wife at the window now, holdin' her arms out to you. Gemini! but she's a stunner!"

The extended arms caught the weeping girl and drew her into the house as soon as Mr. Skillet opened the door. Kind, loving Nell Gaston was sister, mother, friend—everything. She kissed away the tears, laughing with delight and thankfulness.

"Don't cry, my darling!" said Nell, "but help us all to rejoice. We thought our boy was killed. But he is safe and getting well. And we have found you, my poor child! Oh, how could you leave us in ignorance of your fate so long? Tige went to Chicago to look for you, and we have been so unhappy about you. Here, Tige! Mr. Gaston!"

Her husband came in answer to her summons, and greeted Helen, his handsome face covered with cheerful smiles.

"My dear Miss Helen," he said, "things are not so bad as you think. I can promise you deliverance from all that troubles you. Darcy is sleeping, wife. Come, Mr. Skillet; come, Miss Helen; let us all go into this room, and exchange stories. You shall tell the first, and I will follow. We can hear Darcy if he wakes. Begin, Miss Helen."

CHAPTER XLV.

Helen's Story.

"It is not possible to tell you, dear friends, how I shrink from the task you have set me."

Tige took her hand in his, and Nell, passing her plump arm around Helen's slender waist, drew her head down upon her shoulder.

"You should know, first," resumed Helen, "that my life at Mrs. Crowder's was one long misery. I did not appreciate my orphanhood in Lexington, because everywhere I met with ready sympathy and kindness. My only trouble was in resisting the gentle charities that were offered me. You know, Mr. Gaston, that you came to take me to your house, pretending you owed my poor father money. Dr. Graves was eager and earnest in his invitations to make my future home with him and his children. Judge Hammond sent his carriage, with peremptory orders to his coachman not to return without me. So, when I crossed the river with Mrs. Crowder, I felt that I was leaving everything that I loved in the world, and thenceforth could expect nothing beyond the mere human interest of mere strangers.

"But I did not know how bad it was. Although I worked as well as I could, Mrs. Crowder contrived to remind me constantly that I did not nearly earn the little sum she paid me. I was ostensibly the teacher of her children, but the time spent in hearing recitations and in directing their studies was the only time in which I rested. She apparently had long arrears of work to gather up, and I was really her seamstress. I do not complain of this, however, and it may be true that the small wages she paid me more than equalled the value of my work. But the constant pressure of her piety makes me shudder when I think of it. There was something ghastly about it. Always pronounced and always ghastly. The earth was one vast cemetery, and the joys of life one combined delusion. She required me to attend her church, where I sympathized with nothing I heard, except the brief portion of Scripture that was read or quoted. She required me to read some printed sermons, called "Lies for To-morrow," preached by Professor Hang, and I, who had been so carefully instructed in theology, was less horrified by the profaneness of the heresy he taught than by his sickening emptiness of matter, and pretension of style. But she made the book a text book for her children, and when my conscience compelled me to dissent from his conclusions she severely lectured me for my presumption, and that before my pupils.

"Mr. Crowder spent his life in hunting for disagreeable things to say. I am sure I never heard him utter one sentence to his family that had not a sting in it. And the three girls I professed to instruct were worthy children of these parents. I am ashamed to say these things of a household where I was fed and sheltered so long, and I shall never say them again. But I tell you, dear friends, in order to account for all that follows.

"One night a stranger came to Mrs. Crowder's pew and sat by me. I remember now that I glanced at him as he took his seat, and instinctively shrank away from him. I turned my head away, and then I knew that he was watching me. I *felt* his eyes; bold, black, bad eyes! And ever since that night, when he has been near me, I have had the same experience. I could always *feel* him looking at me when he chose to make me feel his power. I don't know how he got into Mrs. Crowder's family, but he was a constant visitor there, after that first evening. His name was Rupert Grey.

"He came night after night, always welcomed by Mrs. Crowder, and especially welcomed by her eldest daughter, sixteen years old, and to her he professed a special attachment. He kept up a kind of playful courtship, with just enough appearance of sincerity to charm the girl, while he carefully maintained the air of playfulness, as if to warn every one else that he was only in joke. But he succeeded in making Jane so madly jealous of me that another affront was put upon me, in her petulant and passionate appeals to her mother to send me out of the room when Mr. Grey called. I learned afterwards that this was part of his plan, and also that he insisted upon my presence whenever he was in the house. He told Mrs. Crowder, with—to use his own words—" with gushing candour," that he would discontinue his visits if they drove her governess out of the room. He told me this, himself.

"If you ask me how it was possible for this man to gain so strong an influence over me, I cannot answer you. Since I have been delivered from his presence I have thought there must have been some occult power in his wicked eyes, that subdued my will and overcame my repugnance. When his attention was attracted to others in the room I would find the feeling of restraint and compulsion wearing off, but if he suddenly turned his eyes towards me, which he frequently did, I would be conscious of a vague sense of his domination, and of the reality of my miserable submission."

"Poor child!" said Tige, "it was a clear case of animal magnetism. If a hideous snake can charm and capture the beautiful bird, why should not a worse reptile possess a similar power? My belief is, that this unnatural ability is inherited directly from the original snake that beguiled Eve in the garden!"

"Mr. Grey met me one day in Main street," resumed Helen, "and after a few introductory remarks, informed me that 'it was necessary that he should have my photograph, to perfect certain business arrangements.' He was so masterful that I could not resist him. After the picture was taken he dismissed me, saying, 'I would have to accompany him to New York, shortly, as I was a party to the arrangements he had in hand.' When I got back to Mrs. Crowder's my original horror of the man returned, and I suddenly resolved to quit Cincinnati and return to Lexington at once. A small satchel contained all my property, and was soon packed. My departure was hastened by an unusually stormy interview with Mrs. Crowder, who charged me with going out to seek Mr. Grey, and who also referred to my father, the sainted gentleman, as the very offspring of Satan, because he died in arms against the Government. I was provoked out of my customary silence, and replied with scorn and wicked anger."

"It was a case," quoth Mrs. Gaston, " in which you fulfilled the Scripture injunction—' Be angry and sin not!' You need not mind repenting of *that*, my dear."

"It was snowing when I left the house. I walked down to the station, and found I had to wait three hours for the train. I sat in the waiting room, reading my Testament—yes; this one—

when I was suddenly conscious that Mr. Grey was near me. I looked up and saw him at the door. He beckoned me out, and I was compelled to follow him. I am only able to recall this much of my sensations. The shuddering repugnance I felt when he was absent—that I feel this moment—was so far modified that I experienced only a dull indifference about him. There has never been an instant when I was *attracted*, even when I most promptly obeyed him; and the events that occurred in quick succession seem to me, now, like the dim memory of an awful dream! I cannot conceive it possible that I really did the things and spoke the words he commanded with his demon's eyes! I remember that he took my satchel and led me to the street, and that the snow was falling thickly. He handed me into a carriage, followed, and sat beside me, and the driver, closing the door, mounted the box and drove off.

" 'So!' said Mr. Grey, 'you meditated a flight, it seems?'

" 'Yes,' I answered, indifferently.

" 'Well, it was unwise. First, to attempt to thwart me; second, to run counter to your own interests.'

" 'I have no interests,' I said; 'where are we going?'

" 'Not far; you will know shortly. Would tobacco smoke offend you?'

" 'Nothing offends me.'

"He smoked in silence until the carriage stopped at the Burnet House. He gave me his hand as I left the carriage, and led me in, I following him mechanically. We entered a handsome parlour, on the second floor, when he took my waterproof cloak and shook off the snow flakes, while he pointed to a chair near the grate. There were three men in the room—one an Episcopal minister and the others apparently servants of the hotel. Mr. Grey sat opposite me, and took my hand in his, looking into my face with his cold, cruel eyes, until I found my eyelids drooping. I felt as I did once before under the influence of opium: no inclination to resist anything, or choose anything; just helpless and indifferent.

" 'Helen,' he said, slowly and distinctly, 'I have prepared, as you see, for our marriage. It is not proper for you to travel with me to New York in any other relation, and we are going immediately; are you ready?'

" 'Ready,' I said.

"The minister came forward with a book in his hand, and Mr.

Grey assisting me to rise, we stood before him. I don't remember anything he read, but I recollect noticing that part of one ear was cut off. He put his hand up, as if to pull his hair over the ugly place, once or twice. Then, I remember that Mr. Grey said in a whisper:

"'Say "I will!" Helen.'

"'I will!'

"I signed my name in a book and he signed his, and the three men signed theirs. The clergyman filled up a printed form and signed it, giving it to Mr. Grey, who rang the bell as they retired, ordering the servant to bring in dinner. It came in a few minutes, and he bade me sit at the table and eat. I cannot remember anything, except that a cup of tea seemed to refresh me. In a short time afterwards, while the servants were still removing the dishes, he put my cloak around me, took me down to the carriage, which had his trunk strapped on the back of it, and we drove to another station through the deepening snow. We were soon seated in the car, and the train moved out, as the night gathered around, and I remember a dull feeling of relief came over me, under the conviction that the future certainly could have no horrors in store for me that would be worse than my present desolation.

"He did not talk to me during the night, but slept in his seat, and while he slept, I gradually recovered my senses and meditated upon the distracting fact that I was married to this wretched man. He had the certificate at that instant! I remembered noting how he threw his arm forward, as he dropped the paper in the breast pocket of his coat. I involuntarily turned towards him, and saw the edge of the paper, and, hardly knowing what I did, I drew it out and read it by the light of the lamp overhead. Yielding to a sudden impulse, I tore the paper into small fragments and threw them on the floor.

"During the next day he was generally silent upon any topic except the scenery, the snow storm, the state of the track and other indifferent matters. I was reading my Testament just before dark, on the second day, when he suddenly leaned towards me and whispered:

"'You run the religious machine, I see; I've no objection. The Book you are reading will tell you that you owe me unanswering obedience! Now, listen and remember! There is a piece of property called Ruthven's Folly in New York, and I am persuaded that it can be secured to you by the observance of a few rules.

First, do not speak of your marriage to any mortal; second, do not mention my name, or your own—I mean, your maiden and married name, both or either—until I give you permission.'

"'I have no title to Ruthven's Folly,' I answered, steadily, 'and I would never accept it if I had!'

"'Pish!' he said, rudely, 'do not be so positive! I will see that your rights are secured in due time. Only obey me. On your religion, I charge you!'

"These were the last words he ever spoke to me. The train stopped almost as he spoke, and it was soon announced that we could not proceed. You know the rest of the story."

"Yes," answered Tige, with exulting eagerness, "yes, Helen; and I know a part of the story that you don't know. My dear child, you were *not* married!"

"Not married?" said Helen, her eyes dilating with delirious joy. "Oh, Mr. Gaston, you would not tell me an untruth!"

"Not I!" said Tige. "I know that one-eared clergyman! He is a vile scoundrel whom I defended once in a criminal suit. He told me, three days ago, that he had been well paid by Grey to personate a minister and perform that bogus ceremony, and I have his deposition in due form to that effect, attested by the same witnesses who saw the pretended marriage. It was from him that I learned that Grey was at the spiritualist's—Doctor Lamis, I mean."

Helen hid her face upon Nell's breast, while the latter coo'd and cheered her in her own fashion.

"Cry away, my dear; it does you good! I'm crying myself. Tige! you hard-hearted old wretch, why don't you cry?"

"I'd rather laugh, Nell," answered Tige.

"It's no consequence!" said Mr. Skillet, openly wiping his eyes. "But if I ever get sight of that chap agin, and don't put him out of the notion of gitten married—dern his picter!—you may jest sell me for a quart of peanuts, and cheat the peanut seller when you do it—that's all! Helen, child! will you come home with me, to-day?"

"Friday, Uncle, composition day; to-morrow will be a holiday, and I can help dear Mrs. Gaston, maybe."

"Yes, indeed! Mr. Skillet, Helen is not going until I go! and I am not going until Darcy goes!"

"It's all right!" said Mr. Skillet, "I cave! But I must go to Wall street, and I'll come back at dark."

"And I'll come back after school! Oh, my heart is so light that all my past sorrow and shame seem as nothing. If I could only be assured that this murderous wretch were imprisoned for life I don't think I should ever murmur or repine again. Dear Mr. Gaston, how kind you have been! Oh, Uncle! this gentleman, if I had yielded to his earnest invitation, would have kept me in Kentucky and then I should never have known you."

"Ya-as! It's no consequence, but them Gastons is a bad breed; they want all the good lookin' gals they see!"

Helen blushed, laughed, and, kissing Nell six times, tripped away.

As the shadows lengthened in the evening she returned. Darcy was much better. He had eaten nineteen saucers of ice cream during the day. But his eyes were bandaged up, poor boy.

Might she watch him, while dear Mrs. Gaston got a little nap?

Certainly! He would only want ice cream; it was in the freezer, just outside the door. If he spoke to her, she could just pass herself off for a Sister of Charity.

Tige was in New York, attending to some law business.

CHAPTER XLVI.

THE DARK CHAMBER.

The sleeper in the darkened room, his other senses rendered more acute by reason of his semi-blindness, was wakened by the stealthy footfall of the Sister of Charity, as she approached his bedside. He could only distinguish the outlines of her form, but he could hear the rustle of her dress, as she seated herself in the chair near him.

"Nell! Sister, is it you?" he said.

"No!" she whispered; "Mrs. Gaston is sleeping. What will you have?"

"Light!"

"Ah! the Doctor says you must wait."

"How long have I been here?" he asked, after a pause.

"It is seven o'clock now. You came at eleven last night. You have been here twenty hours."

There was another pause. Darcy was trying to recall the

events of the previous evening. The encounter at the Ferry. Then Helen! When he endeavoured to collect the sequences in that interview, he found himself perpetually overleaping the intervals and reaching the terrible culmination: "His wife! Do you hear?" Then suddenly he remembered the book, and felt in his breast for it. He only found a wound, smarting under a mass of bandages.

"Pardon me!" he murmured again; "are you the nurse?"

"Yes. I am watching you while Mrs. Gaston sleeps."

"Please tell me the truth! Does the Doctor say——"

"The Doctor says quiet is important; and darkness. Your eye is hurt, and he fears inflammation."

"What makes my breast so sore?"

"You were hurt there also. It is not serious."

"I had a little Book in my breast. Did you see it?"

"Yes."

After another short silence, Darcy began to whisper to himself. She leaned forward to listen. He seemed to be reciting a task, with great deliberation.

"A Verb is a word which signifies to be, or to do, or to suffer; as: 'I am, I love, I am loved!'" Then a pause, as though he were meditating upon the meaning of the sentence, and then the repetition of it.

"What are you saying?" whispered the nurse, uneasily.

"I am a Verb!" answered Darcy; "Nell loves me; Tige also. Those are all!"

The nurse was dismayed by this reply. He spoke so smoothly and coherently, that she rejected the first impression his words produced. His mind was *not* wandering.

"That Book!" said Darcy; "is it here?"

"Yes."

"May I see it? Only a moment."

"You cannot see anything," replied the nurse, after a momentary hesitation; "your eyes are bound up. A few hours' patience is all that is required of you. The Doctor says he will take off the bandages to-morrow, if there are no new symptoms."

"You whisper all the time!" muttered he, fretfully. "Nothing ails my ears! Why cannot you speak out?"

"I must not."

"I cannot tell whether I dream or no!" said Darcy. "I remember a savage fight. I remember drawing my weapon, and Helen pulled it away! But *that* was an old dream, I swear! But I could not shoot *him*, so I shot the other one. His wife! do you hear. O monstrous fraud! There are certain propositions which the mind cannot entertain, even when supported by indubitable proof; and this is one of them. I have dreamed all that wild story. I did not see her. I did not steal her Book! Ah! kind nurse, let me hold the Book in my hand!"

The nurse's eyes were overflowing. She drew the Book from her bosom and placed it in his hand. He felt the shattered covers, with tremulous fingers, and then slipped the volume under his pillow.

"Common honesty, you know," he whispered, apologetically; "I took it without her knowledge. I must get it back to her somehow. That was in the dream also. Darcy Ruthven Gaston stealing a book! Ha, ha! But it's no consequence. I beg your pardon. Do you know Mr. Skillet?"

"Yes. He's my uncle."

"Ah!" said Darcy, with a sigh of relief; "that accounts for your kindness, then. For he is the kindest man alive. And you are in the—the Institute! He told me he had two nieces there. His brother's daughters."

"Yes."

"Then you know Miss Harding?"

There was no answer. He had pushed back the bandage that covered his eyes, and she was leaning over him, readjusting it. She handled him tenderly, but with resolute hands.

"You *must* keep your eyes covered," she whispered, as she resumed her seat; "Doctor Chase left that as his parting injunction."

"To hear is to obey," said Darcy; "but, Miss Skillet, please tell me how you happen to be here."

"My uncle brought me."

"Kind uncle! Do you know that a tear dropped on my cheek while you were leaning over me? Ah! I offended you, ignorantly, by imitating your excellent uncle just now. Believe me, I honor him as truly as yourself, and I did not mean to offend."

"It's no consequence," she answered, with a little ripple of a laugh, in a whisper.

"By George!" exclaimed Darcy.

"Say 'By Gemini!' That is the way Uncle Skillet swears."

Darcy put out his hand, groping in the dark for hers. She drew shyly back out of his reach.

"I beg pardon," said he, withdrawing his hand; "I only wished to shake hands as a token of my gratification. I did not think you were able to laugh."

She leaned over him again, and wiped his pallid cheek with a napkin, and then put her soft hand in his. His fingers closed upon it, and then came to pass one of those inscrutable phenomena that baffle the investigations of philosophers. As he held her hand a faint color spread over his face, and he felt the thrill that passed through his body accelerating his pulses and deepening his respirations.

"Oh, Helen!" he murmured, at last; "is it, indeed, you?"

The little fingers trembled in his grasp, but she did not answer.

"I should call you Mrs. Grey," he continued, "but I cannot yet."

"I am not Mrs. Grey," she whispered; "I am only Helen Ruthven."

This youth of quick perceptions, endowed with that prompt decision of character which is the prime factor in mental dynamics, rushed to a swift conclusion.

"You are kind to me," he said, "because I lie here helpless, and perhaps dying; and you tell me anything to quiet me. I did not dream all that horrible scene last night. Here is the Book!"

"Yes, with the covers shattered," she replied. "The bullet that would have killed you was turned aside by these broken shells!" and she furtively kissed the Book.

"And you told me just now," continued Darcy, "that you are Miss Skillet——"

"No."

"You said Mr. Skillet was your uncle."

"Yes. That is true. He says so, and I believe him."

"And you told me last night that you were Rupert Grey's wife?"

"Yes. But I was mistaken. He pretended to marry me a few minutes before we took the train, when I met you. I will tell you when you are well enough. You are not dying."

"Oh, Helen! I can never be well enough! You must have loved that man——"

"Never!" she answered, vehemently. "I never looked at him or thought of him, except with abhorrence. And when you told me on the train that he was killed, I could have wept for joy. In all

15

the world there is no reptile that I hate, as I hate that wretched man! Love him! Ah, how could you say such cruel words to me!"

He still held her hand, while his own trembled.

"Do you not understand?" she continued, softly. "By some witchcraft, he controlled my will. I felt as one feels who is drugged, or somnambulic, led along without even the desire to resist. His object was to gain, through me, possession of the property he expected me to inherit, and he deceived me by the pretended marriage, knowing that my conscience would compel me to obey a husband's authority! Ah! Do you not see *now*, why I could not listen to you last night!"

He turned towards her, hurting his wounded breast horribly, without heeding it, and drew her head down upon it. It seemed to him that the wounds healed rapidly.

"If I dare understand you to mean this," he whispered, "my life will not be long enough to tell you the story you interrupted last night. May I tell you now, Helen?"

"It's no consequence!" said Mr. Skillet, who had entered the darkened room softly, lest he should disturb the patient; "but it seems to me that you are gitten along pooty smart!"

"Yes, sir," replied Darcy, while Helen shrunk back into her chair; "I am well enough to get up, if the doctor will let me."

"Not to-night," answered Mr. Skillet. "Chase says your eyes must be kept covered. Hay! Hello! Is it you? I thought it was Mrs. Gaston."

"Mrs. Gaston sent me in, sir," replied Helen; "she did not sleep at all last night, and she——"

"All right!" said her uncle; "it's no consequence. Seems to me you looked some sleepy yourself. Wa'nt you a leanin' over like?"

"Yes, sir. Mr. Gaston was asking a question——"

Mr. Skillet beckoned her away from the bedside, to the opposite corner.

"Did he git a look at you?" he asked, eagerly.

"Oh, no. His eyes are bound up. Besides, the room is quite dark."

"Then he don't know you? He! he! That's prime!"

"But I told him I was your niece, sir," said Helen, deceitfully, "and he called me Miss Skillet."

"Did he?" said Mr. Skillet, delighted; "bully for Dassy! And did he ask if you was at the Institoot? I told him my nieces were at the Institoot."

"I think he did, and I said, yes."

"That's right. Let her set, and go about your business, please! You can come back after a while. I want to talk a little to him. Might ask him su'thin you hadn't ought to hear."

"Yes, sir. I left my handkerchief there. I'll get it, and go." She walked softly across the room, and bent over the blind youth.

"I must go now," she whispered; "but I will come again when I can. Give me my Book."

"I won't!" replied Darcy. "Excuse me! I mean I can't. It is in the old place over my heart. My darling!"

"Hush!" and she put her hand on his lips. He kissed the dainty fingers, and she did likewise, as she whisked through the door.

"Can't see nauthin?" observed Mr. Skillet, drawing near.

"No, sir. I think the last thing I saw was the ugly face of Rupert Grey. Mr. Skillet, I found out that he was the man who followed me in New York."

"Did you? Ah, well! He's gone! No sign of him anywhere. Skedaddled. Your brother and me went for him last night; and he had got a bad knock in the head, and we thought he would keep till mornin'. But he was off before daylight. Clean gone!"

Darcy waited to hear more, but Mr. Skillet paused for a reply.

"I thought you might say what you said about old Brown, sir, the other morning—something about his picture."

"Certainly," responded Mr. Skillet; "cuss his picter! Dern his picter! if that makes you feel better."

"Thank you, sir," said Darcy, faintly; "you see I don't like to swear while I am so ill! When I get well, I'll——"

"Better let him set. The other robber knocked him in the head, and stole his watch and pocket-book. It's no consequence about him. You'll be all right to-morrow, I guess?"

"I am quite well now, sir," replied Darcy; "only a little weak. If they would let me get up, I think I could walk out."

"No use to walk out, now. Night. What did you do with the Norman papers?"

"All in my drawer at Mr. Camp's. I gave brother Tige the key to-day. He has gone to New York to settle that business. I see, now, all that Miss Norman desired to do. She is a noble woman, Mr. Skillet. I admire her greatly."

"You do! Well, it's no consequence, but mebbe you'd like to spark her a spell?"

"Oh no, sir!" said Darcy; "I could not think of such a thing. Miss Norman can go to Europe and marry a duke. Do you think I would have the impudence to court such a lot of money?"

"Money don't make a grain of difference, if there's plenty of love," said Mr. Skillet. "She's got it all in her own right, and nobody could say a word agin it, if she wanted to marry an alderman."

"Marriage is a very serious business, Mr. Skillet," replied Darcy, after reflecting a few minutes. "I must wait until I make some money of my own, before I think of matrimony."

"When you first come to," observed Mr. Skillet, cautiously, "you was a ravin' about some Helen. Mebbe you have been doin' some courtin' unbeknownst like? You did not say who Helen was. You seemed to want her saved though, pooty considerable."

"Yes, sir. But I was not thinking of courting then."

"The dickens you wan't! What was you so anxious about then?"

"I thought the—the devil was after her," said Darcy.

"Well, you was not far wrong, I guess. The devil is after most people that I know. Who was you talkin' to when I came in just now?"

"Oh!" replied Darcy, "that was—she said she was your niece, sir. She was very kind, indeed. But I would have known that, if I had known she was related to you, Mr. Skillet. Since I have been lying here, all in darkness, I have thought of all your kindness to me, many times. You took me into your office, though I was totally ignorant of the commonest business rules. You did not scold, though I made so many blunders; but you have patiently endured my ignorance, and have encouraged me in a hundred ways. And you make me think, sometimes, that I shall really learn to be valuable to you. And when that time comes—"

"Gemini!" interrupted Mr. Skillet, "you'll talk yourself into a regular fever! It's no consequence. You're learnin'! Keep your margins up, and don't speckillate yourself. Git your commissions, and bag 'em. If you feel like takin' a flyer in gold or stocks on your own account, jest wrap a wet towel round your head. Them is all the business rules you want. And here is Mrs. Gaston. Good evening, ma-am! Dassy is talkin' quite reasonable to-night. Chase says he may git up to-morrow."

"Sister," whispered Darcy, as Nell bent over him, "I have not seen your dear face. May I take this horrid bandage off? Only one eye hurt! Oh, thank you! Bless your kind eyes. And, sister Nell! Please bring—bring Mr. Skillet's niece in, and let me get one glimpse of her! Oh, you darling sister! I'll make Tige buy you a stunning silk dress to-morrow."

"It's my opinion," said Mr. Skillet, who had overheard the last request, "that you are a deceitful young cuss. Come in, Helen! It's no consequence."

CHAPTER XLVII.

THE PARTITION.

MR. COKE was poring over deeds to the Norman Estate, when Mr. Henry Gaston presented his card, bearing the various legal titles that he had won in his profession, and with it, a note from Miss Norman, introducing Mr. Gaston, and referring Mr. Coke to him for a full explanation of her desires in the matter of the partition of the Estate. The note concluded with the announcement of her wish for an immediate transfer of titles to the Real Estate, and an equitable division of the personal property, as she hoped to sail for Europe in a few days.

"Take a seat, Mr. Gaston," said the New York lawyer, politely; "we shall have no prolonged litigation in this case. Have you any suggestion to offer, relating to the settlement?"

"I wait for you, sir," answered Tige; "Mrs. Bragdon will, no doubt, have preferences, which must be consulted. By the bye, I am instructed to say to you, that Miss Norman entrusts me with the charge of her interests in this division, because she desires Mr. Coke to be entirely free from any embarrassment, in advocating the rival claims of her sister."

"Rival claims?" said Mr. Coke, taking off his spectacles; "there cannot be anything like rivalry. There are two heirs, and they take equal proportions. Have you a list of the property?"

"Yes, sir," answered Mr. Gaston, producing Darcy's list; "please examine it, and correct any errors."

"It needs no correction," said Mr. Coke, after reading the document. "The balance of cash is set down in round figures, and the valuation of some of the bonds differs slightly from mine. But there is really no need of valuations, as each party in interest will take one moiety and pass receipts."

"But you cannot divide houses, Mr. Coke," observed Tige; "and my principal business to-day, is to hear your proposition for the division of the Realty."

"Mr. Bragdon suggests that the separate parcels be put up at a sort of auction——"

"Nothing could be more reasonable," replied Mr. Gaston; "when shall the sale take place?"

"Mr. Bragdon will be here immediately," said Mr. Coke, "and I think he will be prepared to arrange the settlement at once."

"My dear sir," said Tige, "it seems to me that my presence is a mere formality. I am going down Wall street, and will return within an hour. And if you will, in the meantime, get from Mr. Bragdon his bids upon the separate parcels, I will obtain Miss Norman's bids also. The whole business can be settled to-day, if you will examine this deed of partition, which includes all the property, leaving only the names in blank. No doubt you will find some blunder in it, as I am more familiar with Kentucky forms, than with those of New York."

"Let me understand you, Mr. Gaston," said Mr. Coke, as the other put on his hat; "you propose to make separate bids——"

"No, sir. I thought that was *your* proposition."

"Ah, well! no matter. It is all in the family," said Mr. Coke.

"And therefore should be the more carefully guarded. If Mr. Bragdon—or rather Mrs. Bragdon—approves, let her fill up the list, affixing the amount she will pay for each parcel. Miss Norman will offer a similar list. And when we compare the two papers, the highest bidder will take the property, piece by piece. Of course the balance on either side will be settled by the cash and bonds at an agreed valuation. Mrs. Bragdon may desire some special parcels, and will therefore bid higher for them, or *vice versa*. Neither will know the other's estimate, and therefore the partition must be entirely equitable. Good morning! I will be back at noon."

"Now," thought Mr. Coke, "this Kentucky man has constructed the very scheme that Bragdon suggested! It is very curious that they should agree so thoroughly."

In due time Mr. Bragdon arrived. He was charmed with the method of settlement suggested, and to make assurance doubly sure, requested Mr. Coke to "fix a document" that would make the bids equal to a regular transfer of title. When informed that this could not be done, by any forms known to New York lawyers, he suggested that an agreement might be drawn up, binding each of the high contracting powers to abide by the result of the bidding, under a penalty to be decided upon when the ladies arrived.

Notwithstanding Tige's modest depreciation, the partition deed was found to be correctly drawn. Mr. Bragdon drove up town for his wife, and at noon, Mr. Coke introduced Mr. Gaston, as the representative of Miss Nina Norman. Mr. Bragdon's first question related to the amount of the penalty.

"I have a paper here drawn by Miss Norman, and duly attested," said Mr. Gaston, "by which she binds herself under a penalty of one hundred thousand dollars to accept the results of this bidding. If Mrs. Bragdon will sign a similar paper, it is already drawn, and only needs her signature—and Mr. Bragdon's. Mr. Coke and I will witness the signatures, and we will then exchange the papers. Miss Norman has made all these preparations, because she is eager to make a prompt settlement."

"And the bids?" said Mr. Bragdon.

"Miss Norman's bids are in this sealed envelope," said Tige. "There are nine separate parcels enumerated, and she bids on each. Here is the duplicate paper, with the amounts in blank. Mr. Bragdon has only to affix the amounts he is willing to pay, and a few minutes will settle the question of ownership."

"Miss Norman is not coming, then?" said Mr. Bragdon.

"No. She requests Mr. Coke to present the deeds at the hotel to-day or to-morrow."

After a brief consultation with his wife, Mr. Bragdon filled in the blanks, and all the preliminary papers were signed, and handed to Mr. Coke. The envelope was opened, and the slips containing Nina's bids taken out. Mr. Coke read aloud from the separate lists. "Number One! Mrs. Bragdon bids one hundred thousand dollars for dwelling on Fifth Avenue. Miss Norman bids fifty thousand. It is therefore Mrs. Bragdon's."

That amiable lady heaved a sigh of relief. Mr. Bragdon ground his teeth.

"Number two!" continued the lawyer. "Mrs. Bragdon bids seventy-five thousand dollars for the Wall street offices. Miss Norman bids eighty thousand. It is therefore Miss Norman's." Mr. Bragdon ground his teeth again.

"Number three! Mrs. Bragdon bids fifty thousand dollars for the Canal street store. Miss Norman bids thirty thousand. Number three goes to Mrs. Bragdon. Number four! Mrs. Bragdon bids fifty thousand dollars for the store on Bond street. Miss Norman bids thirty. It goes to Mrs. Bragdon. Number five! Mrs. Bragdon bids two hundred thousand dollars for the stores on Broadway. Miss Norman bids two hundred and ten thousand. They go to Miss Norman."

"Curse the Broadway stores," muttered Mr. Bragdon.

"Number six! Mrs. Bragdon bids fifty thousand dollars for the Newport house. Miss Norman bids ten thousand. It goes to Mrs. Bragdon. Number seven! Mrs. Bragdon offers one hundred and fifty thousand dollars for the farm near Yonkers. Miss Norman offers fifty thousand. It goes to Mrs. Bragdon. Number eight! Mrs. Bragdon bids forty thousand dollars for the house in Saratoga. Miss Norman bids thirty-five thousand. It is Mrs. Bragdon's."

"Cursed dear too!" muttered Mr. Bragdon.

"Number nine!" continued Mr. Coke; "Mrs. Bragdon bids two hundred thousand dollars for Ruthven's Folly. Miss Norman bids three hundred thousand. It is therefore Miss Norman's!" And Mr. Coke took off his spectacles. "That is the last."

"Three hundred thousand," said Mr. Bragdon, starting to his feet; "the girl is insane! I really protest against so reckless a proceeding! Three hundred thousand!"

"It is only one hundred thousand more than Mrs. Bragdon's bid," observed Tige, as he collected the slips. "I fancy it is cheap! The rumour now current is, that the city will condemn this property very soon, and add it to the Park."

"Who says so?" said Mr. Bragdon, furiously.

"Oh, several well informed people! And now, Mr. Coke, there will be one hundred and fifty thousand dollars due the common fund, from Miss Norman; that is, she will have to transfer seventy-five thousand dollars from her moiety of the bonds, to Mrs. Bragdon. She instructs me to offer Mrs. Bragdon her choice of the bonds at the assessment, and if you will appoint the hour for the exchange of titles, we will be ready."

"At four o'clock this afternoon," said Mr. Coke, "if that hour will suit Mrs. Bragdon. The deed is ready now: or, if you please, I can fill in the spaces, and take Mr. and Mrs. Bragdon's signatures now, and get Miss Norman's this afternoon."

"That will be the better plan," said Mr. Bragdon. "I have no desire to encounter that peppery young lady——"

"Who is not present," said Mr. Gaston.

"I do not need any hint from you, sir," said Mr. Bragdon, white with rage; "Miss Norman is the sister of Mrs. Bragdon——"

"Who *is* present," interrupted Tige, "and we therefore cannot discuss any questions that might provoke intemperate controversy. I am at the Fifth Avenue Hotel, and will be happy to meet you there, or elsewhere, at your own convenience. I beg your pardon!" he continued, with a sweet smile, "but in my country gentlemen never have altercations when ladies are present. I will give you all the opportunities you desire, to—to compare notes."

Mr. Bragdon looked into Tige's handsome face, so placid and friendly, and saw danger. Darcy had told his brother something about his meeting with Mr. Bragdon, and Tige remembered it. Mrs. Bragdon, deceived by the dulcet tones of Mr. Gaston, saw nothing of the devil that was in his eyes.

"John," she said, "I hope you will not make any trouble. Do let us get this business settled, and be *done* with it."

Mr. Bragdon subsided.

In the interval between this meeting and four o'clock, Mr. Gaston went to Brooklyn, and had a long interview with Helen. And when he waited upon Nina, in the afternoon, he took Mr. Skillet with him. Miss Norman received them graciously. Tige had sent her a telegram directly after the meeting at Coke's, containing only two words, "property yours."

He gave her a list of the bids, but said nothing about Mr. Bragdon's comments. Nina does not know to-day how sorely she had disappointed her brother-in-law, who had learned under the seal of confidence that the City would purchase the property known as "Ruthven's Folly." He had also learned that the assessment would be over the amount of his bid. But Tige had ascertained, as he supposed, the highest possible sum it would command, and by Nina's orders added fifty thousand dollars to that estimate.

"I believe all your wishes have been accomplished, Miss Norman," said Mr. Gaston, shaking hands with her; "I mean, relating to the partition of the property. You have obtained the parcels you desired, and you have paid much more than Mrs. Bragdon bid for them. Her bid for "Ruthven's Folly" was one hundred thousand dollars less than yours."

"Hi!" said Mr. Skillet; "'Ruthven's Folly!' Gemini and Gosh! It's no consequence, but Bragdon has been pumpin' me about that same property, forty times. And now, Miss Nina, you've got it. Gemini! Jest let it set."

"I saw Miss Ruthven," continued Tige, " and conveyed all your messages. She was greatly touched, but inflexible. She refuses to accept the property, positively, saying her father would rise from his grave to rebuke her if she did; and she declares she will instantly transfer it to the Hospital in Lexington, if the ownership comes to her in any way."

"Then I will carry out my original plan," said Nina. "I will give the property to your brother."

"I am afraid you cannot do that either, Miss Norman. Indeed, I am sure you cannot. The Gastons never accept gifts! I have not spoken to him on the subject, but I am quite sure he would decline as obstinately as Helen does."

"Has he ever spoken to Miss Ruthven on the subject?" said Nina.

"Possibly. The boy is over head and ears in love with her!"

A paleness overspread Nina's face. Tige saw it, but, being a gentleman, turned away and addressed Mr. Skillet.

"Mr. Skillet," he said, " cannot you devise some plan by which Miss Norman can accomplish her desire?"

"Nauthin' easier!" said Mr. Skillet; "jest you go about your business about half an hour. I'll manœuvre 'em all. You can come back at four o'clock."

CHAPTER XLVIII.

BLAKE AND BLOKE.

IF Dutchy had known that his friend and patron had two "places of deposit," his soul would have been filled with shame and self-abhorrence, as he sat in the smoking car on the New York Central Railroad, that frosty morning. He would have lamented—more than did Lord Ullin over the loss of his daughter —that he had not "gone through" his late boss, while he lay senseless on the floor. The pocket-book he secured contained two or three hundred dollars, but Mr. Grey had a larger sum, buckled around his body in a money belt; and with this capital he began a new career in Washington. The New York *Herald* gave a graphic account of the murderous assault upon "Mr. Dossie Gaskins," with an accurate description of the locality, near the old church, where the murder had been attempted; and the paragraph concluded with the announcement that Mr. Gaskins' hurts were slight, "the bullet having been deflected by his watch case." All this Mr. Grey read a day or two after his arrival. With his native hardihood, he decided to run the risk of arrest, if Darcy should make complaint, and boldly resumed his proper name, and began business as "claim agent," with one client. This was an impecunious army contractor, whose demands upon the Government were not properly drawn up, and who offered Mr. Grey a moiety of his claim for collecting the total.

He had an extensive acquaintance among the officials, and his success with this initial claim brought him more business. Within a month his office was fairly organized, and he was beginning to be known as the most successful lobbyist at the Capitol. The memory of his altercation on the old church pavement was fading away, when two gentlemen presented themselves in his private office, one day, and brought all the events vividly before him. The visitors introduced each other——

"Mr. Timothy Skillet."

"Henry Gaston, Esquire."

"Ah! take seats, gentlemen!" said Mr. Grey, with charming politeness. He kept two supplies of cigars in different drawers of his desk. One drawer—the upper one—contained fragrant weeds, made of Connecticut tobacco, and perfumed lavishly with valerian. The lower drawer contained genuine Partagas. He usually presented his visitors with native growth; on the present occasion he proffered the imported article. The gentlemen declined, and Mr. Grey, with a word of apology, selected and lighted one for himself.

"We have some private business," said Gaston, gravely, "and, perhaps, it would be better to have no witnesses."

"It's no consequence!" said Mr. Skillet—"that is, to us. But I guess you might as well send out your clerk, and let him shet the door after him!"

"Certainly," said Mr. Grey, nodding to his clerk, who vanished.

"We only want your signature to this document," began Mr. Gaston, handing a paper to Grey; "it is a full account of your adventures in Cincinnati, and of your subsequent attempt at murder in Brooklyn. We require your signature, which we will witness, and, perhaps, a notarial seal also."

While he read the paper, which he did with great deliberation, Rupert performed his accustomed cigar exercise—throwing his arm forward, elevating his chin, and blowing out the smoke-rings. Gaston regarded him with cold gravity; Mr. Skillet watched him with growing admiration.

"May I inquire," said Grey, "what use you intend to make of this piece of romance?"

"We need it at present," replied Mr. Gaston, "to satisfy a lady who was almost your victim, and who still remembers you with unspeakable loathing. We cannot say whether it will be used against you in legal process or not. Probably not, unless you should be troublesome hereafter."

"And if I decline to sign?" said Mr. Grey.

"Then we will obtain the same facts from the records of the court, which will answer our purpose."

"The court?" said Grey, his face flushing.

"Yes; the Criminal Court," answered Gaston, coldly. "We have the necessary papers with us to secure your attendance. We have all the witnesses we need—Lamis, Brown, of Cincinnati, who officiated as clergyman for you, and one of the witnesses to the bogus ceremony; we have Miss Norman's and Miss Keith's testimony in legal form; we have the offer of the testimony of John Dutchy, *alias* Bloke, for a price—moderate enough, if we need it—and we have Darcy Gaston and Helen Ruthven, ready to complete the case, whenever you desire the trial."

"Quite a formidable array of names!" said Mr. Grey.

"Quite formidable," replied Tige.

"It appears to me, gentlemen," said Grey, after some deliberation, "that this paper is very much like a dying confession. If I sign this interesting narrative I take away its present fictitious character, and give it the force of veritable history. If I refuse to sign——"

"If you refuse to sign," interrupted Gaston, "you will please prepare for a journey to New York by the afternoon train. The policeman, who pulled your red beard off at Fulton ferry, waits outside—first, to identify you, and second, to escort you northward. Personally, I shall be gratified if the affair takes this course. I make the other proposal in deference to Miss Norman's wishes, and also to save Miss Ruthven from the notoriety that will follow your trial and conviction."

"And you offer me no guaranty that this paper will not be used against me hereafter?"

"None!" answered Tige, with cold ferocity.

"Not even a promise?"

"Not even a promise. The word of a Kentucky gentleman would be all the guaranty you would demand; but you cannot have that."

"Then I throw myself upon the honour of the Kentucky gentleman," said Rupert, "who will make some allowance for the violence of my passion, even though hopeless, and my consequent jealousy——"

"Be silent!" said Tige, sternly.

Rupert shrugged his shoulders, then took up his pen and signed his name with a flourish. The others affixed their signatures as witnesses.

"Mr. Skillet," said Tige, "will you please call in the notary? The legal formalities had better be complied with." Mr. Skillet nodded his head and retired. "If you and I ever meet again," continued Gaston, in measured accents, "where any pretext will excuse the act, I will kill you!"

"There may be an opportunity," replied Grey, smiling.

"And if Darcy Gaston ever gets near enough to cover you with his pistol, he will not wait for a pretext! I pray you, go out of the country and begin a new life. A life-long repentance will not atone for your past wickedness in this world, but you may modify the retributions that will find you in another."

The entrance of the notary, with Mr. Skillet, prevented a reply. The customary certificate was added to the document, Mr. Grey sworn upon a little Testament produced by the notary, and the gentlemen prepared to depart. Mr. Skillet lingered a moment to pay his parting respects.

"If you ever visit N'Yauk," he whispered, "come to Number fifty-five Wall street and ask for Timothy Skillet, and if I am to home when you call, there will either be a funeral to my heouse, or I'll put sich a head onto you that will make the dome of the Capitol look like a pimple! Dern your picter! Good mornin'!".

To escape the rigours of a northern climate, Mr. Grey removed to Mississippi very shortly after the interview above recorded. The long war had impoverished that State, but Mr. Grey picked up a livelihood by playing poker (draw poker), after the most approved rules. His name was Martinbird, and he bestowed this euphonious name upon a widow lady, three or four years ago, who was fourth cousin to an official who dispensed gifts. This lucky marriage secured him the appointment to a foreign post, with small salary, but with large opportunities, and, under a tropical sky, Mr. Martinbird dispenses princely hospitalities to wandering Americans to-day. Those of them who learn draw poker, under his tutelage, swell his revenues; and there, as Mr. Skillet would say, let him set!

In parting with this man, it is proper to say a word touching the peculiar power he sometimes exerted over persons of sensitive organism. Psychological phenomena are of such a character as to elude scientific scrutiny, and the asserted facts of animal magnetism are not so well established, or so accurately described, as to give it a place among the exact sciences. But there are certain analogies that are well known, relating to the domination of one will over another, which, being exaggerated, form the staple of sensational stories. Rupert Grey, being endowed with an iron will, and being utterly remorseless, exerted so much of this occult power as he possessed, whenever he encountered a new victim; and it is probable that he relied upon this influence to keep Dutchy in subjection.

But Mr. Dutchy not being sensitive, was restive under restraint. He also was born to "take things," and it was not possible to keep him for any long period out of his natural habits. And when he "went West," with a certain snug capital, it was with the intention of finding some locality where stealing was the chief occupation of the inhabitants.

He spent a week in Cincinnati, reading New York papers diligently every day. The escape of Gaston from bludgeon and bullet was totally inexplicable. And he was devoured with anxiety to know the manner of his patron's death, as he had an uncomfortable suspicion that he was poison-proof, and totally invulnerable. And as the papers were silent upon this topic, Dutchy was ill at ease.

One day, when he was standing at the newspaper file, in the reading-room of the hotel, a man touched his arm. It was Doctor Lamis.

"Hardly knew you," said the Doctor. "How long have you been here? I've been looking for you."

"Have you? Well, what do you want?"

"Why, how you've changed! Nobody would know you, since

you've shaved! I have been studying you ten minutes, and was about to give you up, when you tossed your arm out—so!—with your cigar in your fingers; and then I knew you were imitating Grey. You see I have known Grey so long."

"Yes," replied Dutchy.

"Well. I saw Grey's pants on you. I thought I could swear to them. The figure is peculiar. Very!"

"What do you want?" said Dutchy.

"I may want your testimony about that little affair where you lost your fingers. Mr. Gaston has got your fingers, in alcohol. But all I want is the facts about Grey; the shooting, and the arrangements you made before you started. Grey has skedaddled!"

"What do you want?" repeated Dutchy.

"I tell you I want—or Mr. Gaston wants—your deposition, telling where you met Grey, and all that he did."

"A hundred dollars!" said Dutchy, stolidly.

"A hundred dollars?" replied Doctor Lamis. "Why, he can get all he wants by arresting you."

"Werry well!" said Dutchy, obstinately; "let him try. I can be found here, I s'pose. If he wants me to squeal on the boss, he's got to pay a hundred dollars. That's all!"

"Well. I'll telegraph him," said Lamis. "Wait here for me."

"All right," said Dutchy, resuming his study of the newspaper. And as Doctor Lamis passed into the telegraph room, Dutchy passed into the street. Heroically resolving to sacrifice his personal property, he left his new satchel, containing the paper collars, the hair brush, and ten or twelve cigars that had cost him three cents a piece. His anguish was modified by the reflection that he owed about twenty dollars at the hotel, which the urgency of his present business forbade him to pay.

He concluded that safety was not to be found in any northern State, and he therefore decided to settle in the devastated South. He wandered through Kentucky, down into Tennessee, and finally reached the low country of South Carolina, travelling in the track of General Sherman. The war was over, and the people were impoverished. Nothing left for Dutchy to steal, so he bought a plantation, paying three hundred dollars in new bank notes on account, and leaving a mortgage debt upon it. He got a crop planted, working early and late, and compelling the negroes he employed to work also, by the sheer force of brute pluck and indomitable perseverance. Before his crop matured, he sold his plantation, taking cotton in payment, and actually doubled his investment. He was pronounced in his loyalty, and the negroes followed him blindly, and at last sent him to the State Legislature. Here he was a great success. He catalogued the votes that were purchasable, and farmed them out, selling his bonds for whatever they would bring in ready money; and by the time the work of reconstruction was accomplished, he was ready for a larger field of usefulness. He announced himself a candidate for Congress, and was triumphantly elected.

The honourable gentleman from South Carolina was very quiet during the first session. Pay and mileage sufficed for his moderate needs. When the second session began, he was known to the lobby as the one member who had a price, and who could "arrange" with several other members for a consideration. If the lobby did not respond to his just demands, he was wont to shake his mutilated fist at it, referring to the two fingers " he had left at Gettysburg," and finally clawing the considerations that came in, with the remaining digits. He was " long," as Mr. Skillet would say, in Credit Mobilier, Back Pay, and other Congressional enterprises. When election time arrived, he stumped his district, flourishing the same honourable scars in the faces of his black constituents, and secretly dispensing large charities in exchange for votes.

The name he bears is neither Bloke nor Dutchy; but he has found a level where his genius is manifested. He does not bore the House with speeches, but he is looked upon as a rising man. He is surrounded by competitors who give him more uneasiness than the cops who threatened the peace of Dutchy's mind in the forgotten past; not that he dreads detection and exposure, but he keenly feels the loss of the two fingers he left at Gettysburg, as he can only steal with one hand while his competitors can steal with two.

So, as he passes out of this history, the reader, who has followed his fortunes thus far, can safely leave him in the service of his country. Republics are proverbially ungrateful, but while this untiring public servant has one finger left, he can "point with pride" to his prowess at Gettysburg, and can steal more and lie more than any ten men in the ordinary walks of life. And if his towering genius shall ever lead him to attempt the theft of a red hot stove, and he should fail (which is not probable) and perish in the attempt, the unanimous voice of his country will invoke peace to his " ashes."

CHAPTER XLIX.

AND LAST.

IN Paris, June, 1872. The beautiful city, scarred by the Commune, but full of attractions. The broken column in the Place Vendome fenced in, looking grim and desolate. The ruins of historic palaces a little lower down, with spruce soldiers on guard, and busy sight-seers prowling around them. But all the boulevards thronged with passengers. A grown man on a bicycle, darting along the Rue de la Paix, avoiding carriages with French dexterity, and making great time. All the shops gay and brilliant. Along the Boulevard des Italiens multitudes of cafés, with little round tables on the pave, two chairs to each, and most of them occupied by idlers, sipping eau sucré, or Vin Ordinaire.

A little after mid-day. For three or four hours the Bois de Boulogne will be a solitude. With a pocketful of cigars, and no care to vex the soul, one can loiter about the shady drives in blissful idleness, hearing the distant note of the cuckoo, and the warbling of unnumbered nearer birds, darting about in the green canopy. Go down into the Rue Scribe, just below the new Opera House, and select your carriage.

"A l'heure, Monsieur?" said the driver.

"Oui! Just one o'clock—stop! Who is this coming up the Rue Scribe? Mr. Skillet!"

"Is it you?" said Mr. Skillet, joyfully; "wa-al, this is a treat! Where are you goin'?"

"To the Bois de Boulogne. A dozen cigars in my pocket, and three hours of quiet. Come and talk to me. I am starving for the sound of a friend's voice. Come!"

"Sackery blew!" responded Mr. Skillet; "now that's cur'ous! But I was this minnit wishin' for some fellow to talk at. Got dejunny at noon, ben down to Munro's, and was jest goin' back to sleep till dinner time. It's no consequence! I'm in!"

Through the Champs Élysées, with fountains playing—then long streets, then the dusty road. We smoked in silence as we bowled along. But at last came the cool green woods, with flowers all along the roadway, and finally the little waterfall, and the grotto with grotesque carvings on its sides. So we halted here.

"Now Mr. Skillet! It has been seven years since I left New York, and I do not know one item of American history since the close of the war. Begin!"

Mr. Skillet propped his body up carefully in his corner, put his long legs on the front seat, lighted a fresh cigar and threw his hat on the grass.

"Fust of all, then, the Normans. Nina went to Europe."

"Yes. The 'China.' I came out at the same time. But she was not visible during the voyage, and we only exchanged greetings as the ship passed Sandy Hook."

"Wa-al then, she jest fixed up her property in two days, took her old school-marm with her, and skedaddled! And she has not been back since! I have charge of her stocks and rents and bonds, and I jest remit her a thousand pounds every three months, and buy Gov'ments with her suplus revenue. She lives to Mentone and Rome all winter, comes to Paris in June, and spends the summer in Switzerland. Don't write a word to nobody 'cept to me, and then she only says, 'I received your note of sich a date, with the enclosure, and beg to return my thanks!' She might as well have 'em printed. Do you know that I can't make up my mind to call upon her? She is in Paris now. Found her address at Monroe's to-day. But I kinder draw back from seein' her, because she mightn't like to be reminded of the old times! She is smart as a steel trap, but she and her school-marm have sot up a private spiritooal shop, and they have a hull lot of tomfoolery all to themselves. I have heard that she can git a revelation whenever she likes. It's no consequence. But it is a cussed shame that so smart a woman should be sucked in so easy. But let her set.

"Tige Gaston? Certainly! Got a letter from him this very day. Here it is. May as well read it to you. No secrets! It's my belief that Tige Gaston couldn't keep or have a secret five minnits at a thousand dollars a minnit! 'Taint in the breed. Dassy can keep his mouth shet, because I've learned him; but if he heard two fellows talkin' about the locality of a gold mine, where anybody could go and fill their pockets for nauthin', instead of listenin' like any other man, he'd jest pin his ears down and whistle out loud! But I'll read the letter:

"MY DEAR MR. SKILLET: I was delighted to hear that you had really sailed for Europe. Darcy wrote me, enclosing your kind note, and, this being the first day I have had since its arrival, when urgent business did not occupy me fully, you will excuse the delay. Nell, who sends you kind greetings, says I shall quit law and settle down to plain farming; but I have grown so fond of my profession, and am getting so penurious and grasping, that I think

I shall continue the practice a little longer. My country home is a perfect paradise, though. When you return, I intend to have you here to spend six months at least. I used to think this quiet country beautiful seven years ago, when the best music I heard was the songs of the birds; but my two youngsters, Darcy and Helen, aged respectively five and three, fill my house with far more delightful music. My friend, there is no such thing as life for human beings, in its full development, except where the voices of children are constantly heard——"

"Guess that's enough for Mr. Tige. He jest keeps on writin' about them two brats, as if the sun and moon rose and sot for them! Sackery blew! I never met a man that was so swallowed up as Mr. Gaston. Two more pages here and nauthin' in 'em, but Dassy and Helen! It's no consequence!

"Grey? Ah, now you've got me. I called onto him down to Washington a month after you sailed. He was a claim agent; but he didn't seem to like our visit. Mr. Gaston was with me. We kinder give him a hint that we thought he ought to be hung, and we got some documents that he thought might be troublesome. Anyway, he left for parts unknown. Nina told me he was a kind of mesmerizer, and she was afeard of him. She never let him come where she was, without having somebody else with her. He was a rare devil! Cuss his picter! I believe the old he Boss Devil jest carried him off, as nobody could find hair nor hide of him.

"The Norman property? Oh, it was all divided fair and square. Nina had set her heart on a patch o' land that joined the Park, and she bid a cool hundred thousand more than old Bragdon would pay. I beg pardon! Is Bragdon a relation o' yourn? No? Well, you're lucky! So, when she got the deed, the fust thing she started was a transfer to Helen—my niece; but she was spunky and wouldn't have it. The reason why Miss Norman was so set was, fust: an old will that had been superseded by a later one; and second, some devilish spiritooal humbug, that made her as obstinate as a muel. Then, when Helen positively refused, she tried to give it to Dassy, because he was named after the proper owner. But that was wuss! You had ought to have seen that whelp when she made the offer! He was settin' up. It was the day after he was wounded, and she drove over to Brooklyn to see him. He delivered a moral discourse to her about receiving gifts. It was beautiful! I thought he was a tarnation fool all the time, mind you! but there was su'thin grand about the way that boy talked! So we went back to N'Yauk, her and me, and then we manœuvred 'em! Sackery blew!

"How was it managed? It's a secret, but I can trust you! She jest sold Ruthven's Folly to Timothy Skillet for three hundred thousand dollars, receipt whereof is hereby acknowledged, and cetera, though I did not pay her nary cent, and I signed my will in her presence, leavin' the same sum of money to Dassy Ruthven Gaston and Helen Ruthven, either or both, or the survivor of them, and to their heirs, administrators, executors and assigns. And that will is sealed up and in the hands of Philemon Coke to-day. It's no consequence, though!

"Why not? Because I've made a new will!

"The city took the property and paid me three hundred and forty-two thousand dollars, in seven per cent. bonds. The papers raised Cain about Mr. Skillet's foresight and so forth. The *Herald* said Mr. Skillet was the only man in N'Yauk that knowed the true value of property! I wrote to Nina tellin' her I had made a new will, jest leavin' them same bonds, instead of the even money. And I have ben creditin' Dassy's account with the interest ever since, and he is worth a hundred and forty thousand dollars on my books this day! I am payin' him a salary of twenty-five hundred a year, too!

"Dassy? Sackery blew! I don't know how to tell you about Dassy. As soon as he sot up, after that murderin' hound had shot him, dern his picter! he says, 'Mr. Skillet, I want to marry your niece, and whenever I am worth enough salary, please give me enough to get married on!' That's his style! I gave him fifteen hundred on the spot, and he went for her the next minnit!

"I tried to manœuvre 'em, but 'twant no use. They was too heavy for me. Helen refused to quit schoolin', because she had agreed with Miss Keith to keep the Institoot for a year. And she didn't give up till Miss Keith wrote to her from Florence, six months after, to hand the Institoot over to one of Dragger's members, who was spiritooally-minded. And she is runnin' the Institoot this minnit.

"Married? I should rather think so! Got married in September, and went to Kentucky for a weddin' tower. And they are jest as big fools over one another to-day as they was in the honeymoon.

"But, Jerusalem! I mean Sackery blew! that ain't the wust

of it! They live to my heouse, of course. I'd a sot it afire without insurance if they hadn't come, and they knowed it. And the Boy was born there! And he lives all over the heouse, and he owns everybody in it, and if he should take a notion to howl for the moon, cuss my buttons if Dassy wouldn't git it for him!

"His name? Ho! ho! Timothy Skillet Gaston! Sackery blew!"

Trieste Publishing has a massive catalogue of classic book titles. Our aim is to provide readers with the highest quality reproductions of fiction and non-fiction literature that has stood the test of time. The many thousands of books in our collection have been sourced from libraries and private collections around the world.

The titles that Trieste Publishing has chosen to be part of the collection have been scanned to simulate the original. Our readers see the books the same way that their first readers did decades or a hundred or more years ago. Books from that period are often spoiled by imperfections that did not exist in the original. Imperfections could be in the form of blurred text, photographs, or missing pages. It is highly unlikely that this would occur with one of our books. Our extensive quality control ensures that the readers of Trieste Publishing's books will be delighted with their purchase. Our staff has thoroughly reviewed every page of all the books in the collection, repairing, or if necessary, rejecting titles that are not of the highest quality. This process ensures that the reader of one of Trieste Publishing's titles receives a volume that faithfully reproduces the original, and to the maximum degree possible, gives them the experience of owning the original work.

We pride ourselves on not only creating a pathway to an extensive reservoir of books of the finest quality, but also providing value to every one of our readers. Generally, Trieste books are purchased singly - on demand, however they may also be purchased in bulk. Readers interested in bulk purchases are invited to contact us directly to enquire about our tailored bulk rates. Email: customerservice@triestepublishing.com

You May Also Like

ISBN: 9780649066155
Paperback: 144 pages
Dimensions: 6.14 x 0.31 x 9.21 inches
Language: eng

Heath's Modern Language Series. Atala

François-René de Chateaubriand & Oscar Kuhns

ISBN: 9780649639663
Paperback: 188 pages
Dimensions: 6.14 x 0.40 x 9.21 inches
Language: eng

The Lost Found, and the Wanderer Welcomed

W. M. Taylor

www.triestepublishing.com

You May Also Like

The Credibility of the Christian Religion; Or, Thoughts on Modern Rationalism

Samuel Smith

ISBN: 9780649557516
Paperback: 204 pages
Dimensions: 5.83 x 0.43 x 8.27 inches
Language: eng

Results of Astronomical Observations Made at the Sydney Observatory, New South Wales, in the Years 1877 and 1878

H. C. Russell

ISBN: 9780649692613
Paperback: 120 pages
Dimensions: 6.14 x 0.25 x 9.21 inches
Language: eng

www.triestepublishing.com

You May Also Like

Report of the Department of Farms and Markets, pp. 5-71

Various

ISBN: 9780649333158
Paperback: 84 pages
Dimensions: 6.14 x 0.17 x 9.21 inches
Language: eng

Catalogue of the Episcopal Theological School in Cambridge Massachusetts, 1891-1892

Various

ISBN: 9780649324132
Paperback: 78 pages
Dimensions: 6.14 x 0.16 x 9.21 inches
Language: eng

www.triestepublishing.com

You May Also Like

Three Hundred Tested Recipes

Various

ISBN: 9780649352142
Paperback: 88 pages
Dimensions: 6.14 x 0.18 x 9.21 inches
Language: eng

A Basket of Fragments

Anonymous

ISBN: 9780649419418
Paperback: 108 pages
Dimensions: 6.14 x 0.22 x 9.21 inches
Language: eng

Find more of our titles on our website. We have a selection of thousands of titles that will interest you. Please visit

www.triestepublishing.com